THE ECOLOGICAL CITY AND THE CITY EFFECT

The Ecological City
and the City Effect

Essays on the Urban Planning Requirements
for the Sustainable City

FRANCO ARCHIBUGI

Studies
in
Green Research

Aldershot • Brookfield USA • Singapore • Sydney

Published by
Ashgate Publishing Ltd
Gower House
Croft Road
Aldershot
Hants GU11 3HR
England

Ashgate Publishing Company
Old Post Road
Brookfield
Vermont 05036
USA

British Library Cataloguing in Publication Data

Archibugi, F. (Franco)
    The ecological city and the city effect : essays on the
    urban planning requirements for the sustainable city. -
    (Studies in green research)
    1.City planning 2.Sustainable development 3.City planning -
    Environmental aspects
    I. Title
    711.4

Library of Congress Catalog Card Number: 97-74456

ISBN 1 85972 653 4

Printed and bound by Athenaeum Press, Ltd.,
Gateshead, Tyne & Wcar.

Contents

v

vii

Figures, tables and maps

Preface
The ecological city: Reality and mystification

Attention to the problem of the degradation of the urban environment has become particularly intense in recent years. It may be said that this attention particularly exploded on a world scale between the 1980s and 1990s and has represented a sort of turning point in the history of environmentalism, which - as everyone knows - was born as a mass movement and with a strong hold on public opinion around the end of the 1960s. But up to a few years ago, environmentalism had touched on the city, and thus the urban environment, only indirectly.

***

Emblematic of this, is what happened in the European Economic Community. The birth of an environmental policy in the EEC (which was more or less contemporary - at the beginning of the 1970s - with what was happening on an international scale and in the main Western countries) ignored the city as a specific environment to safeguard and organise. As elsewhere, the environment to be protected - at the beginning of environmentalist policy - was felt to be the natural environment: made up of green spaces, water resources, the atmosphere, natural assets to protect (flora and fauna), and the 'natural' landscape in general. It is only in an indirect way, in as much as damage to the natural environment influences the city as well, that the latter was taken into consideration.[1]

In brief, attention was focused at the beginning mainly on the factors creating pollution and devastation in the 'natural' environment, and the 'effects' on the city were measured. It was not taken into consideration, however, that much of the deplored pollution and degradation of the natural environment derived from the city itself: i.e., from bad planning and

1

management of the city and development which was incompatible with the environment.

Naturally, the first victim of bad city planning and management was the urban environment: a mixture of natural environment (water, atmosphere, greenery, etc.) and the socio-cultural environment (the urban landscape, cultural assets, sociality, social deviancy, etc.). Much atmospheric pollution derives from heating and urban traffic, and a lot of water and soil pollution from solid and liquid waste coming from the city. But the factors of bad urban and territorial planning and management have their origin in the imbalance of settlements and in a poor distribution of urban functions in the territory.

Nevertheless, the awareness of this tight relationship between environmental degradation and bad urban planning has yet to penetrate the technical circles.

* * *

It has been said that what has happened in the European Community is emblematic of what has happened elsewhere. In the United States as well, for example, the EPA (which from 1969-1971 represented the operational instrument of federal policy for the environment) had no official responsibility for urban problems, and never took an interest in these, not even in its studies. In fact, urban problems, rather than representing an occasion for the greater strengthening of urban policies and urban planning with their approach, which was fragmented and by single project (on which the single obligation of the environmental impact assessment was applied), have, for many reasons, contributed to demolishing the fabric of analysis and assessment of the overall and co-ordinated use of the territory and cities.

In other countries as well - apart from exceptions which I would be curious to know and assess - it could be said that more or less the same has happened. The multi-year plans for the environment of some European and non-European countries, such as the Netherlands, Japan, France, Great Britain, Canada and others,[2] do not contain any specific programme for the urban environment. An exception is the Italian Ten-Year Plan for the Environment of 1992,[3] which contains some specific programmes for the urban environment. But this plan has had little follow-up in the country's environmental policy, and has remained in a primitive and strongly provisory state, almost as if it had never taken place.

In short, a serious vision of urban policy on a national and international scale is still far from being manifested in a complete form.

***

Notwithstanding this slow awareness of the tight relationship between the environmental crisis and urban planning, the movement for an 'ecological city', as mentioned, has expanded greatly.[4] This movement has developed for the study of urban problems from the 'ecological' point of view. Many of the initiatives go under the name of 'ecological city' or 'sustainable city'. What these notions consist of is however very unclear. Mostly technical measures are proclaimed, which should be taken in every city in order to mitigate pollution, speed up traffic, organise the recovery of the urban landscape, etc.[5]

In these terms, it is thought that any crisis of overloading or any pressure on the city brought about by the most varied factors of development of the same (demographic, industrial, traffic, etc.) may find its particular effective technical response. Technology is conceived as the panacea for any problem spontaneously arising.

However, our opinion is that this is true only in part. Certainly technology has an important role to play in resolving some problems. And certainly this role would be even more important if there was - given the problems - a more direct connection between environmental problems and technological research.

But, understood in this way, technology risks being the instrument of always insufficient solutions: 'cures' rather than 'prevention'. The mitigation of the uncontrolled effects of development, obtained with the instruments of technology, makes the latter simply an occasional hole filler of an anarchic development. As such it will never be enough and always inadequate in itself.

On the other hand, for as much as it is mobilised for certain ends, technology always needs long periods to repair emerging problems. When it does finally mitigate them, the damage has increased and scattered in different directions from those for which the same technology was conceived and applied. It is like a greyhound chasing a mechanical hare. The paradox is in the fact that the dog will never catch the hare.

In this the role of environmental and territorial planning emerges, for the creation of preventive equilibria, which are planned in advance, in land-use, in an overall comprehensive vision including both the development and conservation of the environment and the territory itself.

But, surprisingly, an awareness of the role had in environmental, urban or regional planning for the balanced development of the territory, is not found even in many experts on the 'ecological' or sustainable city. They have succumbed - so to speak - to dealing with the various problems in a sectorial way, with recourse in particular to technological solutions (which have the dubious results indicated above).

3

Difficulties are had almost in recognising that the real 'ecological city' is obtained only with the same techniques and ways of traditional land planning, which (if correctly understood and technically and professionally advanced) has always been, or should have been, the instrument for the study, design, and realisation of the 'equilibrium' between pressure and availability of land, between 'activities' and resources, in short, between the supply and demand of 'environment' which makes up the base for ecological equilibrium.

And difficulty is had in recognising that if measures of intervention are not studied and realised on the scale of a territorial unit which constitutes an appropriate ambit of equilibrium, these measures are destined to not achieve this equilibrium, and thus to fail.

***

The chapters contained in this volume are based on a series of interventions which the author has carried out, on different occasions and from different angles, in recent years, with the exact intention of focusing on the fundamental condition necessary for the success of policies for the 'ecological city', and to re-examine methods and criteria for environmental and territorial planning in order to allow these to respond, in a correct way, to emerging political demands in this field.[6]

All these chapters are based on a unitary conception of the development and conservation of the urban environment, and aim also at denouncing the mystification surrounding the subject which has become very fashionable. This mystification, in fact, tends to perpetuate the problems rather than resolve them. The hope of the author is only that this book will warn people against proposing and implementing solutions without first solving some critical and methodological nodes; measures which may represent - if put into action without the appropriately set out planning requirements - only a huge waste of resources and initiatives.

***

The author would like to acknowledge the contributions of several people who have helped him in the editing of the work.

Neil Campbell has contributed to a not unreadable English translation of a text that, at the same time, has been faithful to the author's thought and style: a doubtful and heroic venture. Joseph King has given advice on the intelligibility and the communicability of the work. Ruth Duffy took care of the expressive and typographical consistency.

My colleagues Phil Cooke and Peter Nijkamp, notwithstanding their, on the whole, encouraging assessment concerning the contents of the book, also gave precious suggestions on the readability of the text that the author has tried to adopt, without knowing for certain whether he has been able to implement them.

Fulvia Banchi and Marcela Bulcu, together with other collaborators of the *Planning Studies Centre* of Rome, have helped to make feasible and tidy the access to the bibliographical documentation of the PSIS, the "Planning Science Information System", that the Centre itself has developed and maintained for some time with funding from the (Italian) National Research Council.

Although the book reflects - as said - a series of interventions relatively recent of the author, it also represents a distillate of a long experience of work and reflection matured within the Planning Studies Centre of Rome since its foundation (1963) until today; work which has its roots in other past works. For instance, some important roots can be found in the collective book on the "city-region" published in 1966 (see Archibugi ed., 1966), in the territorial scenario of the Progetto '80 (see Ri, Ministero del Bilancio e della programmazione economica, 1969 and 1971), and in a further series of other works oriented to urban, regional, and territorial planning in Italy at the national scale (for example: Ri, Ministero per il Mezzogiorno, etc. 1983). Thus, it is correct to recall and acknowledge, at this time, my colleagues and friends who have shared that work experience in its different phases, from the oldest to the most recent. Apologising for sure forgetfulness, I would like recall: Bruno Ferrara, Vincenzo Cabianca, Roberto Cassetti, Annalisa Cicerchia, Rosa De Rosa, Maurizio Di Palma, Maurizio Garano, Franco Karrer, Alberto Lacava, Giuseppe Las Casas, Claudio Mazziotta, Piero Moroni, Calogero Muscarà, Massimo Pazienti, Valeriano Pesce, Sandro Petriccione, Giorgio Ruffolo, and Umberto Triulzi.

Finally, all the anonymous interlocutors - mostly the author's students, but also colleagues and friends - who have stimulated the author's thinking and therefore the development of the reasoning of the book, and without whom the necessary intellectual stimulus would be lacking, deserve an acknowledgement.

Notes

1   For example, in the first four 'programmes' of action of the European Commission for the environment (1973-76, 1977-81, 1982-86, and 1987-92), the city as such is never mentioned. We have to wait for the

fifth programme (1993-2000) before the Commission takes the initiative to elaborate a 'green paper' on the urban environment, on the basis of which the Council of Ministers then decided to launch an urban policy, or urban environment policy, on a Community scale. In the operational structure of the Commission, a Directorate was formed for the Environment (DGXI), but only recently has there been a service instituted aimed at the problems of the urban environment. Urban problems, in the Community services, have continued for a long time to be treated in a scattered way, in various 'Directorates': that of 'Regional Policy' as responsible for everything happening in the territory; that of 'Social Affairs' for urban problems considered essentially social problems and relative to the social environment. If problems of urban transport or research into urban management technologies, the Transport or Research Directorates were directly involved. But despite recent attention to urban problems, a unified European policy relative to these is still to be achieved. The elaboration of such a policy, entrusted to a Committee of inter-governmental experts has still not reached a clear direction: it is somewhat sacrificed, with respect to the traditional 'naturalistic' approaches, within the same Directorate for the Environment; the other Directorates have continued to follow their policies without recognising the importance of co-ordination, partly because of an absence of good criteria of co-ordination (the 'inter-services' co-ordination proclaimed is the least implemented in the history of Community activities). The urban environment continues to be relatively ignored in the fifth Community programme of environmental action.

2   See on this the bibliographical references: Nl (Government of the Netherlands) (1988-89, 1990); Jap (Government of Japan) - Environment Agency (1986); Rf (Secretariat auprès du PM chargé de l'Environnement...) (1990); Gb (Government of Great Britain) (1990); Ca (Government of Canada) (1990).

3   Ri (Ministero dell'Ambiente) (1992): we will discuss this plan in Ch. 8, and in more detail about its 'programme for the urban environment' in Ch. 9.

4   In the first place, some important documents have been prepared by the OECD and by the European Community (now Union). The following should suffice: OECD (Urban Affairs Group), Environmental Policies for Cities in the 1990s (OECD, 1990) and EC Commission, Green Paper on the Urban Environment (EC Commission, 1990). Among the

international conferences which have proliferated, the most important in our opinion are: a) the OECD conference on 'The Economic, Social and Environmental Problems of Cities' (Paris, 18-20 Nov. 1992); b) the international conference promoted by the OECD-EC-Berlin Senate on 'Urban Environmental Improvement and Economic Development' (Berlin, 24-26 Jan. 1989); c) the 'international forum' promoted by OECD-UNEP on 'The Global Environment and the City' (Osaka, 2-3 July 1990); d) the European Community Conference on 'The European Future of the Urban Environment' (Madrid, 29-30 April 1991); e) the 'workshop' of the 'European Foundation for the Improvement of Living and Working Conditions' on 'Land Use Management and Environmental Improvement in Cities' (Lisbon, 6-8 May 1992); f) the International Symposium on 'Urban Planning and Environment' (Seattle, 2-5 Mar. 1994), promoted jointly by the Universities of Washington (USA) and Groningen (Netherlands); and g) the more recent European Conference 'On Sustainable Cities and Towns' (Aalborg, Denmark, 24-27 May 1994), promoted by the European Union.

5   On the subject, the literature, both scientific and popular, is reaching enormous quantities. Concerning the scientific, or presumed scientific, we select some works that, it seems to us, are most informative and exhaustive, even if not oriented specifically to the problem that animates the reflections of this book. See the essay by Douglas (1983); the set of essays edited by Nicoletti (1978); by Elkin et al. (1991); by Stren, White, and Whitney (1992); the Gaia Atlas of Cities edited by Girardet (1992); the handbook by White (1994). For the policy of interventions aspect, see Waste (1989).

6   See the list at the end of the volume.

1 A strategy for the modern city:
Research lines aimed at the identification of 'optimal centrality'

1 The definition of the current urban problem

1.1   The terms of the modern urban question

The main problem today for cities and urban organisation in Europe (and also in other economically developed parts of the world)[1] can be summed up (with all the imperfections of any summary) in the tendential conflict between two fundamental goals of urban settlement, which become two contrasting goals of urban policy:

1   Ensuring a high level of access to the functions of 'superior' urban services that produce the city effect, which no modern citizen is prepared to give up (or which would be a policy goal guaranteed for all citizens).
2   Guaranteeing that the concentration of urban services (necessary for the city effect) does not produce such an overloading of functions as to make liveability unacceptable or unsustainable from the environmental and social point of view.

The two contrasting goals pervade the current 'urban question', characterising:

– on the one hand, the contemporary tendency for a 'total' urbanisation of the population;
– but also, on the other hand, the current effort to clean up the urban environment, which is compromised by pollution, traffic congestion, social separation and disintegration, the degradation of the urban landscape, etc.

It is the second of the two objectives (that of 'liveability') which has captured the attention of town-planners and the public in the debate on the future of the city.[2]

The first objective, that of *city effect* - to be ensured for all citizens - has been considered the automatic result of the urbanisation tendency, understood as a tendency of all citizens to live in cities (whether large, medium, or small) or near to them; or at least as the result of a general tendency not to give up, as happened in the past for important portions of the population, the city's superior services, i.e., those which produce the *city effect*.

If anything, this first objective has been considered achieved automatically, not only with the tendency to urbanisation mentioned, but also with the effect of modern telematic technology, which greatly reduces the need for the spatial concentration of urban services whose access can be reached aspatially or telematically, i.e., making the city not a physical fact or system of 'distances', but rather a system of abstract communications via cable (the 'wired' city).

Moreover, in the current debate on the city, there is a tendency to consider that telematics modifies the actual concept of 'city effect': not by eliminating it completely, but by eliminating the way in which it was seen to be produced only by the proximity of the urban services and the catchment mass.[3]

Thus, not only is urbanisation considered the main factor, achieved automatically, of the solution of the need for the city (or of city effect), but it is also considered likewise that the city effect is transferred in this way to another territorial scale other than the urban one; more precisely to a meta-territorial, meta-spatial scale. In this way, either the need for the city disappears (it is considered a physical fact), or it is automatically resolved by the progress and application of technology.

From this conception, which considers technology prevalently exogenous to the development of the city, it results as well that the said technology not only makes the objective of achieving the city effect superfluous, but also tends to resolve automatically, or 'naturally', the second fundamental objective mentioned, that concerned with the recovery of the urban environment or 'liveability', or ecological city, as is said nowadays. If the city effect is not of a physical nature, if the city is not going to be a 'non-city', then the effects on liveability and on urban degradation (congestion, pollution, etc.), which today are essentially produced by spatial, territorial 'overloading' of the urban services, are eliminated with new technology; it is sufficient to give the time and means to apply it.[4] The wired city is also a clean or ecological city and vice versa.

Naturally, this vision of a given automatic tendency on the part of technology to resolve both the aforementioned fundamental town-planning objectives, rests on the postulate that the need for the city, of for the city effect, may be satisfied in an aspatial way, or over distance, with telematic means. If this was not completely true, or at least only true in part, the expected automation (or the action limited only to promoting it, or rather to accelerating the application of the wired city, as the main - if not only - solution to the problems of the city) would be translated into a seriously negative factor for the achievement of the two basic objectives under discussion.

In fact, if the implementation - on which efforts would be concentrated - of the wired city were not to satisfy fully the needs for the city and did not achieve the city effect, then the physical factors would subsist in favour of urban concentration and the demand for 'centrality'. Nothing would have been done to achieve the city effect (the first objective), and thus doing, the factors which - in seeking the city effect - create the overloading of the city and consequent degradation, would be left to operate unhindered, and without an alternative strategy. At the same time, the achievement of the second fundamental objective would be delayed: the recovery of the urban environment.

Leaving aside, nevertheless, whether telematics and information technology reduce, or replace, the need for the city,[5] the same over-attention for the problems of the urban environment (the second objective) - which today are manifested in such a widespread and redundant way - when accompanied by an equally widespread lack of attention for the problems of the city effect, tends to realise a negative effect with regard to its own objective of recovery and city liveability. In fact the logic of systems, which is the logic of inter-dependencies (which commonly tends to be ignored), tells us that in this case, if it is true that the overloading of the cities is favoured, or rather determined, by the citizens' desire for the city effect, the equilibrium of the load could be obtained by trying to produce the city effect in another way (or elsewhere), and not by ignoring it.

In conclusion, what we wish to emphasise here is that the two objectives in question are inversely dependent in their pursuit: i.e., the tendential actions which pursue one, create damage in the pursuit of the other. And that, consequently, a correct policy of territorial achievement of the two fundamental objectives of the current urban question must at the same time deal with one and the other, without preference. In fact, the greater chance of obtaining results in one relies on the success of the other. Otherwise, the efforts aimed at the success of one risk being inefficient and inane.

1.3 The role of the city effect

This joint attention for the two objectives is relatively absent in the current debate.[6] Today the 'ecological' city and the single city liveability factors are examined in essence.

Enquires into tables indicating the liveability of cities, which use 'liveability indicators', recurrently point out that the most liveable cities are small and medium-sized, and definitely not the large metropolises.[7] But these enquiries never tell us, or they never ask, why, despite their decidedly higher liveability standard, they are not chosen as preferred locations, even by their most dynamic citizens (the young, the 'brains', etc.). The most obvious answers (often of a deductive and not inductive type) are that in these cities suitable work opportunities do not occur. But we should ask ourselves then why these work opportunities are not developed. And why, all things given, are the unliveable cities preferred to the liveable ones, both in terms of contemporary production settlements (jobs) and for homes. The most obvious answer, and also most ignored, is that in the first the city effect is enjoyed, whereas in the second it is not.

We will never manage to make the unliveable cities more liveable, on the one hand, and the liveable cities more appetising on the other, if we do not manage in a different way the city effect in the unliveable (because they are overloaded) cities, and if we do not create a city effect in the liveable cities. In short, in each case it is the city effect which constitutes the key to sustainable urban development, and liveability is a function which must be considered a variable dependent (and not independent) on this.

We repeat: this inter-dependency, which from being negative must become positive, between the two objectives of contemporary urban development, is not always present in the current debate. On the contrary, it tends to be neglected even when the separate terms are understood well. The objectives of liveability and/or local identity[8] are not necessarily in contrast with those of sociality. They are in potential contrast however (and unfortunately widely practised, judging from almost all the European urban experiences) with the objective of the city effect. This occurs also because the latter is strongly conditioned, as said, by a demographic urban dimension (with the constraints of commuting accessibility)[9] and by a catchment area which is important enough to ensure the co-presence of all the superior urban services which are indispensable for its production. We can call it the 'critical mass' for obtaining the city effect.

2 Two situation typologies in western urban geography

2.1 Large cities and medium-small cities

Despite noteworthy differences in the urban history of European countries, and of the derived urban framework, the 'urban question', as we have briefly indicated above, is emerging in a substantially uniform way both in Europe and (with some differences which we will discuss later) in the entire western world.[10] This may provoke, or allow, a remarkable convergence of approaches in urban policy on the European or American scale, founded on the development of 'new urban concepts'.[11]

In the urban geography of nearly all western countries (we are referring to the European countries and also to the United States), a situation is arising which can approximately be summed up thus:

1 On the one hand, we have important and larger cities *which have reached the highest levels of the city effect* (the great capitals, metropolises), but which, exactly because of this, are the object of a growing overloading of functions, with respect to their territory; this overloading is degrading any urban quality and factor of liveability. We can call these LC type urban situations.

2 On the other hand, we have small and medium-sized cities which, despite once being important cities and having recently recovered functions and population increases (because the overloading crisis of the great cities has placed them in an advantageous position), *have not yet reached sufficient city effect levels*. We will call these SMC type urban situations.

The two situations must be analysed separately, because they present a somewhat different phenomenology from many points of view. But they must also be analysed in their mutual relationship because they are largely interdependent in any concrete national reality.[12]

13

The LC type cities already enjoy the city effect; they may have too much of it, in the sense that often the necessary 'critical mass' is over-abundant in relation to the territorial resources available and the degree of concentration inherited from the past.

In fact, because in the past this agglomeration took place by spontaneous gravitational force, an overloading has normally been seen of the 'historic' centre, and a sprawl-like expansion, with the creation of 'peripheries' which, albeit autonomous, always depend, for the city effect, on the congested historic centre. The result of all this is the loss of human sociality ('sociality'), of a sense of belonging and identity ('identity'), and environmental liveability ('sustainability').

The SMC type cities, whilst suffering sometimes in some central points from traffic congestion, or pollution, or urban landscape: degradation, have in comparison to LC type cities a liveability or an urban quality which is decidedly higher. In recent times, the shortening of distances (due to the lowering of transport technical times) and the telematic technologies have strongly increased the chances of these cities as places of settlement, both for residential and production purposes.

Recently, the SMC type cities have drained the exodus from the country - where it still persists - to a greater extent than the LC type cities; this has given the impression of a larger expansion of the same and of a sort of 'de-urbanisation', as has often been said.[13] However, all this, in the majority of cases, is rather the product of the statistical error in not considering the increase of residents of the municipalities of the first, second and third band around the central band of LC type cities (hit by the spill-over phenomenon) as belonging, in the comparison, to that of the sprawl-like expansion of these cities.[14]

Therefore, the cities of SMC type certainly enjoy greater sociality ('agora'), 'global-local relationship' and/or 'local identity': but have unfortunately also the defect of not reaching the critical mass for producing the city effect. This simple effect makes them vulnerable in comparison to the general increase in urban quality. They will continue to lose more sophisticated strata of residents (the 'brains' or class leaders) with a damaging effect on the quality of the sociality itself. A good part of the pre-existing fixed social capital (health, education and cultural infrastructures), will be under-used, discredited and abandoned by sufficient maintenance: with the effect of not indifferent environmental degradation. The residents, despite the environmental liveability, will become more and more frustrated by a sense of marginalisation, in as much - we must not forget - at the levels of the city effect of the past, that many of these SMC type cities, enjoyed a good and satisfactory position.

All this is translated into a great waste of territorial and urban resources, and in a persistent flow of functions towards the LC type cities, with a further aggravation of their overloading crisis, which will worsen even more the environmental crisis in the sense mentioned above.[15]

3 The potential alternative solutions

3.1 The two goals of urban policy: the city effect and liveability

Thus, city effect and liveability - whilst both representing two unrenouncable goals (as said at the beginning) for any modern urban policy, which is common to the conditions of any urban situation - are presented in such a way as to lead to two different town-planning strategies in the two city typologies, even if they are nevertheless very complementary and interdependent strategies.

In the LC type cities, which are rich in city effect but lacking in liveability, the problem is posed of finding the ways and means to resolve the problems of liveability ('sociality', 'identity', 'sustainability'), without compromising the existence of the city effect.

In the SMC type cities, with good liveability standards, but which are lacking in the city effect, the problem is posed of finding the ways and means to realise the city effect, without compromising liveability.

3.2 The interdependency between the two policies

The two policies - which are somewhat different, and which will probably suggest very different operational solutions, and merit anyway being studied in a very different way - have something in common (besides the two general goals mentioned): they have in common the fact that they are strongly interdependent. The success of one, in fact, will inevitably depend on the success of the other.[16]

It is unlikely that a policy aimed at resolving problems of liveability in the LC type cities will be successful if the settlement flow continues in these cities well over the critical mass levels which have conferred on these cities the level of centrality that they enjoy. As said before, it would be like greyhounds chasing after a mechanical hare. The liveability desired would never be reached, and the environmental, social and technological policies (enacted in order to lighten or better distribute the overloading of these great cities) would not have the capacity to be last over time; and therefore they would represent an irrational and disordered waste of resources. Their level of effectiveness with regard to the goals would be very low.

This flow of settlements would be destined inevitably to continue if in the cities and territories in which these flows originate the city effect is not produced which is able to hold on to the citizens who now desire more and more to enjoy modern urban life to the full, without restrictions (as happened in the past). Therefore the success of overloading 're-equilibrium' or 'depolarisation' policies, to be implemented in the LC type cities in order to improve liveability, depends strictly on the success of policies to improve the city effect in SMC type cities.

Vice versa, it is unlikely that an increase of urban functions could be realised in SMC type cities (wherever and on condition that the indispensable critical mass to obtain a city effect) if we continue to invest means and resources in the strengthening of LC type cities, spontaneously growing, and if we continue to invest in the accessibility of these cities on the part of ever more distant territories as an apparent answer to a spontaneous demand, which today is justified only because real alternatives are lacking. The success of an attempt to increase polyvalent urban functions in these SMC type cities, and a sort of alternative 'polarisation' to that of the great cities (of which we will outline the requirements in the following paragraphs), depends only on the success of a policy of depolarisation in the LC type cities.

In this sense, the two policies - although different in their contents - are strongly complementary and synergetic.

Notwithstanding this, it is very important that the diversity between the two policies - whilst supported by the same principles or criteria - is substantial. It gives rise to very different subordinate strategies.

3.3   The typical strategy for the larger cities (LC type)

In the appropriate policies for LC type cities, the strategy must respond to the question 'how to decongest, loosen up, lighten the hypertension towards the single, historic, city centrality in question?'; or, in other terms, 'how to decentralise the functions?' In fact, it seems that without this decentralisation of loads, which go above the acceptable loads for liveability, any environmentalist policy is destined to be precarious, based on chance and unsuccessful.

In the history of any LC type city is found some attempt to decentralise functions; but these attempts have rarely been successful: in the direction of suitably alleviating the (more or less historic) centre, the 'downtown' area, of its hyper-functions, and thus of its environmental degradation, and at the same time creating peripheral alternatives capable of being self-sufficient with regard to the centre.

The whole history of town-planning as a discipline since its first steps at the end of the last century and at the beginning of this one (for example, the intervention by Ebenezer Howard and his disciples, Raymond Unwin and Thomas Adams, who were the first theoreticians of modern town-planning) is marked by the problem of 'decongesting' the spontaneous centralities of the large cities.

The garden city by Howard, Unwin and Adams; the *ville radieuse* by Le Corbusier; the rebuilding of the city by Gropius; the Brodoacre City by Wright; the innumerable urbanism 'charts' (starting from the famous one of 'Athens' by CIAM of 1933); and almost all the guiding ideas which town-planning has brought with it - despite their different solutions - have not done anything, other than rotate respectively around the same problem: how to decongest the city from its concentric pressures and from its excessive pressures with regard to the available territorial resources, and how to ensure an environmentally 'liveable' character? From this point of view, the contemporary excitement about the 'ecological (or sustainable) city' seems to be only the current version - more banal than innovative - of the eternal town-planning problem.[17]

3.4   The typical strategy for medium and small-sized cities (SMC type)

With a suitable policy for SMC type cities, the strategy must answer the question: 'how to increase the urban functions of the city to the point of reaching such an effect as to adequately withstand a comparison and competition with the quality of the services provided by LC type cities?'. In other words, 'how to create a centrality which is sufficiently important and competitive?'.

In this case as well, attempts are not lacking. Rather, a tendency is common to almost all SMC type cities to take on - in one way or another - new functions which enhance services and image. Each centre tends towards 'parochialism'. And each 'parochialism' reaches some goals. But much more often it achieves such a dispersion of resources, that it nullifies the apparent advantages, without reaching any strategic result. In the worst cases, the local initiatives, unless they are supported by an economic rationale, tend to fail after making initial progress. In this case as well, the waste of resources is great and the effectiveness of the policies is very low.[18]

4 The dossier of parameters to be transferred in terms of reference

4.1 The need to provide the two policies with greater cognitive instruments

The knowledge of constraints in each of the two policies is often lacking, i.e., of the conditions which have to be respected for the feasibility of a strategy such as that indicated. These constraints must be the object of study, research and experiment.

In the traditional experience of town master plans in European cities, more plans have been faced without any knowledge or definition of these constraints (and, moreover, without them even being taken into serious consideration) than those which have taken them into serious consideration.

The studies envisaged by the EU Commission[19] seem to constitute a wonderful opportunity to proceed to an initial greater knowledge of such constraints and parameters of an urban strategy, on the European scale.

We start from the conviction that the research aimed at the action must above all be oriented towards providing the planning operators involved with cognitive instruments in order to work, respecting the constraints mentioned above. Any action aiming at resetting the city balance concerning the overloads on the one hand, and an absence of centrality on the other, must be able to start from an assumption of parameters (of accessibility, loads, performance, cost, etc.) which the research must supply.

The studies carried out up until now, although imperfect and insufficient, tend to show that now the urban centrality which counts does not differ much from city to city, whatever their historic origin (administrative, industrial or port, etc.). Thus it is very probable that the proposal will give, as a result, rather similar answers, notwithstanding the differences between the cities empirically examined.

4.2 The necessary cognitive instruments postulated

In particular, these cognitive instruments may, it seems, be treated and developed (for the purpose of obtaining the first technical-scientific answers) in the framework of a traditional approach to urban and regional planning: as instruments to promote the city and its regional basin as local interactive networks.

For this reason, we will develop considerations on the specification of the arguments presented in the introduction, in the form of questions - and consequent potential answers - which the research desired should propose, in any implementation of the approach suggested.

5 The suggested approach: searching for the optimal centrality

It has been said that the strategy applied to the LC type cities should answer the following question: 'How do we decentralise the great cities?'.

And the first answer expected to such a question (we have also already said) is: 'to make sure that decentralisation takes place by "units of decentralisation" which represent alternative centralities to the current overloaded centre, and which are sufficiently strong and important to compete with the centre to be counterbalanced'. Otherwise the action is destined to fail from the outset.

Likewise, the strategy applied to SMC type cities will have to answer the following question: 'how do we produce the city effect in the small and medium-sized cities?'.

The first answer expected for this question is: 'to make sure that such centres reach in some way (linking up between themselves, becoming agglomerated, interacting with appropriate networks and systems, above all of privileged intercommunication, etc.), a "critical" mass which is sufficient for them to compete with the force of attraction of the great cities'. Otherwise any effort to increase the coefficient of city effect within such centres will inevitably be not enough for the aim pursued, and consequently ineffective and unsuccessful.

In both cases, nevertheless, the work must be based on a concept of sufficient or, rather, optimal 'centrality', and of a sufficient catchment 'critical mass' or threshold, in order to produce the indispensable city effect: this concept is hardly known however. Neither are the effects which various technologies may have on it, or on its single components, such as telematic and information technology which are expanding at such a great rate.

Thus the first aim of urban studies today should be to examine such a concept of optimal centrality in depth, and how this concept can be a support for urban planning choices, and finally how it can be determined by a range of already available technologies, or which are to be promoted.

19

The qualitative and quantitative definition of optimal centrality is therefore a preliminary goal of research (formulated in the aforementioned way) which is indispensable for the support of both strategies and policies to be pursued in the large cities and small-medium ones.

The problem of optimal centrality, as posed here by us, recalls a sort of relationship with one of the classic themes of the so-called 'urban economics' (which is nothing but an application to the economic relations of the 'aggregate-city' of the general theorems of economics *tout court*). We are referring to the theme of 'urban size', or that of 'equilibrium city size' and the 'optimal city size' of cities.[20]

This relationship which undoubtedly exists is, however, so weak in the epistemological approach that it begs a brief interlocutory comment. In order to make it more directly aimed at its purpose: the search for the optimal centrality for which we have postulated the necessity for the formulation of a policy guideline for urban systems on a national scale.

6 The search for optimal centrality and the abstract 'theories' of urban economics

On the optimum size of cities - if it exists in the first place, and what conditions determine it - there are dozens of theoretical analyses which have added up to a very vast literature which we have no intention of summarising here.[21]

We would only like to point out that the explanatory or interpretative models of the urban phenomenon, and in particular those connected to the 'positive' identification of the optimal city size[22] - models which aim at the definition of the existence of a city, or of the city agglomerate, 'equilibrated' or 'optimal' - have little pertinence to our problem. In fact, admitting, although not completely accepting, that they can be useful for understanding urban organisation for what it is, as it manifests itself to us, it is likewise our opinion that they have little usefulness - given the operational[23] problem with which we are faced today - to determine what should be the optimal urban dimension.

All this implies a question of approach to the problem (which we are dealing with) of optimal centrality, on the subject of which it is obligatory to give a brief clarifying comment, at the risk of deviating from the argument.

By 'sophistication' of the reference models, we mean the procedure of reasoning, usual in neo-classical economics, which starts from functions (models) that are simple, rich or loaded with 'assumptions' (concerning both the number of variables in play, and their dynamic stability which is expressed in the well known expression '*ceteris paribus*'), then gradually 'relaxes' such assumptions, by introducing new variables and new relations (relaxations and extensions which - as it happens - are always introduced in the name of 'greater realism').

6.1 The 'ballet' of assumptions

Taking for example a procedure which is pertinent to the regional and urban economics,[24] we can summarise it in the following stages or steps:

A.   A start is made from a simplified function of a single object (let us say the household) which chooses its place of residence. It is supposed (and/or taken for granted) that this choice takes place on the basis of certain factors. An attempt is made to classify such choice factors in an exhaustive way and it has been proposed that these are included in the following four categories: 1) accessibility (to goods and services); 2) space (habitational area of the land or dwelling); 3) environmental amenities; 4) distance from the town centre; and that this choice has two constraints: a) budget and b) time available.[25] Already, the selection of such (but also any other factors and constraints) implies an assumption: that these are exhaustive.

The function-model which derives must rest - from the start - on a series of assumptions:[26] 1) that the referred-to urban area is monocentric; 2) that there is a relatively important radial system of transport; 3) that the territory is flat. Other assumptions necessary for such a simple model will be: 4) that the family (although later all the institutional subjects at play will be introduced) intends to maximise its function of utility (in a way subject to the constraints of budget indicated), understood as the sum of goods and services to which access is possible (apart from the territory, because otherwise the whole pack of cards of spatial economics would fall!) and the consumption of territory (for example, the size of the residential lot), which implies that the function of utility is continuous and growing to any increase of the above-mentioned consumption (goods and services and residential space), which is not always a valid assumption; 5) that there is an ever-increasing cost for transport, etc.

B.   But then, such a model (defined as 'basic') may be made more sophisticated, relaxing it from the assumptions of the few variables on which is has been organised: for example, introducing into the model: 6) the 'time' factor (cost in commuting time).[27] In such manner, the maximisation of the utility - by the single household - becomes subject also to access times constraints. Therefore, there can be introduced: 7) the 'structure of the household' factor, which - while assuming supposed 'rational' behaviour - may also make possible behaviour that is very divergent whilst in the same preceding framework of functions (by structure, for example, as variables to take account of, the number of components and the number of active persons who work in the family).[28]

C.   Thus, to the 'basic' model (concerning the behaviour of each single household) is added the more 'realistic' circumstance that the household is never alone in deciding a localisation, but in fact competes with all the other households: for this reason the concept of 'competitive equilibrium' in land-use is introduced, which refers to the fact that the decisions (theoretical and rational as supposed) of all households, taken under the constraint of a given curve of land rents, must be mutually coherent and compatible; and in particular that there are the conditions for equality between the supply and demand of land-use. And, since the balance between supply and demand does not seem necessarily to be a desirable condition, although indispensable, the concept of optimal allocation of the land-use still needs to be defined.

But, already the condition of equilibrium of the territory assumes the concomitant presence of other particular conditions (thus of other assumptions) which alter the validity of the starting model: for example, 8) the perfect information of all the operators (households and owners) of the land rents in the territory itself (in our case the city). Furthermore, 9) that no participant, or selected group of participants, may exercise a monopolistic power. As an alternative it should be assumed that each operator will receive the land rent in the city as given (which constitutes a further assumption).

D.   But this is not enough. Subsequently, the equilibrium model, in order to function, needs to choose between two other cases: 10) if it is applied to a population 'exogenous' to the city (for example the model itself could be called the closed-city model), or, 11) if it is applied to a population (households) of the city which are free to move without excessive expenses within the confines of the city itself (open-city model).[29] Furthermore, some other important variables which condition the functioning of the model (and which link in particular with the two preceding ones but obviously interfere also with all the others) are: if there is a case of 12) absent land ownership, or 13) public land ownership.[30] In the first case - still with the assumption that all households are similar - the assumption is in force that the supply of bid rent varies in a decreasing proportion to the distance from the centre. In the second case, the possibility is introduced that the determination of the supply of rent is not the individual utility of the land owner but an undefined 'public utility'. By itself, this hypothesis renders insignificant the entire construction of a model of this type, even if it obviously does not dismantle its intrinsic logical-mathematical consistency (which draws on other factors, which, however, have nothing to do with the object of urban economics).

In any case, because of the presence alone of this possible extension of various hypotheses, which follows a sought-after 'realism', there arises a 'casuistics' of crosses between assumptions which multiply the formulations of adaptive models (which are called, euphemistically, 'refinements').

E.   But, even if the equilibrium is assumed to be possible - at the condition of respect for the set of assumptions and/or specification or 'casuistics' above mentioned - the analysis continues to be made more sophisticated through other cases or hypotheses. Leaving aside the hypotheses that are being born from alternative objective functions[31] (that are obviously the basis of measurement for the optimality and that would be valid, even in any case of a decisional model, which we will come to again below),[32] we recognise that the land-use equilibrium can even be influenced by other parameters (and parameter changes) as such: 14) agricultural rent, 15) population, 16) household income, 17) transportation costs, 18) estate and land ownership taxes, 19) zoning. How could we forget these elements within our model?

But, to take account of these elements complicates, terribly, the calculability. If the intervention of these other factors is analysed, one by one - while the model keeps its simplest form or while the extensions are also dealt with, one by one - it is possible to achieve a theoretical configuration that in some way is effective, although abstract. But if all of these variables enter the field simultaneously, a free-for-all is created of which we cannot assure the governance, even through the most advanced and potent of the analytical and mathematical formulations and formalisations.

F.   Despite all of this, the reality is still much more complex, and it escapes any effort that to capture it easily within a framework. With all of the variables introduced, we have worked with the assumption (in this case it would be more correct to call this a premise or postulate) that all individuals or households be of only one type: all similar and of similar behaviour (a postulate that is also less realistic).

In this way, it restarts from the beginning toward the introduction of the model and in its formalisation of the 20) typological multiplicity of the decision-makers.[33] The function of the 'bid rent' of the household type has been displayed according to a 'curve' of the same bid rent based on testing (as in the case of the unique subject) the existence and uniqueness of the equilibrated and optimal land-use.

However, all this has required other assumptions, for instance that 21) of bid rent functions are ordered and obedient. The problem seems to be only by itself, mathematical:[34] at which 'formal' condition the bid rent function and the related lot size function, can be acceptable as determinants of locational choice, and in this way, of the theoretic validity of the model?[35]

G.   The desire, in any event, to fix the law of development of land-use on the basis of theoretical assumptions related to the subject behaviour[36] has not stopped here. In fact, the reasoning coming from the behaviour of the household and firms with respect to land-use and locational choices has assumed an enormous quantity of hypotheses and simplifying assumptions all founded on that assumption (quite abstract and unrealistic) of only one 'centre', in a world without competitive centres. It is the monocentric hypothesis. In such a way, it has been obligatory also to introduce the principle of spatial aggregation by itself, or of the 'city function'.

Here the theory of urban economics approaches our problem a little bit more. An explanation of the city through the principle of the economies of scale and the externalities produced by it has begun. In relation to what? Who knows! In relation to the non-city,[37] or - more reasonably - to a range of many possible and effective centres of different sizes that produce economies of scale and different externalities: so that we have a curve of economies of scale and externalities for each type of cost and benefit taken into account (or in other words, we have as many curves as we have types of costs and benefits taken into account).

From a substantial point of view, this side of the path of 'regional science' approaches, as we have said, the problem of optimal centrality as we have posed it. But, even here, it is necessary to clarify in which sense and with what limits this connection could be acceptable.[38]

6.2   The standard theory of the agglomeration and of the urban size

The standard theory of the advantages, or benefits, of agglomeration tend to group such advantages in the following categories:

1 Advantages in the field of available resource and transport;
2 Economies of scale;
3 Externalities and costless interactions; and
4 The variety of choices in consumption and production.

Each of these categories constitutes, for the theory of urban economics, a component of the 'urban function'.

Normally, such advantages are counterbalanced by the disadvantages or costs that the urban agglomeration produces in terms of time, and nodes of accessibility, and thus, in terms of transport costs. One of the more current assumptions is that the transport cost increases proportionally to the commuting distance between residences and the 'urban' central place.

Usually, it is assumed that the presence of localised natural resources (minerals, natural harbours, natural beauty, etc.) favours (but, it would be better to say that it favoured, in the past) the formation of urban agglomerations. We cannot ignore, in fact, that by now - in front of the pre-existence of cities in the urban structure of the territory (and this is valid overall for the western countries but it is also valid for those non-western countries that have new territories to develop) - these factors are strongly superseded by other factors, most importantly the simple fact of urban pre-existence; and their (natural resources) impact has almost completely vanished.

The economies of scale (in consumption and production) are, instead, the most important factors. And, it is well known that such economies of scale pertain, essentially, to the indivisibility of certain exchanges of goods (persons, residences, factories, infrastructure, public utilities). The indivisibility of persons produces a labour specialisation; and the infrastructure cannot be used effectively if not on a large scale. The efficient co-ordination of many specialised persons, of infrastructure, and of production processes requires the proximity of all such factors, always improved by communication services and helped by the savings in transportation of products and raw material. From all this, it follows that the median, comprehensive, production cost of a good will be less to some extent if it can be obtained on a large scale and within contiguous localisations. And, even the relationship of productive 'interdependencies' between different sectors can give advantages through the proximity of the productive process. Furthermore, even many public services (such as schools; hospitals; electricity, water, gas and other utilities; and even roads) are factors that are susceptible to economies of scale.

Even the 'technological externalities' represent an important urban function. It is a matter of advantages that are collected without paying a price. And the same is true for those intangible externalities that come from the larger quantity of cultural and recreational exchanges; in a word from a higher social interaction that the scale of the city offers.

Finally, the variety of opportunities and choices that the scale of the city offers is another important and recognised factor of agglomeration. The higher freedom of choice produces (at equal price) a greater utility for consumers; and thus, a greater income (to the extent to which 'utility' means 'income': which it is not always wise to assume).

All of these 'factors' of an increasing utility intervene in the production of a 'complementary effect', economically advantageous, which - along with others that are by nature also intangible and always more present in determining the behaviours and motivations of the users of the city - can be called, as we have done, the 'city effect'.

In urban economics more in-depth study, of course, has been tried regarding the city size under the profile of the functions of economy of scale and externalities. For simplicity, we will speak only about externalities.[39] And, even in this case, the use of the expressions certainly is not satisfying if we do not also clarify the reference framework of the analysis.

Indeed, since the institutions of the economic system are (from the point of view of modern system analysis) interdependent, what is an 'externality' for one institution can be an 'internality' for another. This fact is often neglected in the use of the expressions, neglecting, also in this way, to make explicit from which (institutional) point of view we are proceeding with in the analysis.

Since we have internalities and externalities that are reciprocally both positive and negative, we know well that a positive externality from the point of view of a firm can be specularly negative for the household or for the community and vice versa. But, it is not necessarily the case: we must see case by case. In fact, a complementary effect can occur which operates, not only for the benefit of the individual unities of each institution, but even between unities belonging to institutions that are not only by nature competitive as normally are those of the same institution (household vs. household, firm vs. firm, community vs. community) but even conflicting as happens to the unities belonging to different institutions (households vs. firms, and firms vs. communities).

Besides, even overtaking in a certain way the logical semantic problem mentioned above, there continues to be even more substantial defects of approach in conventional urban economics. Even accepting that it could be possible to set (and at the same time to solve) the problem, making explicit the concept of positive externality (that we have called city effect) and the concept of negative externality (that we have called overload); and even taking care to make explicit the institutional point of view from which we are looking; until we have defined the positivity and negativity thresholds of the externalities, it will not be possible to confront the operational problem of giving an optimal size to the city. And, neither will it be possible to evaluate the policies of intervention or the corrective measures to restore eventual theoretical condition of equilibrium.

In such manner, operationally, we must define the optimal level of the city (always in conformity with the objective function that must be predefined as in any elementary scheme of operational research) at that level of urban goods for which it would be meaningful to research the complementary effect that we have called city effect.

In the abstract models of 'explanation' of the city, for example, attempts have been made to introduce - as said above - the externalities.[40] But on this point, the concepts are not at all clear in the literature, and poor references are made to the contents and the empirical correlatives that we have called indicators. At this point, it seems to be very necessary to make a bridge between the urban economics and the empirical analysis of the indicators (and their relative selection).

6.3   A policy-oriented (planological) approach to the definition of the optimal size of the city

At this point, in effect, we can pose questions to ourselves regarding the standard path of urban economic theory.

The first question is the following: given the current modelling[41] and taking into account all 'principles' of the spatial economy, already abundantly elaborated,[42] would it not be better (in the sense of more useful and more practical) to start from objective functions or preference functions, based on the real conditions in front of us, and directly expressed by the decision-makers, without making a 'theory' about them founded on abstract assumptions?

And obviously, is it not better to adapt the procedure to the future decision-makers concerned (households, groups, responsible politicians); and adapt it to the environmental and spatial level at which we are studying such choices and decisions (programming, projecting or planning)?[43]

This last approach, that I will call policy-oriented (or programmatic, planologic, or decision-oriented), marks a turning point in the traditional and dominant approach in economics, an analytical/positivistic approach, since it legitimises this process only within the limits of an intellectual exercise which - if prolonged without critical spirit - becomes superfluous and without exit, i.e., sterile.

27

This type of approach produces, what elsewhere I have been pushed to call (with a certain amount of roughness), the syndrome or neurosis of casuistics.[44] Starting from elementary functions, people are induced - from their evident incapacity to represent reality in its complexity - to introduce even more numerous complications in the attempt to trap reality in its multiple manifestations and 'cases'. But this process, by its nature endless, never will be able to give reliable answers. What is tried, in effect, is to trap (or 'explain') reality within interpretative models which try to give an account of all cases that have not been included in the basic (simplified) model, until finally, the result is a proliferation of models, complicated and sophisticated, which are used only to decree, actually, the dissolution of every model.

Moreover, the tool of mathematics is today at our disposal to give to the language the aspect of a logical rigorousness in this endless and circular cognitive process, achieving the maximum scientific appearance with the minimum of operational utility and truth.[45] Two profound connoisseurs of mathematical epistemology and its applications to the social sciences and especially to economics, Frisch and de Finetti, irreverently, have called this syndrome: 'playometrics' (which de Finetti translated into Italian as 'Baloccometria').[46]

The trouble is that in the evolution of economic thinking (and in the other social sciences), this syndrome is increasing, perhaps because of a scarce familiarity with economic studies that have foundations in logic and philosophy; and it is not by chance that the most sceptical regarding to the theorems of the neo-classical economics have been just the mathematicians that have occupied themselves with epistemology.

Little attention has been given, in contrast, to the fact that the variables on which any function or modelling is based in the economic and social sciences are variables relative to 'human' behaviour subject to the liberty of evaluation and choice: i.e., behaviour unpredictable enough *ex ante* in positive terms, but determinable *ex ante* only in decisional terms.

In sum, in the social and economic sciences, the most important variables (on which all modelling is based) are those of the human preferences (individuals, groups, cultures, nations, etc.). And, these preferences are determinable only as functions of value judgements, which change with time, and which it is possible to assume as effective only in the moment in which they are expressed and influence concrete decisions. It is doubtful that rational behaviour could be determined (by who?) on the desk through abstract hypotheses in the models, and it is doubtful that these choices can prejudice, in the decisional phase, the choice between alternatives that the models themselves put on the desk.

The structure of the variables in play, and therefore the structure of the models in use, must reflect - in the selection of the variables themselves, or in the selection of the relationships between those variables, or in the assumptions of the parameters on which basis are registered such relationships - the nature of the problems on the field; and must reflect, overall, the values on which basis the decision-makers (of whichever kind and level) make their decisions, given the constraints that those values will represent.

From this, it follows that our problem of the search for an optimal centrality, albeit assimilated in the logical formulation to that of optimal urban size developed in urban economic theorems, diverges from it strongly, because it is taken for granted that the search itself will implicate the search of the welfare indicators not in the sense of possible variables of a positive analysis, but in the sense of possible variables of a decisional analysis. In this way, they will be indicators which some hypothetical decision-makers must, in a certain way, select and apply in order to achieve the plan objectives.

7 The imperative research approach

Thus the most important line of research for urban planning should firstly be devoted to examining what are the constraints and conditions necessary so that strategies and planning interventions (in each situation given) have a possibility of success for the following: realising an adequate centrality and acquiring an adequate catchment area critical mass.

Since both the strategies and policies of 'decentralisation' (for the LC type cities) and 'centralisation' (for the SMC type cities) would be founded on the notion of 'optimal centrality', or rather on feasible and sustainable centralities, it is imperative to carry out a number of phases of research:

1 To study and define, with appropriate 'qualitative' and 'quantitative' indicators, what the essential components are which ensure and produce such an 'optimal centrality' and what critical mass can constitute its efficient justification.[47]

But, since any conceptual study of the components of centrality, however irreplaceable in a study which aims at action, and not only at the mere recording of past phenomena, cannot but arise from theoretical reflection, nevertheless this too deserves to be supported with empirical observation. A research programme, therefore, should also propose:

2   To study and illustrate what are the essential functional components which have produced today - or which are currently clearly producing - centrality, in a vast range of urban cases and situations.

Having gathered and defined sufficient information and knowledge for these first two phases, the programme should then proceed:

3   To examine the urban framework, in order to research concretely what 'solutions' could be proposed for a reorganisation of this framework, in a coherent way with the results of the previous two phases.

8   The definition of optimal centrality and its constituent parameters

The first operation, the definition of optimal centrality as outlined above, must be developed along lines and sectors of analysis which will be listed here in brief.

As mentioned, in the first place the 'components' of such a centrality would have to be defined and the role that each of these has, for itself and in relation to others.

8.1   The demographic component

First among these is the demographic component, i.e., the area of potential users of the centrality in question.

Much has been written and said on the production of urban services which produce the city effect, but we are still far from having formulated threshold evaluations which are adequate to support a homogeneous strategy, such as that at which the studies are aimed. The urban studies would therefore have to arrive - by means of a screening of the most important literature on the subject - at a statement relative to the minimum threshold catchment area to achieve the city effect.

8.2   Frequency of use of superior urban services

The other essential component of centrality - which interacts with the demographic component - is the frequency of use of superior urban services, which normally is a function of income, and of the availability (per capita) of opportunities and resources.

A variable which is quite influential on the said frequency of use is the lifestyle of the interested populations, even if the growing homologation of lifestyles in advanced western societies is noticeably reducing any such differential. It would be convenient in future urban studies to develop these aspects and arrive at some conclusive judgements concerning the effect of such factors on the average behaviour of the consumer or user of urban services.

8.3   The accessibility to superior urban services

Another component of centrality is represented by the accessibility to superior urban services and is expressed in terms of access times and costs.

Here the parameter within which the acceptable thresholds of access to such services can be measured is that of 'dailyness', i.e., a parameter linked to the acquisition of such services within the time span of a day and the return to one's home at night. This is the parameter which may concern the city effect, and the actual concept (however wide) of the 'city'. Other territorial 'accessibilities' which involve travelling and transport in the life of individuals, do not concern 'urban' accessibility, but rather the accessibility to other forms of spatiality use (holidays, business, professions, politics, etc.). They have an 'inter-city' dimension, rather than an 'infra-city' one, and cannot be considered as indicators of urban functionality. Naturally accessibility linked to dailyness does not imply that the access to the single service must be daily: it is enough if - when desired - it has the potential to be acquired by the user in the daily time span. Some services, whose frequency of use is very rare for any user, can be judged as not constituting the city effect, and are therefore excluded from the list of services whose presence produces the city effect (whatever their frequency of use by the citizens). For example, is the presence of an ordinary season of symphonic concerts or that of an adequate number of philately shops or art galleries to be considered essential to produce the city effect?

In conclusion, the accessibility (or presence) of superior urban services is an essential component (to be specified) to characterise centrality, of which this type of research would need to map the features. For brevity's sake, these have been defined as 'superior', in order to distinguish them from other services which - however important and essential (perhaps more essential than the superior ones) - are not necessary indispensable for the city effect (e.g., secondary schools, hospitals, cinemas, sports facilities, etc.). The aim which this type of research should pursue is to examine the definition of 'superior' in depth, and to discuss, with a wealth of argument, the importance of the services which make up centrality and define it. In particular we will discuss for each of these, what its predictable future will be on impact with the new technologies, in particular telematics and information technology: will this impact result in the substitution of daily spatial accessibility, or in simple 'integration'? Or will there be no impact? This discussion will take place, case by case, but always with an eye on the problem of 'centrality' (which produces the city effect), and its new face, with its consequences on the parameters sought, which are to be provided for town-planning.

8.4   Sufficient public spaces

Another fundamental component for centrality (which is very bound up with that of accessibility to superior services) is that of sufficient public spaces. Since such spaces (open, closed, monumental or otherwise, formal and informal) constitute, nevertheless, an ingredient which characterises centrality, as a factor of potential convergence with social and public life, in this case as well, its characteristics and necessary dimensions should be better defined.

As has been said, such an enquiry is strictly linked to that of superior services, many of which are also public or imply the occupation of public space.

8.5   Mix of fundamental spatial functions

Another essential component for the territorial delimitation of centrality is the existence of a mix of fundamental spatial functions. The research in question should pay attention also to this intuitive requirement, which is often used in order to contest a particular traditional approach to the 'zoning' of activities (which in past town-planning experience was perhaps applied in a too schematic and dogmatic way, but which is unlikely to be avoided in the future, even if production technologies have clearly modified the terms of the question), not in order to suggest architectonic solutions which achieve the 'mix' of spatial uses on a building scale, as much as to qualify (and quantify) the requirements of centrality, in the spirit of the method and reasoning followed up to this point. Such requirements in essence concern:

1 The physical possibility of locating any typology of production installation, without which the feasibility of centrality and its functions is substantially compromised;

2   The physical possibility of absorbing, recycling and 'metabolising' pollutants and waste within the space and catchment area of the centrality itself (apart from specific cases in which appropriate technologies allow for the management of such pollution on a meta-urban territorial scale);

3   The physical possibility of satisfying, with adequate quantities of 'free' nature and greenery, the 'urban' needs for outdoor recreation of the users of the said centrality.

8.6   Urban structure and morphology

Among the components to be described and analysed is urban structure and morphology which is capable of guaranteeing efficient functioning.

By structure we mean here, for example, the presence and definition of a 'load-bearing axis', of an 'intensive area' and of a 'free area' (which can be assigned specific coefficients of differentiated density); of lines of development in conformity with its morphological articulation (for example: 'linear', 'stellar', 'reticular') on which the future territorial organisation can be conditioned coherently.[48] Standard values should be expressed for all these elements from theoretical judgements or from surveys of satisfactory situations.

8.7   The communications network

A final component for the territorial delimitation of centrality should be a description, with a wide breadth of vision, of the communications network which is essential in order to ensure the efficiency of the centrality in question, having explored - service by service - the appropriate nature and technology for its accessibility.

Among the communications 'networks' discussed is placed first the traditional one of urban transport in its multiple forms (public and private, individual and collective, goods and persons). A research strand should examine what technological opportunities are offered to each of the components, examined above, of centrality - having a role in producing the city-effect - from the point of view of future technology. But, it should be dedicated above all to exploring the technological instrumentation of transport and communication available for the needs of the city (or city effect), identified in social integration, in local identity, in environmental compatibility, which are the postulates of the planning approach indicated above.

It can be gathered, from this list of components of optimal centrality that such centrality is based anyway on a 'basin of a sustainable catchment area', which is self-sufficient and not a mere collection of urban architectural monuments. All the studies would thus be oriented towards the vision of a territory (region, or otherwise) which acts as a basin or system for a set of inter-human or inter-social relations, which are explicated in that 'dailyness' which produces the city effect.

In short, there is a need to 'qualify', and also 'quantify', with suitable indicators (of load, state, meaning, result, achievement, etc.), all the components of the city effect as they are developed in the said basin, or area or region; and which on their part have been chosen as having an effect on the city effect and on the function of centrality which allows it.

9 The components of centrality as found in the current western urban situation

Based on the definition of optimal centrality as developed above, the next phase should aim at gathering an appropriate dossier of information through the survey of current 'urban situations', from which can be verified the state of things, in relation to the centrality, of which we will attempt to configure the standard values.

The urban situations which could be examined and evaluated, will vary from case to case and from country to country.

To give concrete results to this line of research, these 'surveys' should have relatively common approaches. Without a common approach it would be difficult to compare the results. This is why the selection of the urban situations to be examined and evaluated should be influenced by common criteria, and the survey should be based on equally common questionnaires.[49]

The common selection criteria could be the following:

– the selection of urban situations on the basis of the representativeness of some general factors in common to all centralities (for example, classes of width, or other differential geographic factors, as the case may be: e.g., climate, for the indicators of heating emissions;
– the selection of urban situations on the basis of possibly different lifestyles which deserve to be borne in mind;
– the selection of urban situations also on the basis of the need to highlight (by their exclusion) specific factors not having an effect on the theoretical

centrality sought (e.g., some specific roles: capitals or particular administrative centres).

10 Configuring an articulation of optimal centralities

A third phase, based of results of two first phases should be an attempt to distribute, in the territory, a reorganisation of the centralities which bear in mind the two goals given in para. 1:

1 Elimination of the possible overloads of the centralities acquired by the great cities;
2 Modes of acquisition of centrality for the medium- to small-sized cities.

Together with the reorganisation of the centralities of the type indicated above, it would be useful to proceed to the concrete formulation of initial proposals for the strategy of urban transport to be adopted in each of the urban systems 'designed'.

A scenario would be thus configured of a future organisation of the urban framework of a country, region or supra-national territory, etc., which could give rise to political evaluation and decision-making procedures; but it would start from some technical assumptions of parameters and indicators inspired by a largely common evaluation.[50]

Once this has been acquired by the political decision-makers, the said scenario could carry out a set of functions which are commonly assigned to these scenarios: a) freely guide the actions of the designers on various scales, sectorial and territorial, in which they happen to work; b) orient the decisions of a number of bodies which operate in the territory, for the purpose of conforming to situations which are tendentially convergent and, therefore, synergetic; c) constitute the appropriate territorial reference for further operations of research and evaluation.

11 Conclusion

In this first chapter, we have described a particular approach to the study of urban policy (and in particular to that of policies aimed at the improvement of the urban environment, and at greater equilibrium in urban development with the use of the urban resources available). This approach is distinguished by the attention given to the constraints considered unavoidable for the 'city effect', understood in the modern sense. The general basic thesis of the approach is that any effort aimed at improving the urban environment which does not bear in mind these constraints is useless, and destined to fail.

Town-planning, despite its long evolution (in this century), and its many schools of thought, has not gone beyond the 'minimum units' constituting the city: whether these were 'garden cities', the minimum units of housing (Le Corbusier), the satellite towns and 'new towns', or the 'periphery' units or 'suburbs'. Town-planning has developed arguments for and against concerning how the use of these units might constitute the best form of the city. Town-planning has also assumed the cities (big, small, medium, tiny, etc.) on which it is called to intervene with design, as they offered themselves for analysis. Town-planning has still never either elaborated or discussed the concept of the 'minimum unit' of the city, the minimum requirements so that a city can be had, or real urban life.

Up to now, town-planning has dealt with how to build *in* the city, but not how to build *the* city.

It seems to us, in fact, that - as 'science of the city' - town-planning cannot ignore dealing with the city, starting from the normative concept of the city, as a point of reference for developing its choices and techniques of optimisation of urban space. This seems to be the essential starting point for 'scientific' town-planning.[51]

This chapter has also given the general outlines of an 'agenda' of research aimed at studying and quantifying, with the appropriate indicators, the constraints which we consider relevant to the city effect. In brief, an agenda of research has been developed, aimed at elaborating both indicators of the city effect and indicators of city overloading.

Whilst a vast literature has been produced relating to policies in favour of the sustainable city, with undefined confines, with regard to city effect indicators we know very little, and research is practically at the starting point. Policies and urban plans manifest a clear ignorance of these indicators, and thus of the constraints which they represent for their efficiency.

At the same time, the greater knowledge of environmental impact, better known, has not resulted in the elaboration of indicators of urban loading sufficiently coordinated with those of the city effect; thus with regard to 'overloading' indicators (connected to the presence of indicators of city effect) we know very little. The overloading indicators, or the (complementary) ones related to optimal loading, are an essential ingredient as well for the evaluation and quantification of the concept of optimal centrality. Until we carry out appropriate research in this field, we will not have the necessary instruments available to evaluate optimal centrality, which represents in turn the indispensable guidelines to make the policies for the improvement of the urban environment efficient (the ecological city, sustainable city, etc.).

We will move now, in Ch. 2, to a critical analysis of the problems of a policy for the improvement of the urban environment and for the construction of the 'ecological city'.

Notes

1   For an overview of the literature on how the urban 'question' has matured, see the works by Pred (1977, 1978, 1980 and 1988) and Hirschorn (1979). But for a more relevant and acute approach to the present urban problem, I would like to recommend the works by Harvey Perloff on 'the planning of the post-industrial city' (1980), and by Peter Hall (1977, 1978, 1980, and 1988) on the 'city of the future', the history of planning in the 20th century and the disasters of planning. Other works of a general nature may be interesting as well for an overall acquisition of the current urban problem; for example: Bird (1978); Goldfield and Brownell (1979), Drewett and Rossi (1984); Ravetz (1986); Van den Berg et al. (1989); Herson and Bolland (1990); Perulli (1992); Breheny (1992); Drewett, Knight and Shubert (1992); Simmie (1993); and the collection of essays edited by White and Burton (1983); Gottmann and Muscarà (1991); Getimis and Kafkalas (1993); Perulli (1993); and finally other documents deriving from activities of the European Commission (EC 1990, 1994a, b and c).

2   See, for instance, the initiatives listed in the introduction. A good overview of initiatives taken in many European countries in recent years in favour of and experimenting with innovative processes, is contained in the volume produced by the European Foundation for the improvement of Living and Working Conditions (1993) of Dublin, and in the summary contained there by V. Mega (1993).

3   On the wired city as well, much literature has developed, although the journalistic approach has largely prevailed over the scientific one. Good references to the set of research carried out in this field is in the collective volume by Brotchie et al. (1985), in particular the essay included by J. Dickey (1985) and R.L. Meier (1985). Work should also be recalled by M.J. Webber (1982) and T. Mandeville (1983). I would like also to recall the noteworthy amount of interventions on the subject from Italy collected by Corrado Beguinot, over several years of promotion of studies and debates on the 'wired city' (see for all C.

Beguinot, 1987, 1989; T. Giura, 1992; and C. Beguinot and U. Cardarelli, 1992) at the University of Naples. The specific phenomenon of telematic networks for the innovation of the city has been discussed and evaluated in a large number of works: amongst which we would happily mention Camagni and Rabellotti (1990), Camagni, ed. (1991), Camagni and Capello (1991) and Graham and Marvin (1994).

4   This is, for example, the pervasive attitude which emerges from the majority of works on the 'ecological city' which are proliferating at the moment. On reflection, this in fact was the attitude of the first experts who dealt with the subject in the 1960s: for example, the works of M.M. Webber (1963, 1964, 1982, etc.).

5   A vast panorama of the possible impact of new technologies on the future city is in the collection of essays on the 'future of urban form', already quoted, edited by Brotchie et al. (1985). See also Newton and Taylor (1985).

6   There are naturally some exceptions (for example, Conti, 1990), but still rather tending to see the problem from the angle of technological innovation.

7   See for example a collective work edited by Elgin et al. (1974); an essay by Burnell and Galster (1992); and a work by Grayson and Young (1994).

8   For example, in a recent interesting document for the organisation of a research programme for the EU Commission (called 'City Action Research') (EC Commission, 1994a), three fundamental objectives for a modern urban policy are listed: to create: a) the conditions for greater social cohesion and development ('agora city'); b) conditions for better local identity, in respect to global homologation ('global-local city'); c) conditions for environmental conservation and sustainability (the 'sustainable city'). The agora city can be indifferently considered as analogous to the city effect, since social cohesion in the city may be strongly conditioned by the achievement of a critical mass of events and users which produce this social cohesion (level of human inter-communication; we may recall the studies by R.L. Meier (1962). But it can be considered a fundamental prerequisite of liveability. Thus also the global-local city (or 'glocality' as it has been called with a curious but not pointless neologism) may be considered a requirement both of the city effect and of liveability, according to the point of view chosen (on the concept global/local see also Knight, 1992b; Lipietz, 1993;

Mazzoleni, 1993). Whilst the sustainable city is decidedly an attribute of liveability.

The most important thing to remember are the dialectic inter-relations occurring between the three or two requirements, which produce situations of optimal or dosed choices (trade-offs): 'to what extent are we prepared to lose in sustainability or liveability to obtain the agora or city effect?' and vice versa. And what do we have to do to reconcile to the utmost possible one with the other objective?

9   On this subject see a work by Clark and Kuijpers-Linde (1994).

10 In the 'third world' the differences of urban organisation are very different to those of the 'western' world. And such differences would imply analyses substantially different from those applied to the western cities. The strategies as well could be very different. Such a comparison leaves aside nevertheless the objectives of the present analysis which only concerns the European situation and that of the West.

11 To use the terminology of the terms of reference of the European Union Commission Actvill Programme, mentioned in para. 1.3.

12 This is what has been done in the 'Quadroter' research promoted by the Italian National Research Council as a 'strategic project' in which is hypothesised in Italy the identification of 37 urban eco-systems, founded essentially on the effort to 'franchise' the small and medium-sized cities from the attraction and supremacy of the large metropolitan areas. (See Chs 8 and 9 for more details about Quadroter.) For a more general examination of the relations between centralities and cities, see Bird (1978).

13 On this phenomenon there are many descriptive analyses which have grasped, nevertheless, only some apparent numeric phenomena, and not their substantial meaning. We will return to this subject in Ch. 2 with more extensive reference to the literature on the subject.

14 To the extent that the actual phenomenon of 'de-urbanisation' or of 'counter-urbanisation' would deserve to be called 'hyper-urbanisation'. See for the studies mentioned references in the following Ch. 2, para. 4.

15 Many of the studies recalled above talk a lot about the 'decline' of these cities, of 'competitivity' between these cities, etc. (see for the USA, Bradbury et al., 1982). But these concepts should be revisited in the light of the conceptual parameters proposed here.

16 The interdependency which we are postulating on the scale of an entire country (and which often goes beyond the boundaries of a single country), draws on the logic of system analysis. For more details see a

contribution by the author (Archibugi, 1990b). Many aspects of interdependency (which today are included in the term 'competition') have long since been highlighted by experts on urban problems: see the collection of essays edited by Mesarovic and Reisman (1972). Interesting information is in the volume by Neiman (1975) on 'metropology'.

17 We will return to this point in Ch. 4 with further considerations on the relationship between ecology and town-planning. For more complete information about the views of the author on the entire evolution of town-planning thinking, see the Theory of Urbanistics: Lectures on a Reappraisal of City Planning Foundations (Archibugi, 1995), where an overall review of the foundations of town-planning itself is attempted.

18 It is advisable to remember this type of consideration when support and revitalisation policies are launched for 'medium-sized cities'. See on this subject the results of a meeting-survey promoted by the 'European Foundation for the Improvement of Living and Working Conditions' (European Foundation, 1994). The strategic lines for the medium- and smaller-sized cities will be reconsidered and deepened in this book again in Ch. 3 (paras 4 and 5.2), Ch. 8 (para. 4) and Ch. 9 (para. 4.5).

19 We refer in particular to the Actvill programme already mentioned, but the same is also the case in many other programmes in course or being developed in other EU sectors (urban environment, regional policy, social policy, transport, etc.), and by other international bodies (OECD, World Bank, etc.). For rapid information about these programmes, see some recent EU Commission documents (EC Commission, 1992 and 1994-99).

20 According to the above-mentioned theorems, equilibrium city size in the simplest model is defined by the (diagrammatic) intersection of the curve of population supply with the curve of population demand of the city. And in order to determine the optimal city size the surplus function of the city must be maximised (see, for example, Fujita, 1989, p. 133).

21 Among the first systematic studies there is the well-known contribution by Alonso (1971). Other contributions are in Neutze (1965-68), Evans (1972), Richardson (1972), Knox (1973). See also the more recent approaches in Bullinger (1986) and Begovic (1991).

22 Whatever the complexity and relative sophistication of such models, based on an abstract or 'theoretical' behaviour of the subjects: individuals-families, companies, collectivities, states, etc.

23 The word 'operational' is used here in the usual sense adopted today in 'operational research'; i.e., with the meaning that a problem becomes operational when a multiple number of possible solutions is conceivable, between which one is selected as 'optimal' in relation to a preference function previously prescribed. To the extent to which such a definition is accepted, two things become essential: a) the system must have open goals; and b) a defined preference function must be formulated. But in other senses as well we can understand the use of the word 'operational': a) in the meaning that only observable concepts are used, for which empirical correlates may be determined (in a particular context on the basis of various possible existing or creatable statistical sources), which we will call indicators; and b) that the method of reasoning is quantitative (or also qualitative, but in some way measurable quantitatively), in such a way that the planners and (on the basis of their work) the political decision-makers are helped in the process of the formulation of coherent and feasible plans and programmes.

24 And which corresponds to a large amount of the evolution of 'regional science'.

25 Here we are at the earliest stages of the theory of localisation (Loesch, 1940; Isard, 1956, etc.). The classic and most familiar version - founded in fact on these hypotheses of factors and constraints is that constructed by Alonso (1964).

26 As does in fact the basic model to which we have referred (Alonso, 1964).

27 This extension has been discussed by a great number of authors; it is particularly dealt with by Henderson (1977). By some, the basic model, extended to include the time variable, has been augmented by the introduction of multiple forms of transport (see LeRoy and Sonstelie, 1983).

28 This sophistication has been dealt with, to my knowledge, for example, by Beckmann (1973).

29 It seems that the definition of 'open city' was introduced by Wheaton (1974).

30 The public property model was introduced by Solow (1973), and has been largely dealt with in works by Kanemoto (1980, 1987) on the 'theory of urban externalities', which we will come back to later.

31 In fact, in this case, another general problem is entered into, which extends far beyond the objective-function of localisation: that of the validity of a function of social welfare, as theorised by the modern

'welfare economics'. Without even touching upon the general problem of the function of social welfare (for which we would refer to positions, that are, in my opinion, definitive, such as those of Frisch [1971] and Johansen [1977]), here it is our duty to recall some critical adaptations of the theorems of welfare economics to the case of urban economics (still within the ambit of the route we have set ourselves: the successive sophistication of models of spatial-urban development). In fact, whilst in welfare economics, the function of social welfare is considered the sum of the utilities of the single families (but here also in the assumption of the non-pondered sum of identical families), in spatial-urban economics the levels of utility (and thus of social welfare) of albeit identical families depends on the localisations, and 'an unequal treatment of equals' is produced. Supposing, as is obvious, that we choose a level-objective of utility (or objective-function), and that this is chosen without concern for the various localisations of families, we will have to find the instruments (for example, taxes and subsidies motivated territorially) according to whether the utilities of the families is found to be higher or lower than the pre-established objective level.

32 See para. 6.3 below.

33 And we are still, and exclusively, discussing the household, the institutional decision-maker. But as we have said, there are also 'enterprises' as decision-makers and states (governments), which as well internally are not all equal or do not all behave the same.

34 On this point, see Ch. 4 of the work of Fujita (1989) and Fujita and Smith (1987).

35 But here, the question emerges again: if the theoretical validity of the model (even in itself!) is so difficult to achieve, and only on the basis of very complex mental and formalistic acrobatics, what can we say about its practical validity? And, at the conclusion of this path, emerges another demand: are we aware enough of the point to which we have arrived, dragged only by this mental exercise? We are pushed to ask ourselves if it would not be more reasonable (even if terribly counter-current) to invoke a return to a critical Kantian spirit against what manifests itself as a real meta-physics of the urban phenomenon; against a theory on the basis of which we build models without any capacity to be quantified and that seem good only for academic exercises, useful only to exercise the minds of students through mathematical equation solutions (only symbolic) but certainly with scarce operational utility.

36   Right now, we have spoken about households, but the same criteria could be applied to other subjects, such as firms, or the state or government, albeit for the last there are behavioural problems and choice problems and thus decision-making problems that are much more complex, based on objective functions much less simple regarding those of the institute, household or firm; problems that are less psychological and more sociological.

37   In fact, a good deal of abstract reasoning or modelling of this type has used, antinomically, the concept of 'countryside': but is it reasonable today to think in the western countries about the existence of a 'countryside' that is not part of the city function?

38   Which means a clarification of the way the optimal centrality is conceived in the 'regional sciences' and in 'planology'. For a more extended examination of the relationship between 'regional science' and 'planology', see Archibugi, 1993c.

39   The first functions can be distinguished from the last (in the Marshalian sense of the expression) with the fact the first are 'internal' and the second 'external' to the individual firms. This is less conceivable if the reference is made to the single unities of the institution-household instead of to the institution-firm. (The question becomes even more complex if the reference is made to the institution-state, -government or - community.)

40   This problem has been the subject in the literature of several formalised descriptions: some general, others applied to single portions of territory or urban function. For the general formalised descriptions see, for instance, two essays of Papageorgiou (1978) and all the second part of the work by Fujita (1989) which includes numerous bibliographical references.

41   A very well informed and critical illustration of the modelling developed by urban economic theory is in the second and third part of the work of R. Camagni (1991). Here, the models are grouped as follows: A. Static Model: a) 'of continuous space' (those of which we have made a rapid schematic reference in para. 6.1); b) 'of discrete space' (which are more adaptable for decisional modalities); and c) 'hierarchical'. B. Dynamic Models: a) 'aggregate models' (among them those macro-economic and those ecological/biological); and b) 'disaggregate models'.

42   Also in this case, we recommend the illustration of R. Camagni in the first part of the already quoted work, which enumerates the 'principles' (as he very opportunely calls them, where others might use the improper

term, 'laws' and others, again, the even more improper terms, 'factors' or 'criteria') of spatial economy. Camagni's principles are listed as follows: 1) Principle of Agglomeration; 2) Principle of Accessibility (or Spatial Competitiveness); 3) Principle of Spatial Interaction (or Mobility and Contact Demand); 4) Principle of Hierarchy (or City Order); and 5) Principle of Competitiveness (or Export Base). The modalities with which these principles are interwoven are not discussed, even if many models described later in the second part of the work (see preceding note) are strongly based on one and often more of the above principles. In reality, the effort to enucleate these principles from the spatial economy literature is an end in itself; it is didactic and taxonomic; and as such it is useful to put in order a literature that is somewhat in disorder. Toward this effort, we do not apply the reserves that we have pronounced about euristic (and even less operational) capacity of the behavioural models which try to replicate the functioning of reality. The principles serve not to interpret reality (as the models claim to do), but only to classify the logical categories that govern the knowledge of reality itself; and no more.

43   We mean, choices and decisions: on the goods or services to consume, on times and ways with which to access such goods and services, on the places in which to develop activities, etc.

44   See Archibugi, 1993c.

45   'The utility of this model is purely theoretical and didactic by nature,' the already quoted Camagni states (Camagni, 1991, p. 175), and he acknowledges that the most recent contributions on these themes 'have become often merely exercises of mathematical virtuosoism.' (p. 176).

46   For the special criticism of the conventional 'econometric' approach by Frisch, see some specific contributions (Frisch, 1964, 1970a and b); but for the general planological conception of Frisch, see his last, more meaningful contributions, posthumously published (Frisch, 1976); and for the critical work of de Finetti, largely convergent (and in part referential to) with that of Frisch, see at least two works (de Finetti, 1965, 1969 and 1973).

47   Obviously this examination could not be the object of factual analyses, but rather of conjectural analyses into which behavioural scenarios and life styles will emerge and predominate in the near future. Certainly it could be founded on factual analyses of urban situations in particularly dynamic environments and with a recognised leadership of socio-economic tradition and development. The most advisable technique for

delineating these scenarios is the consultation of experts (with Delphi methods, for example) in the various fields in which urban life manifests itself: from educational services, health, culture, recreation, etc., which characterise in particular urban life and quality. (For some further development of considerations on the methods of research in the field of town-planning, see Andranovich and Riposa, 1993.)

48   Some remarks, but still largely insufficient, on this point can be encountered in the literature. For example, see Breheny, 1992 and 1993.

49   See again, the already quoted work of Andranovich and Riposa, 1993.

50   The attempt at 'design' here suggested and proposed can only start from the methodological intention to provide a scheme of the final result of the set of research indicated. And this - whatever the level of examination reached both by research in operation a and by verification in operation b - must represent in the research stage only a 'first' attempt, which is very approximate, and destined to be subsequently perfected and completed during the territorial planning stage by the competent authorities. The attempt is suggested, as mentioned, in order to exemplify a method. The research processes at the base of the construction of such scenarios have been illustrated by the author with sufficient analysis, in another work (Archibugi, 19791-19822).

51   To which the author has devoted a large part of his attention with regard to urban planology, and whose results are condensed in the quoted work currently under publication on the 'Theory of Urbanistics' (Archibugi, 1995).

2 The degradation of the urban environment:
The planological approach

Before entering into the analysis of the possible strategy for responding in a valid way to the 'current urban problem' (as described and organised in the preceding chapter) - a problem which, as we have said, coincides in its aspect of 'overloading' with the multiple and recurrent aspirations for the 'ecological city' - we would like synthetically to list the factors of urban environmental degradation which most commonly and conventionally attract the attention of scholars, decision-makers and public. Subsequently, we would like to underline how - whatever the way of reading and recording urban degradation - its analysis brings us to identify some priority conditions for a policy of improvement of the urban environment:

– the need to choose a suitable territorial ambit (or of a 'policy-oriented' type) in which any factor of degradation may be adequately 'managed' and contrasted, in the sense of the control and recycling of impact factors (we will call this ambit the 'urban eco-system');
– a method of definition and choice of goals that a policy of improvement of the urban environment proposes (priority, given the constraints, preferences, etc.) by means of the evaluation of the suitable indicators of environmental well-being (a method that we will call the 'planological' or 'policy-oriented' approach).

Naturally, in giving our catalogue of factors which undermine or compromise today a satisfactory urban environment (para 2 and 3), we will sum up what has been described widely by an abundant literature, without dwelling too long on each of these factors (and pointing out where we have drawn our information and where the reader should go for further of the same). Since the purpose of this book is not to inform about factors of urban degradation, but rather to critically relate them with town-planning strategy, we will be likewise critical and succinct in this catalogue.

At the same time, in making a catalogue of possible goals, and linked indicators of control and achievement which concern these goals, in what we have called the planological approach (para 4 and 5), we will refer only to some amongst the best known programme schemes and indicators formulated both internationally and by some centres of study, without considering this catalogue to be completely exhaustive, because it is not the intention of this book to constitute a manual of environmental planning.[1]

In the following chapters, we will proceed to examine in depth on what 'principles' and with which analytical policy-oriented instruments it will be possible to ensure a policy of the improvement of the urban environment.

1   General considerations on the degradation of the urban environment

It is without a doubt that environmental degradation - and in particular that of the urban environment - of cities and towns has become one of the most serious problems of European urban citizens (the 'urbanites'), who represent - one can say with the help of certain statistics at hand - 80% of the European population.

It is difficult to state with certainty whether the seriousness of such a problem derives more from the absolute increase in the level of degradation of the urban environment with respect to other periods of recent urban history, or from the relative decrease in the level of 'other' problems (for example, of income, of consumption, of welfare and well-being in general) which have found a certain relief, allowing, therefore, the environmental problem to emerge. It is a fact, however, that the degradation of the urban environment has become a dominant factor in the social, and therefore also political, malaise of our times (as is, moreover, largely evidenced by numerous opinion polls, amongst which some conducted by the EC itself).[2]

It will be useful to evoke here rather briefly that this malaise in relation to urban environment degradation demands attention from diverse and complex points of view:

−   from the point of view of the different factors that provoke it;
−   in relation to the different types of cities in which it is produced, and
−   and in relation to the different 'stages' of the urbanisation process.

Here, in fact, the very same concept of the 'urban environment' referred to is in question: nonetheless we will not discuss this *per se* on this occasion, but we will treat it indirectly, examining environmental degradation from the three points of view indicated above.

2 The degradation of the urban environment in relation to its factors (or causes)

We propose to classify together the numerous factors of urban environment degradation, roughly in five principal categories: a) physical pollution; b) congestion of urban traffic; c) congestion of activities and paralysis of functions; d) disappearance of the 'urban landscape', and e) breakdown of human communication or 'social segregation'.[3]

2.1 *Physical pollution*

Physical pollution of cities is certainly the most serious factor,[4] above all for its effects on the physical health of citizens. It appears in its aspects of atmospheric pollution, of water pollution, and of waste pollution (liquids and solids).

Amongst all the environmental pollution that is found in cities (air, water and soil), the most widespread, the most serious and even the most insidious is atmospheric pollution. In western cities at least, where polluting emissions into water and soil are generally controlled by works of adduction and drainage, even if insufficient, atmospheric pollution is today definitely the most harmful to the health of urban dwellers.[5]

The atmosphere of urban areas is already notoriously considered as being subject to a meteorology worse than that found in non-urban areas: a lower level of sunshine (calculated at 20%); a great variability of temperature (1-1.5 centigrade on average, 15-20 in summer); low levels of atmospheric precipitation (15%); heavy clouding (100% in winter); a high level of relative humidity (5% on average); a slow wind speed (20-30% yearly average), etc. All of this is due to the different distribution and restoration of heat. It is well known precisely that urban activities, in particular urban heating and automobile traffic, form a 'heat column', that is not easily dissipated and which constitutes a hot air bubble, also called a 'heat island', which represents an important factor in pollution concentration. The suspended materials (called a 'dust dome') that are formed, and for which night-time humidity favours the condensation in mist, are transformed into suspended particles, which, before being able to dilute and disperse, fall back on the city restoring the pollution produced by the latter.[6]

It is well known that the main sources of urban atmospheric pollution are: a) domestic heating; b) vehicular traffic, with combustion engines, and c) industrial plants. It is above all on these three fronts that urban atmospheric pollution must be fought, using diverse and complex means. This does not mean that amongst the factors of atmospheric pollution often noise and bad smells are not of great importance: the first are above all a result of vehicular traffic, the second a result of the location of industry, especially of chemical plants.[7]

Atmospheric contamination, even if the most harmful, as has been said, today goes alongside other emergencies of water pollution and urban waste. In spite of the infrastructure that exists everywhere for these purposes, the absolute and concentrated amount of liquid and solid waste of the city has become such that a sufficient absorption capacity can no longer be found in this infrastructure and in the urban space that it occupies. The same non-urban spaces, in which such waste materials have until now been absorbed, are becoming all the more insufficient. Also because the (peri) urban space has extended, both as a material extension of buildings set up and inhabited, and also for the inclusion in the latter, with the aim of gaining urban access, of many non-urban or green areas, previously rarely frequented, if at all, and today often frequented as a result of the increase in spare time activities that were previously unknown and not practised. Even these green spaces, once considered 'rural' or 'countryside', are today saturated by urban pollution. Therefore, besides the atmospheric pollution problem, there is also the pressing emergency of water and soil pollution as a result of emissions and urban waste.

An emergency which calls for the research of an ecological equilibrium at a correct territorial level for the city, in a space which is precisely urban (even if the concept of urban will have to be redefined precisely to take into account this essential ecological equilibrium).[8]

2.2   Vehicular traffic

The degradation of the urban environment is today greatly caused by the congestion of urban vehicular traffic. This has greatly increased in relation to several factors: to the increase in the number of private cars per urban inhabitant; to the intensification of urban 'journeys' per car (private or public); to the increase in urban distances as a consequence of the absolute and relative increase in the number of urban inhabitants (urbanisation) and of their per capita consumption of land.

All this has produced a sort of 'garagisation' of cities, as well as a chronic personal 'traffic jam' in city traffic, which produces clear disturbances for psychic stress. Today a chronic and diffuse situation of 'time wastage' (or stupid employment of time) is accepted as a result of urban traffic, a situation of malaise whose solution has been found in personal adaptation, which, as a result compromises the same traditional 'advantages' of urban life: intensity of interpersonal relationships and exchange efficiency. In reality, such a situation causes one to dream of the return to decisively less 'civil' and less 'civic' forms of life than those that have been achieved mainly thanks to the historical development of cities.

In particular, European cities, especially those built on a Medieval and Renaissance structure, but also those planned with farsightedness on a structure of wide avenues by the eighteenth and nineteenth century monarchies, are unsuitable to support, for mere physical reasons of space, vehicular motor traffic in the dimensions it has reached. Every infrastructure and road intervention designed to adapt the dimensions to the traffic (one-way systems, urban motorways, fast lanes, by-passes, high-level and slip roads, underpasses, circular roads, co-ordinated traffic lights, and other such pieces of engineering wizardry) has caused and does nothing but cause serious and unacceptable damage to the urban landscape, producing, on the contrary, exactly the urban degradation that is to be opposed. [9]

2.3   Congestion of activities and paralysis of functions

Urbanisation, that is to say the striking growth of the urban population with respect to the non-urban population and the constant increase of urban functions compared with those of the cities of the past, has occurred without a proportional expansion of the urban infrastructure; rather it has occurred through a massive utilisation of the pre-existent and ancient structures (in particular the historical urban centres inherited from the past). This has congested beyond measure all the urban activities conducted in these old spaces: offices, hospitals, schools, shops, recreation and amusement centres. Even the pavements are congested and difficult to walk along (from which derives the growing 'pedestrianisation' of some parts of ancient cities, this also constructed work with a disproportionate access infrastructure).

Congestion has provoked a situation of paralysis of urban functions to which the reaction has been a search for new spaces for activities and for the reactivation of functions.[10] There has thus been achieved a spontaneous 'decongestion': the transfer of several city activities to the peripheries.

But while the old urban centres, as long as they conserved a certain equilibrium between activities and the spaces at their disposal, guaranteed a certain mix (non-congested) of functions, the new locations have achieved decongestion, but they have lost the mix. For this reason, there has come about - as a result of the congestion of activities and of the incipient paralysis of functions - a loss of 'complexity' of urban functions, a complexity on which urban quality has always been based. This quality loss is a further factor of degradation of the urban environment, which has been compromised by congestion and is further compromised by the decongestion that follows it.[11]

Certainly urban quality which is talked about here, furnished by the complexity of functions, is to a large degree an inheritance from the past, and it is difficult to reproduce it through new settlements. But it could have been possible and could still be possible, through simultaneous and, at the same time, preventive planning on urbanisation tendencies, to create new alternative 'centres' (without accepting the degradation of quality by congestion of our historical centres) with sufficient dimensions and complexities in their functions so as to constitute a real alternative to the historical one. These new centres should become, in a short time, with a minimum 'patina' of time, good examples of balanced urban functions, without therefore having to degrade their urban environment. Indeed, without starting off already degraded, as has almost always happened when such centres or areas are brought into existence without an adequate complexity of urban functions.

All this without considering the case (it is surely the case of Italy, but also of many other European countries built on an ancient urban structure) in which the urbanisation that has created the congestion of activities and paralysis of functions, has developed parallel to the emargination, if not even the decline of a great number of small and medium-sized cities; cities that would have rather been able to conduct the role - with a preventive planning policy - of these new and alternative centres of decongestion for which we are searching; conserving, and indeed updating their historical 'patina'.

But to do this it was necessary, and it is still necessary, to have a conception of urban policy at a national (and today supranational) level for the protection of the urban environment, which still must penetrate the conscience of political and administrative action; and of which there is still no tangible sign, either in Europe or in America.

2.4   Loss of the urban landscape

It is difficult to imagine that in the past cities displayed environmental degradation of their 'landscape' (understood in terms of a visual pleasantness of both their internal spaces as of their external perspectives) analogous to that which they display today. An empirical confirmation of this thesis derives from the observation of how well the 'urban landscape' has been nonetheless safeguarded in all those European cities (for example, East European cities) that have not been influenced (for amongst the most diverse reasons) by the phenomenon of economic development and by a considerable urbanisation (although these can have been on the contrary degraded by other factors different from those which are only 'aesthetic'.[12]

In cities which are quickly undergoing a process of urbanisation, in spite of the presumed technical progress in town-planning, land-use plans have only been able to control and to influence to a small degree urban space and land-use.

These urban spaces have been everywhere at the mercy of spontaneous, casual, deregulated, illegal intervention. (Without talking, moreover, about 'programmed' interventions - especially in matters of urban transport infrastructure - which, as has been said, in aiming only at the single 'function', have deliberately ignored the aesthetic criteria: we mean those which are possibly sheltered from changes in taste and therefore from the value judgements which time produces.)

All this has happened - we wish to emphasise - in spite of the fact that never, in the history of cities (except in the case of wartime destruction), have there been recorded so many factors which converge against urban conservation and against the harmonious growth of civic volumes and spaces (and therefore in favour of creative town-planning), as have been recorded in the past decades.

2.5   The breakdown of interpersonal communication

The physical degradation of the urban environment, including that which affects the physical and mental health of urban inhabitants, has been moreover accompanied by a sort of 'social' degradation - or of 'sociality' - of the urban environment, due to a breakdown in interpersonal communication: a breakdown born from the congestion already referred to above, time loss, loss in the complexity of functions of various places and of the specialisation of places and spaces.

In the traditional (and even conventional) opposition between 'city' and 'countryside', one can say that the breakdown of interpersonal communication in cities has turned the latter into a 'countryside of reinforced concrete': that is to say spaces where the same scarcity of interpersonal relationships are reproduced; such a scarcity that was once the sociological appanage of the countryside.

Information rather than communication has certainly improved thanks to the different technologies of telematics and computing: especially television and the incipient tele-video-communication (such as the video-telephone, the video-conference). But has 'sociality' improved in like fashion? This seems rather to have worsened, at least compared with the level of needs manifested by today's generations, needs that today's urban organisation seems incapable of satisfying.[13]

3 Urban degradation in relation to any city typology

One of the most surprising aspects of the degradation of the urban environment today is that it is revealed almost with the same seriousness independently of every urban typology: in other terms, whether large metropolitan or small and medium-sized cities are concerned; whether ancient, modern or even 'new' cities are in question; whether it is a case of 'pole' cities, or of 'satellite' cities; whether we are concerned with 'industrial' cities or cities whose activities are prevalently commercial or touristic.

Although the urban typology can influence the way in which different factors or aspects of degradation are presented and united, more precisely it may influence the 'mix' of the factors of degradation, the main part of the factors mentioned are present nearly everywhere; to the point that it makes one think that degradation is produced beyond narrowly urban conditions, but which by now represent a condition of every type of territorial agglomeration.

On the other hand, the 'urban condition' (as was once said, when it was not so generalised as today) tends to totalise the population, and therefore to englobe in its indicators and parameters each form of location or stable installation of people. The objective of a national (and even supranational) 'urban' policy can only be that which will assure an urban lifestyle acceptable to each citizen of the reference community and to make this community benefit from the 'urban effect'.

It is therefore a matter of restructuring the urban framework so as to englobe in a general urban function 100% of the citizens. The urban 'pattern' which results from this is a derivative of this constraining objective, linked - case by case - to the distribution of the pre-existing territorial agglomerations.

In this manner, the problem of urban typology must be 'revisited' in the light of the role that different city types can play in a general and 'finalised' rehandling of the urban framework.[14]

4 Urban degradation in relation to the stages of urbanisation

The ascertainment of urban environment degradation offers itself also independently of the current stage of urbanisation particular to each country, or to each agglomeration, which is in question.

In other words - adopting some classifications already in use - degradation is evident:

- in the presence of a phenomenon of 'urbanisation', defined as the rapid expansion of urban zones and a parallel residential decrease in rural areas;
- or in the presence of a phenomenon (normally successive to the preceding one) of 'sub-urbanisation', defined as that in which residences and work places transfer to the peripheries of the city;
- or in the presence of a phenomenon of 'de-urbanisation' (some have even spoken of a 'counter urbanisation'[15]), defined as that in which urban agglomerations lose residents and jobs overall;
- or finally, in the presence of that phenomenon which we begin to define as 're-urbanisation', when the 'heart' of the cities (above all of the most ancient ones) undergoes a residential recovery and, at the same time, a building restoration (the phenomenon defined also as 'gentrification').[16]

Yet no fixed relationship between the degradation of the urban environment and these stages of urbanisation can be found. On the other hand, these stages can in reality present themselves jointly on different territorial layers or in different regions of a same country. And this happens even if each stage is characterised in a country or in a city by their own dominant phenomena, linked essentially to a demographic indicator with its own precise sign.

This mix of stages, besides this 'indifference of effect' in terms of environmental degradation, reinforces the opinion that we are in the presence of a largely generalised phenomenon of degradation of the urban environment that is connected more to factors of general socio-economic development than to typology and urban pattern.

If anything, we must note a close relationship between the progression of the stages indicated above and the stage of economic-industrial development.

As such, it seems that urbanisation is remarkably contemporary to a primary stage of 'industrialisation', which has seen everywhere residents and jobs concentrated in already existing urban areas. This still occurs in all countries which are still in a more or less rapid industrialisation process in both Asia and Latin America (countries with urban histories considerably different from those of European cities).

It also seems that the stage of sub-urbanisation corresponds very well to a further stage of industrialisation, that of 'advanced' or 'excessive' industrialisation, in which the per capita product increases, and there develops a greater demand for more spacious and comfortable housing (perhaps with a private garden).

It seems, finally, that the stage of de-urbanisation corresponds well to the stage succeeding advanced industrialisation, that of de-industrialisation, that is of the absolute reduction of jobs in industry, and of growth, on the contrary, of tertiary activities; a stage, besides, in which the public infrastructure network of every type tends to cover the whole national territory, and the areas that were initially of a high urban density lose their 'comparative economic advantages'. This is also the stage defined by many as the 'post-industrial' or 'information' society.

And finally the re-urbanisation stage, which, in its early days, seems in fact to be a phenomenon which has only appeared on the scene of the cities of the economically richer countries.

It seems therefore that we can conclude that the degradation of the EU is to be linked to the advance of economic development rather than to different urban patterns and structures. And that these patterns and structures - in their current stage of development - are nothing more than a spontaneous and disorganised response to the imbalance that such a development provokes in the use of urban spaces.

This does not prevent, however, the urban pattern and structure - if conceived and planned appropriately - not being able to contribute in the future to the avoidance of the disequilibria that, through successive stages, economic development has produced in the territory, in the absence of planning.

It is only a question of reformulating the problem: that is identifying the appropriate territorial unit in which economic development can take place without creating a territorial and environmental imbalance; and tying each location and every further land-use to its functional modalities.

In short, it is a matter of identifying an 'eco-system' in which all the values of the modern urban condition can be not only respected but also extolled, that is to say an 'urban eco-system'.

And it is a matter also of using such an urban eco-system as a link and reference framework for all the choices of installation and location that any development policy should involve.

In brief, it is a question of adopting a 'planological' approach to the analysis of the urban environment.

5 The degradation of the urban environment from the point of view of the goals of 'environmental well-being'

A last way of looking at urban environmental degradation is that of linking it in some way with the possible goals of environmental urban well-being that may be formulated. In truth, this looking at and classifying the degradation is closer to the planological or policy-oriented approach that has been recommended. In fact, this way includes in its articulation the same problem of the choice to be made. The goals of well-being are implicit in any type of evaluation of the state of degradation. And any policy against degradation presupposes some alternative choices of the use of resources and of the means which are simply trade-offs between various goals. It is this which we will see better in the following para. 7, when we discuss programme structuring as an essential instrument for rational choice between objectives.

A classification of the degradation with respect to the objectives may be considered linked to the lack of some principles of environmental well-being to be placed at the foundation of territorial policy.[17] For example, the degradation may be seen as:

1 The lessening of the potential contacts of the urban man with nature, with other persons, with the works of man himself; which means an overall worsening in personal freedom;
2 Difficulties in the capacity of acquiring the potential and actual human contacts; which implies difficulties and worsening in the utilisation of the most useful way and means to achieve these contacts;
3 The shrinking of the protective space of man; which means the reduction of the distance of man from other persons, or animals or objects, which permit the contacts sought for mentioned above, without sensory or psychological disturbance;

4   The loss of quality in the relationship of man to his environment (nature, society, lodging and communication network); which also represents the psychological and aesthetic order influencing architecture and art;
5   And finally, a reduction of the capacities and freedom to choose an optimal synthesis of all the preceding principles evoked.

As seen, the point of view of the objectives meets up several times with that of the factors (para. 2). Too often a goal coincides with the maximum attention and action assigned to a positive factor for the urban environment, or with the maximum attention and action against the negative factor for the same urban environment.

A more precise articulation of goals leads immediately to the method of territorial planning which will be discussed in para. 7, and which will pervade all the analyses given in the subsequent chapters of this book. But before this, we must clarify some basic requirements for rendering territorial planning efficient, in particular that which takes into consideration urbanity, urban well-being. The basic requirement is represented by the appropriate territorial unit[18] to which such territorial planning may be applied: which we would define as the 'urban eco-system'.

6   The urban eco-system evaluation

6.1   A model of an urban eco-system

Let us examine more closely the concept of the urban eco-system as an instrument for the orientation of a policy aimed at the elimination of urban environment degradation.[19]

As has been argued, urban environment degradation is the product of a disequilibrium in the functioning of the urban eco-system. In fact, cities can be considered as systems in which an exchange (relationship) is constantly realised between the 'demand for territory' (for land or environmental resources) determined by the needs of production/social consumption, and the availability (supply) of territory (land or environmental resources).[20]

If the demand exceeds the availability, the territory becomes overloaded with excessive weight, and a disequilibrium is produced which tends to be compensated in some way.

Often the balance is looked for and found again by enlarging the space of the (urban) system and englobing new territorial resources inside. This often carries the imbalance to another territorial level. As with firms, also for cities there is a tendency to 'externalise' the cost of the urban equilibrium. However, if a saturation threshold is reached even in the 'external' environment, a way also has to be found to 'internalise' this cost, to find the equilibrium between the demand and supply of territorial (or environmental) resources internal to each system.

Positive theory, in fact, supposes that in the research for 'environmental well-being' (that is of the equilibrium between activities that require resources and the availability of resources) there is a permanent tendency to 'balance' demand and supply; and from here derive urban patterns and, perhaps, the (spontaneous) optimisation of the urban environment.

That may be true: but in the long term....!

The degradation of the urban environment that is evident everywhere demonstrates that, between the initial situation or equilibrium (which corresponds to any stage of urbanisation and of economic development, as they are evoked) and the new eventual point of 'arrival' equilibrium (in the long term), there is an important temporary and substantial gap, let's say a transitional period of imbalance that produces serious wastage which has to be managed, contested, reduced to the minimum: in order to maximise on the other hand environmental well-being.

Positive analysis (theoretical) is always *ex post*. But to minimise the disequilibrium and its waste (no matter how transitional) we need an *ex ante* analysis and a preventive line of action to follow it up. That analysis must develop the theoretical hypotheses of the factors of disequilibrium and simulate the equilibrium (according to a method which I call 'planological').

In other terms, it is a question of a policy or programming problem: to evaluate the demand and the supply of land and of environmental resources, and to prepare for their 'balancing'; and to promote a selection of priority activities (policies) through the trade-off between different objectives and the accurately studied connection between objectives and means.

A policy for the recovery of urban environment degradation passes therefore through the identification and construction of an urban eco-system model. A model that can be identified as: the space in which the different urban functions can be optimised; the space - above all - in which demand and supply of a community's territory or land resources can find their equilibrium, at least in the framework of its daily needs and of its residential functions.[21]

This model, today, does not exist. Even the attempts to build it, here and there, would need to be compared. The best comparison would be that between sensitively different realities, precisely so as not to risk that the parameters measured are not too dependent on particular historical and geographical circumstances (the urban typology or the urbanisation stage or economic development): which would not render them more constant and significant, because of changes in the urban conditions of the place for which the model was devised.

A common work between diverse realities would certainly be essential to construct this analytical and decision-making instrument for an urban policy.[22]

Of course, such a model should incorporate all the possible factors of urban environmental degradation. It should incorporate not only the direct factors of degradation, but also the indirect factors, those which are, in their turn, at the base of the direct factors.

Let us provide an example: if atmospheric pollution of cities is caused by the level, by the modalities and by the intensity of vehicular traffic, the latter, in its turn, is caused by the demand for activities, by the location of services to which urban inhabitants must have access, and by the purchasing power of the people, etc. It is difficult to exclude the apparently 'indirect' variables of the urban eco-system model, because very often these are the key variables of evolution (degradation or recovery) of the urban eco-system.

6.2   Urban eco-systems and network

In the approach sustained here, it is not even the case of taking into consideration a widespread old position of 'refusing' to consider the city as something which has spatial limits and confines.

This position recurs punctually when the 'urban spaces' for a certain period of time tend to change in surface and population and to cross the old city limits.

This happened when cities became centres of production of goods and services aimed at the entire national and international 'market': for which the concept of 'basic' and 'non-basic' structure of urban and regional inter-relations (a concept which then revealed itself to have limited significance, and be even useless, like many of the theorems of 'spatial economics'). A similar thing is happening with the latest phenomena of growth of information and telematic technology, which seem to guarantee the triumph of the 'non-place' or 'non-spatial' over place and spatial factors. Such phenomena have immediately stimulated the idea that the urban phenomenon could be reduced, almost dissolved, into that of urban 'networks', infra-urban networks and inter-urban networks.

It has been considered useful to dissolve the concept of city in that of 'network' - mimicking currently fashionable computer jargon; this has contributed to a complete loss of any reference to urban policy.[23]

The latest version of this refusal, in the name of the non-spatiality of the city, is based on the incessant reference to the development of telecommunications and information technology. And in fact it is more than obvious that the expansion of telecommunications has provoked (and will provoke even more in the future) the reduction of urban functions physically understood as relations of proximity. But if the human function is always correlated to man, to the real man, this man - unless certain forms of futuristic daily transport do not permit a physical ubiquity (for example, a sort of personal air transport), or physical needs are not satisfied in a telematic (or 'virtual' form, as is said now) - will have for a long time to come in the city in which he lives a sure point of reference for his personal identity.

As has been well stated by an Italian colleague concerning the sustainability of the city:

the absence of certain confines is that which denotes the lack of identity, clarity of belonging, defined and recognisable form. And it is in fact that which denotes primarily the unsustainable city, built on spontaneity and short-sightedness, allied also with speculation, in the years of growth without form. Wishing to reach a sufficient level 'urban quality' means then also looking for the confines of the real city, of the human city, of the historical city. And it means also intervening in the shapeless and faceless outskirts, and redesigning there the confines - the structure and forms - of a city of today and tomorrow, in which everyone can recognise themselves, find their identity and a common 'citizenship'.[24]

It is that which we have called long since, without particular emphasis, the 'city effect'. This is a city effect which we must seek not only by requalifying and redesigning the urban 'peripheries' of the large cities (which have grown 'without a face and without form'; perhaps by redesigning - in fact - new more appropriate confines for the 'city of today and tomorrow'. But we have to look for this city effect also by redesigning 'new confines' for those scattered small and medium-sized cities, which once had an urban quality whilst they are losing it today (if they have not already definitively lost it), exactly because of that spontaneity (perhaps very much analysed by the theorems of regional economics, and supported by the theorists of political pragmatism) which makes the cities, likewise, unsustainable with respect to the indispensable city effect, i.e., to the 'real', 'human' and 'historical' city (which cannot but be also the 'city of today and tomorrow').[25]

7 The planological approach: programme structure and urban indicators

The modelling of the urban eco-system,[26] as has been defined above, needs to be preceded by the determination of the variables and parameters that must be considered. This determination corresponds to the list of social concerns that an urban and/or national, and why not supra-national, community can express[27] on the subject of the improvement of the urban environment.

These social concerns can be expressed in the shape of a series of 'objectives', to which can be connected - after the appropriate studies and evaluations - a series of means and instruments suitable to attain these objectives. As is well known, objectives, and likewise means, are sometimes compatible, sometimes not. They can be directly 'synergetic', but they can often enter into conflict, both in the ends and in the means employed and in the resources to be drawn upon.

The objectives are linked together on different hierarchical levels. An objective at an inferior level can be a means to attain an objective at a superior level; and vice versa, a means at a superior level can be an objective to an instrumental inferior level.

The logical framework (or simply 'logframe') of the system of objectives and of concatenated means is usually called, in planning science or planology, the programme structure.[28] It therefore seems essential that every reference policy against urban environment degradation should use the instrument of a programme structure to put order into its series of problems, concerns and aspirations.[29]

The system of objectives organised in a programme structure must be made evident through quantitative and/or evaluative variables, that is through vote or judgement. Each social concern or objective concerning the urban environment (as likewise on the other hand with any other factor of community social well-being) must be measurable and measured by one or more indicators. These indicators (or measuring instruments) indicate the degree of satisfaction or dissatisfaction in relation to the above-mentioned concern or objective, or the degree of achievement on the topic of that concern or objective.

As an example, we will refer to some programme structures and indicators of objective and achievement, arising out of some studies that have already attained a certain international consensus: we refer to the OECD studies (mentioned in para. 2.1), conducted at different times. Tables 2.3 and 2.4 (found at the end of this chapter) reproduce the OECD indicators as far as they specifically concern the urban environment, which are drawn from a specific OECD work (1978). The OECD work has not received great political application: this would have required a certain consistency over time, accompanied by appropriate pressure on governments, at least to establish a periodical data gathering in the direction indicated. Moreover the whole work would have been much more valid if, rather than coming to a standstill, it had continued through the elaboration (as a further step) of an urban eco-system model: this model being built on the same variables expressed by the indicators, but with more accurate findings on the inter-relation existing between the said variables.[30]

To develop some initial general thoughts in the direction indicated, we will recall here - amongst many other works existing in the literature on the subject - two schemes which seem to us to be the most worthy of attention. A first - already mentioned - and by now outdated work, going back to the end of the 1960s, and carried forward by Resources for the Future, the well-known American organisation for the study of environment problems (a work directed by the late colleague Harvey Perloff). A second, extremely up-to-date work, proposed by a study group of the Town Planning Institute of Montreal (see Institut d'Urbanisme, University of Montreal, 1988).[31]

The sum of documentation quoted testifies in the first instance the unoriginal nature of approaches suggested here, and the possibility to start from a level of research and reflection which is not completely at zero. Besides, it is noted that the oldest studies (1960s) conformed perfectly with today's needs, which demonstrates that scientific approaches - if they are good and pertinent - grow old gracefully and remain valid in time, if only they are given a frequent follow-up and updating.

There arises, however, the regret that even if having advanced well in methodological reflection, there has not been, on the part of national or international public bodies responsible for this work, an adequate follow-up; such that it gives one the impression that we are always restarting from zero. (Sometimes the same researchers are negatively influenced by the behaviour of public decision-makers, and they reveal themselves as even being little informed on the work of their preceding colleagues.)[32]

In Ch. 3 - before examining in later chapters some technical aspects of the instrumentation which we have indicated for an appropriate organisation of a policy for the improvement of the urban environment - we will give a general account of the most current themes in this type of policy, in the light of the approach adopted and discussed here. We will focus in particular on the problem of the relationship between centralities and their peripheries, mainly in the contemporary larger cities.

Notes

1   For this we would refer to a work in course of completion by the author which constitutes in fact an *environmental planning methodology.*

2   According to a survey promoted by the EC Commission in 1983, in all the member states of the time, the index of 'sensitivity' to malaise relative to the six factors selected in the context of daily life (the closest to the familiar urban reality of everyone), i.e.: 'purity of drinking water'; 'noise', 'air pollution'; 'lack of access to green spaces'; 'disappearance of good agricultural land'; 'degradation of the landscape', - the latter factor is that which is recorded relatively with the highest index in the average of the countries involved in the survey; and then noise, air pollution, and so on (see the publication, Les europeens et leur environnement, EC Commission, 1983).

3   Some taxonomies have proposed different aggregations: for example, Deelstra (1993) lists 'six themes of sustainability' in urban design: 1) water; 2) energy; 3) waste; 4) greenery; 5) infrastructures (buildings, roads, etc.), and 6) traffic. And he lists four 'indicative points' for a better design at a local level for sustainable development: 1) making good use of the possibilities and quality of the area itself; 2) multiple use of spaces; 3) building decentralised systems in the city, and 4) making optimal use of the infrastructures.

4   Even if - judging by the EC survey just mentioned - physical pollution is not at the top any more of the sensitivity index of the average of the European citizens surveyed, but only in third place. Evidently the urban landscape and noise are considered more serious problems in European cities; or at least problems against which policies are in use which are more effective than those against atmospheric or water pollution. Probably the 'urban landscape' - as a factor of degradation - includes also the sensitivity for problems of urban traffic (not otherwise indicated among the factors selected) but seen only in its aspects of atmospheric pollution.

5   A general picture can be had in a study by the World Health Organisation (see WHO-UNEP, 1992).

6   Further information can be found in a type of technical literature that is not very accessible, and not very usable for overall evaluation. A relatively old work by Oke (1973) provides good information on these aspects, comparing them to the 'size' of the city. A good source is represented by some works of L. Mammarella (1976 and 1978) of the

University of Rome, and President of the 'Italian Association for Environmental Hygiene'. But see also the more recent evaluations of the Lawrence Berkeley Laboratory (Garbesi et al., 1989). For a general picture of the problems of the impact of atmospheric pollution, we recommend a vast essay, which is almost a book, by Gary S. Samuelsen in the collective work edited by J.G. Rau and D.C. Wooten (1980), an essay by Carpenter in a collection of essays edited by Carpenter and Sani (1983). The level of technical knowledge has not been so greatly improved in recent decades, and neither have strategies for the reduction of emissions, if we take into consideration the more recent works on the subject (see for example the collection of writings edited by Harrison [1990], the work by Davison and Barnes [1992], and, for an overall view which the author would call 'holistic' - abusing this word which is beginning to become misleading - the 'manual of environmental management' by S.O. Ryding [1992], in particular Ch. 5.2 concerning the 'urban approach'). See also a vast exploration of the more recent scientific acquisitions in urban pollution and its factors in R.R. White (1994). On the energy balance of the city, see the excellent work by Douglas (1983). Finally we can recall that a 'course for environmental planning' is currently being published (which was prepared for a post-graduate curriculum), edited by the author, which collects information which is hopefully the most up-to-date on the subject.

7   This is not the occasion to confront what policies and what 'battles' must be faced on these various 'fronts'; besides the already mentioned work by Samuelsen, see, for the specific problems of acoustic pollution, a work from the OECD (1971a) and an exhaustive essay by Mestre and Wooten (1980). And for pollution caused by automobile emissions, see the OECD study (1986) in the framework of the 'Compass' project. See also Part IV of the OECD study (1988b) 'Transport and the Environment', dedicated to the 'assessment of technical changes to reduce air pollution and noise emissions from motor vehicles'.

8   A good review of the conditions of contemporary urban malaise, and of the ways, on the basis of which, it can be measured (measuring thus the "quality of the Urban Environment") is the now classic work by the Harvey S. Perloff from 1969 (Perloff, 1969b). Here, in Table 2.1 we reproduce, the extremely "comprehensive" "picture" of the various "elements" making up the urban environment, and of the various indicators for assessing its costs and benefits. In Table 2.2 is reproduced another table on the policy measures - and the possible actors of such

measures - to manage and improve the urban environment as classified by Perloff. This table was elaborated by Richard J. and Beverly F. Frankel and published as an appendix to Perloff's work (1969b). More recent works have only provided modest improvements with regard to data, and no improvement in concepts, in comparison to Perloff's work (see Kuik and Verbruggen, 1991). Important schemes of Urban Quality Indicators have been subsequently proposed, on several occasions, by the OECD: in Tables 2.3 and 2.4 the taxonomy and structure of such OECD indicators arc given, of which we will speak again in Para. 3. See the OECD publication on urban environmental indicators (1978).

9   Despite the fact that for a long time the planners profession has acquired the elementary principle that transport flows cannot be thought out, planned or managed, apart from the conception, planning and management of land-use, urban traffic continues in almost all cities to be managed only with 'traffic engineering' methods, usually with disastrous results, since they are totally illusory, in the medium and long term. Few modern western city town plans are thought out and planned in strict correlation with the effects on traffic demand that they themselves generate. And few 'traffic plans' are studied and proposed with an eye to the settlement effects that they induce, and thus the town-planning problems that they create. The OECD has dealt often with urban traffic (in the old ECMT works - the European Committee of Transport Ministers - but also outside the ECMT), but its works have not gone, on the subject of the relationship of land-use/transportation, beyond general appeals for the adoption of policies that pay attention to the problem, which deserve to be recalled if only for the importance of their source and nothing more (OECD, 1988a and b). These studies are usually rich in data and information, but all reflect situations that have come about in the absence of an appropriate urban traffic policy, such as that, for example, delineated by previous studies again by the OECD, in which there was at least the attempt to outline the fundamental requisites for a planning policy of urban transport (see OECD, 1971b and 1979). The second of the OECD works (1988b), which examines the relationships in general between transportation and the environment, contains a chapter on 'assessment of innovations in urban transport management'; but this chapter too is limited to examining and discussing (in a very interesting way, however) a vast quantity of single technological measures and innovations, but it does not frame them in an overall general strategy of the land-use/transport relationship. For further elaboration on the

subject, see the works of Blunden (1971) (Blunden and Black, 1984, for the 2nd edition). See also Appleyard (1986) and Appleyard and Lintell (1986).

10   On this subject, see the work of Booth (1976).

11   There is not a specific literature on the subject that can be recommended, even if it is underpinned by the vast production on town-planning which has developed in recent decades. A general overview of the literature of the 1960s on the subject can be found in a highly recommendable book by G. Simoncini on the problems of urban prediction. Some well-known collections of writings by the most authoritative experts are in: the journal 'Daedalus' (Fall, 1961), edited by L. Rodwin, on the 'future of the metropolis'; those promoted on the occasion of the 50th anniversary of the American Institute of Planners (Ewald Jr. [ed.], 1967 and 1968 a and b); those edited by Warner (1966); Anderson (1967); Eldredge (1967 in two volumes), and Frieden and Nash (1969). Among the collective works mentioned above, should be included the already discussed work edited by Elgin (1974) on the relationship between urban dimension and quality of life. In this framework, among individual works we should recall the well-known work on the 'death and life of American cities' by Jacobs (1977); the study by Elkin et al. (1991) on the revitalisation of cities, and finally the essays collected by Goodland, Daly and El Serafy (1992) on the relations between population, technology and life style. Also interesting are considerations on the argument contained in an essay by Loeckx (1993).

In comparison with this literature, that is critical in a balanced and appropriate way of contemporary urban degradation, there is a vast, plaintive and complaining 'jeremiad' of numerous architects, sociologists, historians, and every other type of lover of arts and letters, from which everyone may draw for his or her personal experience. Of this generalised and confused lament, this inexhaustible laudatio temporis acti, which is a bit 'one way', the disturbing fact is the limited critical-analytical capacity, but also the stubborn non-recognition of the progress that the same arts and cultural activities have made in the modern city, despite the undoubted faults and deficiencies to which we are dedicating, in this chapter, our attention. Exactly: we would not like our work of denouncement of the problems and worries about environmental degradation in the modern city, which is motivated by the intention to identify the feasible ways and means to fight it, to be confused with that type of historic superficiality to which we have alluded. Among the most noble and authoritative of this jeremiad, we can recall authors such as: Simmel, Howard, Chambart de Lauwe, Wright, Riesmann and perhaps even Mumford. An old debate on the 'myth and reality of current urban problems' (held at the beginning of the 1960s at the Joint Centre for Urban Studies, between MIT and Harvard, in which such figures as Charles Abrams, Edward C. Banfield, Lloyd Rodwin, Martin Meyerson, Charles M. Haar, Raymond Vernon, etc., participated, had a much more acute critical penetration than the repetitive, ephemeral, disorientated and inconclusive debates of today (Vernon [ed.], 1962).

A comparative study (with a joint contribution of the EC Commission and of the German Government) - carried out at the 'WissenschaftZentrum' in Berlin (WZB) on the 'policies of decongestion of urban cities in the EC) (see R.W. Wettmann and W.R. Nicol [eds], 1980) - is limited to classifying some typologies of territorial urban order, and gathering information and data on measures taken by various governments (national and local) in Europe to protect some congested areas from further overloading and installations (especially of industries); but there is no trace in it of any operational model of reference on which a suitable territorial policy could be hinged.

There is something planned in the history of the French amenagement du territoire of the post-war period onwards (above all as regards the studies carried out by DATAR), whose central attention was aimed at decongesting the Paris area. But the scale, i.e., national, of the problem was only seen - in the opinion of the author - in its suitable dimensions much later, at the conclusion of the following campaigns for the villes nouvelles of the Parisian basin and the metropoles d'equilibre (V Plan, 1965), and then for the villes moyennes (VI Plan, 1971), and finally for the more 'contractual' forms (contrats de pays, contrats etat-regions) of development (VII and VIII Plan, 1975, 1979) after the official creation of the 'Regions' (1972) and, finally, with the technological fantasies of Urba 2000 (IX Plan, 1983). Only after 1988, it seems to us, does an adequate conception of the organisation of the urban framework make itself heard, by means of the idea of the reseau de villes, but the real functionality of these nets is still not very clear. See on the subject the Lettre de la Datar, special number (Aug.-Sept. 1988) on the theme 'Cities and Territorial Planning' (DATAR, 1988).

Neither can one consider as an appropriate policy of 'decongestion' that to the English satellite towns (or 'new' and 'expanded towns'), which began with dimensions that were incapable of representing a real alternative to urban congestion, and have represented only a rather modest, localised (but in our opinion failed) attempt at urban 'decentralisation'.

A satisfying approach (albeit only in the approach, which had no actual implementation) to the problem was had in Italy with the Progetto 80, proposed (at the end of the '60s) by some sectors of the Italian government (the Ministry of Budget and Economic Planning), which included a genuine plan for the re-equilibrium of urban functions in the territory, articulated in 30 'metropolitan systems', co-extensive for the entire territory (see Ri, Ministero del Bilancio e della Programmazione Economica, 1971). This plan has been reproposed on subsequent historic occasions: a) in 1983, by the Ministry for Southern Italy, to re-orient the development of highly unbalanced 'urban systems' in Southern Italy (Ri, Ministero per il Mezzogiorno, 1983); b) in 1985, among the studies of orientation of the General Transport Plan; and finally it has been currently reproposed, with suitable updating of content, by the Ministry of the Environment, in the work for the construction of a territorial framework of reference for a Ten-Year Plan for the Environment (called 'Decamb') (Ri, Ministero dell'Ambiente - Consiglio Nazionale delle Ricerche, 1991a and b).

In Germany, a country whose urban framework is the most balanced in Europe, the *Raumordnung Bundesprogramme* of 1975 (later not applied by subsequent governments) does not give particular indications on methods of urban decongestion, simply because such a problem did not present itself in that country as of priority importance (although it will become so more and more there as well in the opinion of the author).

It is time that at the European level a suitable study was made, with a great effort of co-operation between Community and national structures, in order to construct an urban framework of reference on the European scale, and adequate guidelines for criteria and common indicators of measurement for a standard quality of urban life. See, on the subject, the information collected in the study promoted by the EC on 'integrated planning of urban areas and its position in the environmental policy of the Community' (Heripret, 1989).

12 This observation qualifies even better the one developed in the preceding note. The urban landscape is certainly degraded and new construction, which is often not regulated by intelligent, cultured, volumetric designs and visual standards (still little known among the architects themselves),

has certainly created rather depressing syntheses of the urban landscape (see the observations of the Prince of Wales, who has dealt wisely with the subject) (Prince of Wales, 1989). But also the conservation of the cities obtained thanks to limited economic development has produced negative effects that cannot be forgotten at the same time that their praises are being sung. It is not understood why development cannot be directed - by means of suitable planning - in respect of certain quality and aesthetic standards, etc. Planning in fact is the only method to obtain both things. A vast treatment of the psycho-perceptive aspects of the city, which the designers of building works and town-planners often neglect, is in the work by Amos Rapoport, which aims at a 'man-environment' approach to urban form and design (Rapoport, 1977). However, in this book he deals more with residential design rather than with urban design proper; and consider anyway the 'environment' of the man, that of his visual scale, in which the urban scale is not necessarily exhausted.

13   On the evolution of the city as a centre of social communication, we cannot do better than recall the well-known pioneering work of Richard L. Meier (1962). See also the critical commentary by Karl W. Deutsch (1971). Note that the same author has sufficiently brought up to date his assumptions, in the light of the important increase in material factors of communication, such as the information technology and telematics revolution. See R.L. Meier (1972, 1974, 1985).

14   In reality, the analysis of the urban pattern in relation to specific phenomena or to urban typologies has been the ground on which the great majority of scholars of 'regional sciences' and urban and economic geography have exercised their brains. A movement has been born (of a 'descriptivist' type) of an uncontrollable vastness; from which have come even more unreliable and elusive consequent theorisations. But it is the approach itself - that of an interpretation of historic phenomena brought to light - that seems to us to be misleading. Today it has been noticed that the phenomena of environmental degradation have little to do with a large part of the positive analyses mentioned; and that a more 'planological' approach is necessary (more oriented towards political choices and decisions) in order to give some sense to the models constructed for the purpose. See, for a vast treatment of the subject, Faludi (1973a and b) and Alexander (1986).

15   See for example, Berry (1976) who has been among the first to highlight and measure this phenomenon.

16 In this case as well there are numerous studies that have aimed at theorising a sort of 'life-cycle' of cities and extrapolating some constant trends (Norton, 1979). The same statistical studies on the development of urbanisation in Europe have been largely influenced by the intention of seeking and codifying constant 'dynamics' (see on the subject, the empirical analyses by Klaassen, 1978; Hall and Hay, 1980; Van den Berg et al., 1982; Bradbury et al., 1982; Drewett and Rossi, 1984; Cheshire and Hay, 1989; Kunzmann and Wegener, 1991; and the overall evaluations of Nijkamp and Schubert, 1985). With respect to the 'planological' approach (which will be better explained in para. 2), this type of research tends to leave things 'as it finds them'.

17 See on this subject the principles of human settlement listed and proposed by Doxiadis as a basis of the 'ekistics', or science of settlements, which seem to me quite useful (Doxiadis, 1968 and 1970).

18 Such an appropriate territorial unit for urban planning is a 'hinge' concept and principle of planning methodology and theory; and it has been the object of recurrent dealings by the author. See, for further depth, Ch. 4, para. 3.1 and Lesson 6 of the work, *Theory of Urbanistics* (Archibugi, 1995).

19 We will do this here with the rapidity and superficiality imposed by the subject of this chapter. We will come back to the concept of the urban eco-system in the following chapters: especially Ch. 4, 5 and 6.

20 On this point greater elaboration will be found in Ch. 7.

21 See on the subject some work by the author (Archibugi, 1979, 1986a, 1990b). From the completely different works of Fox on the identification of appropriate territorial units of well-being evaluation, the FEA (Functional Economic Area), (Fox, 1965, 1967, 1973, 1974, Ch. 12), of Berry (1966, 1972a and b), and of Doxiadis (1966-70 and 1970) on the identification of a space for a 'daily urban system', are gleaned interesting points of identification with that which we have called the 'urban eco-system'. More in general see also two essays by Newton and Taylor (1985) and Klaassen (1985).

22 Would not the best level to develop this model be the level of European Community co-operation?

23 For a vaster and less synthetic account of the problem, see the essays collected by Perulli (1993), and in particular that by Mazzoleni (1993). See also Herson and Bolland, 1990.

24 Salzano (ed.), 1992, p. 15.

25 I would not like to be controversial - it is really not worth it! - but it is devastating to realise that this great short-sightedness has been carried forward just by a large part of the town-planning establishment, political and so-called 'technical', but essentially 'para-political' operators, who, rather than devoting themselves to studying thoroughly the parameters of this 'real city', have been happy to deny this type of study any utility and validity, and thus to neglect its utilisation in design and planning at the urbanistic level. Based on the granted difficulty of applying plans, these pseudo town-planners, these charlatans in petty professionalism and political sub-government, have contributed to make town-planning a widespread 'politological chat' (but, not disdaining however to involve themselves professionally in any sort of study or project, at not feasible scales without a minimum of co-ordination and coherence, and giving up pursuing tenaciously the study of planning and its methods, and the formulation of the constraints of co-ordination and coherence that underpin it - coherence and co-ordination that only an advanced level of organic and integrated may guarantee). In such a way, the practical (expected or presumed) results have not been achieved, and moreover, the chance has been lost to carry out a serious process of education of the experts, decision-makers and perhaps even the public in the science of planning. I estimate that, in the '70s and '80s, around 90% of the town-planning production, academic and otherwise, was affected by this sort of cultural schizophrenia. And this has had an effect that has been culturally and operationally devastating.

26 On the modelling of urban systems, there has been for some time now an abundant and imposing technical literature: in the '50s and '60s urban phenomena began to be modelled, in the wake of the spread of 'systemistic' techniques and operational research (among the most significant works of the time, we can refer to the proceedings of a conference promoted in 1967 in Hanover, New Hampshire, by the 'Highway Research Board', in which the experience of seven models of urban development constructed and used by a number of metropolitan and territorial agencies in the USA was discussed and compared [HRB, 1968]) with particular regard to the contributions given to the conference by some individual authors such as: Steger and Lakshmanan (1968) on the 'methodologies of plan evaluation'; Chapin (1968) on 'systems of activities' as a source of inputs for territorial models; Lowry (1968) on the 'structural comparison' of seven different models, etc. Naturally later ('70s and '80s) the techniques of model construction became more

sophisticated (not too much, however), but they lost those last connections with real planning processes which they formally had(albeit with very controversial ways) with planning agencies (see on this the manual on urban and regional models by Wilson [1977]). Among the more recent works on urban models is the collection of essays edited by Bertuglia, Clarke and Wilson (1994); also rich in contributions is the collection edited by Hutchinson and Batty (1986), where together with essays on the role of models, and developments in the structure of models, dynamic models and the application in models, the door has been opened to 'new directions' (among the latter there are particularly interesting contributions by P. Nijkamp (1986) on the 'qualitative methods for the analysis of regional and urban impact', and by B. Harris (1986) on 'revision of the foundations of post-industrial urban policy'.

We should point out however that all this vast literature - although it is fundamental in the field of model construction - has been little influenced by an appropriate methodology of use of this modelling. The methodology of use in fact concerns the selection of variables on which to construct models, which cannot be made on the basis of 'implicit' visions, but rather on the basis of the preventive explication of the planning goals, which modelling must serve, as an instrument of calculation and evaluation. In this paragraph however we will only rapidly discuss such methodology: for a more extensive discussion of the same see other works by the author (Archibugi, 1979-82 and 1995).

27   See works on social indicators of the OECD (1973, 1982). They have been widely taken up again and discussed in numerous works, amongst which - for the sake of brevity - we recommend that of Fox (1985).

28   For further analysis on 'programme structure', there are numerous writings of the author; see Archibugi (1979, Ch. 7) and Archibugi (1996).

29   It would be more than ever recommendable that such a structure be elaborated on a European Community level, in a joint operation on more than one territorial level of the Community.

30   On the other hand the work of the OECD Urban Affairs Group (of which the author has been a member for several years) has not managed to absorb and develop the studies on urban indicators about which we are speaking. The work so far has been directed to general descriptions of the state of the problems and outlines of general urban policies, from which - without a more precise methodological framework - cannot be gleaned much apart from more generic information.

In Italy as well, the Planning Studies Centre has attempted to advance a more precise definition of urban environmental indicators, using the schemes proposed by the OECD (see Table 2.5) but without much particular success.

It would certainly be very appropriate if such a work (a subsequent elaboration of an urban ecosystem model and a close examination of the system of quality indicators of the urban environment) should proceed also in the European Community on its own initiative.

31   See Perloff (1969) and Institut d'Urbanisme (1988).

32   This is the impression that one gets from the tenor and results of almost all the numerous 'meetings' that have multiplied over the years on the urban environment.

Table 2.1

Framework for evaluating policy measures for the environment

Elements in the environment	Indicators of present condition	Costs of environmental maintenance at present levels		Costs (or other adverse consequences) of environmental abuses and shortfalls		Costs of achieving standards at various levels		Benefits of achieving standards at various levels	
		Private	Public	Private	Public	Private	Public	Private	Public
	(1)	(2)		(3)		(4)		(5)	

A. *The natural environment*
   1. The airshed
   2. The watershed
   3. The open space-recreation 'shed'
   4. Quiet-and-noise zones
   5. Olfactory zones
   6. Micro-climate zones
   7. Sunlight exposure

B. *The spatial environment*
   1. Underground space
   2. Uncovered land
   3. Covered land
   4. Radiospectrum space
   5. Airways space

Elements in the environment	Indicators of present condition	Costs of environmental maintenance at present levels		Costs (or other adverse consequences) of environmental abuses and shortfalls		Costs of achieving standards at various levels		Benefits of achieving standards at various levels	
		Private	Public	Private	Public	Private	Public	Private	Public
	(1)	(2)		(3)		(4)		(5)	

C. *Transportation-utilities environment*
  1. Transportation:
     a) commuting time; b) alternative modes, including mass transit; c) congestion; d) safety; e) stress;
     f) aesthetics (e.g., billboards, landscaping)
  2. Water supply facilities
  3. Sewerage facilities
  4. Solid waste disposal
  5. Electricity facilities
  6. Gas facilities
  7. Telephone facilities
  8. Other communication facilities

D. *Community-neighbourhood environment*
  1. Community characteristics:
     a) mix (e.g., degree of segregation); b) types and condition of structures and land uses; c) community stresses; d) design environment (densities, street lighting billboards, interest points, landscaping, zoning, etc.)
  2. Services environment (measures of quality and nearness):
     a) educational-cultural environment; b) personal safety and protection; c) health facilities and services; d) commercial facilities and services;
     e) recreation facilities and services; f) 'caretaker' functions

75

Elements in the environment	Indicators of present condition (1)	Costs of environmental maintenance at present levels (2)		Costs (or other adverse consequences) of environmental abuses and shortfalls (3)		Costs of achieving standards at various levels (4)		Benefits of achieving standards at various levels (5)	
		Private	Public	Private	Public	Private	Public	Private	Public

E. *Household shelter*
1. Housing condition
2. Crowding
3. Rats, roaches and other pests
4. Plumbing
5. Household equipment

F. *Workplaces*
1. Safety
2. Amenities (e.g., eating facilities, sanitation)
3. Work challenge indicators (assembly line, freedom of movement, etc.)

Source: H.S. Perloff, 1969

Table 2.2

Policy measures for the environment: responses to macro-environmental conditions

Elements in the environment	Attribute of macro-environment	Societal-governmental approach	Private or individual micro-environmental approach		
			Family	Workplace (firm)	
	(1)	(2)	(3)		

A. *The natural environment*

Elements in the environment	Attribute of macro-environment	Societal-governmental approach	Family	Workplace (firm)
1. The airshed	Air quality (smoke, soot, smog, gaseous waste); smells or odours	– emission or ambient air standards – fuel or combustion equipment standards – taxation on emissions	*Self:* shift from outdoor to indoor physical activities *Household:* – ventilation control (air filters, air conditioning in car and house) – greater frequency of cleaning (clothes, household items, car) and earlier replacement of goods due to more rapid deterioration – increase in outdoor maintenance (repairs, repainting and vegetation replacement) – relocation to another neighbourhood *Transport:* more frequent trips (from polluted areas)	– process change or product substitution to reduce waste – waste treatment to reduce pollution – air conditioning of entire plant (closed windows) – relocation of factory
2. The watershed	Water quality (pH, hardness, turbidity,	– water quality standards – municipal water and	*Self:* bottled water or preferences for other drinks	– change in water source (new wells or water intake points)

77

Elements in the environment	Attribute of macro-environment (1)	Societal-governmental approach (2)	Private or individual micro-environmental approach (3)	
			Family	Workplace (firm)
	dissolved solids, BOD, organisms, etc.)	– waste treatment plants – effluent charges or user fees – regional transfers of water	*Household:* – individual wells – home water softeners – greater consumption of soaps, more rapid deterioration of clothes – outdoor vegetation affected (change in types of shrubbery) *Transport:* change in type and location of watersports	– industrial water and waste treatment plants – change in water consumption per unit of output, recirculation and re-use – relocation of industry
3. Open-space-recreation 'shed'	Lack of vegetation, scrubby open areas (due to asphalting, density and buildings)	– urban redevelopment programmes (tree-lined avenues, parkways, play-grounds, shopping malls, etc.) – change in transport system (subways, commuter trains, buses, off-street parking, underground highways, centre-strip plantings)	*Household:* – plants in lobby, entrance ways and around house – more flowers, flower pots, flowery wallpaper *Transport:* – frequent trips to gardened parks – relocation to suburbia	
4. Quiet-and-noise zones	Noise	– zoning regulations (quiet around hospital areas) – muffler standards (car	*Self:* ear plugs *Household:* – air conditioning of home and car	– insulation or heavier construction – 'Musak' or other background music programmes

Elements in the environment	Attribute of macro-environment (1)	Societal-governmental approach (2)	Private or individual micro-environmental approach	
			Family	Workplace (firm) (3)
		inspections, construction equipment, planes, diesel trucks) – flight patterns or routes around cities – laws of nuisance pertaining to noise	– thicker wall construction, more insulation, closed windows – competitive background noise from radio, TV *Transport:* – premiums on certain locations of private homes or high apartment units away from street level – relocation of home (or construction of units at far end of lots, away from street)	– complete air conditioning (closed windows)
5. Olfactory zones (see airshed)				
6. Micro-climate zones	Weather variations (differences in climate between areas and seasons as distinguished from small changes due to air pollution or heat sinks in urban areas)	– building codes or standards for construction materials – school sessions varied to suit weather – snow removal operations – geodesic domes	*Self:* – individual dress - light reflective colour in heat; dark, heavy material in cold – reapportionment of leisure time between inside and outside activities – sports change between indoor and outdoor	– cropping patterns or plants grown varied depending on climate – enclosure of facilities (construction) varied – no. of working days or school days per year varied

Elements in the environment	Attribute of macro-environment	Societal-governmental approach	Private or individual micro-environmental approach	
			Family	Workplace (firm)
	(1)	(2)	(3)	
			Household: – house design includes basement for recreational areas when weather does not permit outdoor playground – stress on indoor activities for family (TV, – reading. games. exercise groups)	*Household:* – more glass construction, increased artificial light – lighter and brighter colours in decorating
7. Sunlight exposure	Amount of sunshine	Building codes (requiring space between buildings. maximum height)	*Household:* – larger window areas – lighter colours in decorating	

B. *The spatial environment* (partially covered under 'D')

C. *Transportation-utilities environment*

1. Transportation	Traffic congestion	– change in transport form (rapid transit, commuter trains, subways, shuttle planes) – easing of traffic situation (traffic reports, roadnet	*Self:* – individual preference for car, public transport or walking *Transport:* – compensation by living downtown or further out	– shopping centres located in sub-urbia to cut travel time – more on-site parking important factor in accessibility – staggered work hours and shifts to accommodate off-peak traffic

Elements in the environment	Attribute of macro-environment (1)	Societal-governmental approach (2)	Private or individual micro-environmental approach	
			Family	Workplace (firm) (3)
		regulations, changing of one-way direction during rush hours, off-street parking, highway programme)	– more mobile public demands increase in recreational area accessibility	
2. Sewerage facilities (e.g. of one of multiple utility types)	Sewage	– sewerage system for collection – municipal sewage treatment plant – reclamation plant for water re-use – conveyance system for disposal – waste treatment plant performance criteria	*Household*: outhouse or septic tank	– tie-in with municipal facilities – wastewater treatment plant – disposal system
3. Law enforcement	Crime Civil riots	– law enforcement agencies (police, FBI) – civil codes of justice – institutions for confinement and correction – military interventions – curfews – licensing of protests	*Self*: – stay in at night – carry firearms for protection – deposit valuables in bank or home safe *Household*: – insurance – house safe, locks	– burglary and protection system installed (including safes, locks, etc.) – relocation of business

Elements in the environment	Attribute of macro-environment	Societal-governmental approach	Private or individual micro-environmental approach	
			Family	Workplace (firm)
(1)	(1)	(2)	(3)	
		(marches or sit-ins)	*Transport:* – travel in pairs or groups – avoidance of dangerous or undesirable neighbourhoods – relocation of home	

D. *Community-neighbourhood environment*

Elements in the environment	Attribute of macro-environment	Societal-governmental approach	Private or individual micro-environmental approach	
			Family	Workplace (firm)
1. Community characteristics	Space	– building codes (height of buildings, distance between structures, vision regulations) – zoning of low and high density areas and uses	*Household:* – idea of living space altered (living-sleeping quarters combined, efficiencies, roll-out beds, one-half kitchens) – physical reshaping of space (dividers for visual spacing, more windows, porches or sundecks to extend space, light coloured walls) *Transport:* – join clubs which offer space facilities (tennis, swimming, gym, etc.) – rent space for parties, recreational activities	

Elements in the environment	Attribute of macro-environment (1)	Societal-governmental approach (2)	Private or individual micro-environmental approach	
			Family	Workplace (firm) (3)
	Population density	– rezoning of low and high density dwellings – birth control programmes – greater emphasis on educational and recreational facilities (impact on services environment)	*Self:* – seek privacy by renting single apartments; – off-hour working schedules – recreational interests indoors (development of the arts - painting, music) *Household:* – limit number of children – social activities within home (bridge groups, etc.) *Transport:* – frequent walks or trips away – greater use of individualistic transportation modes – travel at off-peak hours	
2. Services environment	Education	– federal and state assistance programmes (loans, scholarships, research and development funds, construction grants) – federal and state stan-	*Self:* – education time lengthened (time horizon requiring supplementary income expanded) *Household:* – pressure on children to excel	– job training, schoolwork programmes, apprenticeships – competitiveness for job positions based on education level – higher salaries for higher education levels

Elements in the environment	Attribute of macro-environment (1)	Societal-governmental approach (2)	Private or individual micro-environmental approach	
			Family	Workplace (firm) (3)
		dards (compulsory education, hiring policies) – job training – social work agencies – pay differential in educational systems for advanced degrees	(rebellion, competitiveness of school children) – exposure to media (TV, newspapers) – private tutors – reclassification of job status by education level	
	Health (physical and mental)	– Medicare programmes – physical fitness (other preventive medicine) programmes – health-education programmes – social work agencies – hospitals, clinics, medical centres – pest control and eradication programmes	Self: personal physical fitness (yearly check-up, vitamins, weight consciousness) Household: – medical insurance – accident prevention by safeguards (netting, screens, sprays, protective clothing)	Safety programmes, medical insurance, independent medical staff

Source: H.S. Perloff, 1969

84

Table 2.3
List of concerns about man's urban environment[a]

1. Housing

    1.1   Inside space
    1.2   Outside space
    1.3   Comfort and sanitaries
    1.4   Security of residence
    1.5   Cost of and access to housing

2. Services and work

    2.1   Accessibility and quality of commercial services
    2.2   Accessibility and quality of health services
    2.3   Accessibility and quality of educational services
    2.4   Accessibility and quality of leisure facilities
    2.5   Accessibility and quality of transport services
    2.6   Accessibility and quality of emergency services
    2.7   Accessibility and safety of work

3. Surroundings and environmental nuisances

    3.1   Quality of air
    3.2   Quality of water
    3.3   Exposure to noise
    3.4   Solid waste disposal
    3.5   Exposure to natural dangers
    3.6   Climatic conditions
    3.7   Quality of land and urban landscape

4. Social and cultural environment[b]

    4.1   Social integration
    4.2   Organisation of the collectivity
    4.3   Absence of criminality and delinquency
    4.4   Extent of cultural activities

a   The numbering of the concerns doesn't imply an order of priorities.

b   Indicators are not proposed for social and cultural concerns. Refer to pp. 57-58 for a brief examination of this matter and to the OECD programme on social indicators for a more in-depth study.

Source: OECD, 1978

Table 2.4
Summary of social indicators

Concern	Proposed indicators	Proposed indicators for new research
1. Housing		
1.1 Inside space	% of living units where fewer than X (specified number) people per room live, e.g., X–0.5, 1.0, 1.5	
1.2 Outside space	% of population living in an area with a net density of over X people/km^2	Av. area (m^2) of usable outside space per housing unit – Av. number of public children's play areas per 100 children in the corresponding age group
1.3 Comfort and sanitaries	% of housing with private shower or bathroom	
1.4 Security of residence	% of households owning their housing (including tenants with long-term purchase contracts)	% of households well protected against risk of expulsion for a given period
1.5 Cost of and access to housing	% of households dedicating less than X% of their revenue to a determined type of housing, e.g., X=20%, 30%	
2. Services and work		
2.1 Accessibility and quality of commercial services	% of population with access to a food shop within a radius of X metres, e.g., X=400, 800, 1,200, 2,400 m	Indicator taking into consideration other qualitative aspects
2.2 Accessibility and quality of health services	% of population with access to a doctor within a radius of X metres, e.g., X=800, 1,600, 2,400 m	Av. delay between the awareness of a non-urgent functional problem and the appropriate treatment
2.3 Accessibility and quality of education services	% of pupils with access to a primary school located less than X minutes or metres away, e.g., X=15 mins (on foot or by bus) or 800 m	Indicator taking into consideration other qualitative aspects
2.4 Accessibility and quality of leisure facilities	% of population with access to public open-air spaces within a radius of X metres, e.g., X=800, 1,600, 2,400 m	Indicator taking into consideration other qualitative aspects
2.5 Accessibility and quality of transport services	– Number of road accident victims (killed or injured) compared to the total population in one year – % of population with access to an urban public transport stop within a radius of X metres, e.g., X=400, 800 m	Complementary indicator of the quality of public transport (frequency, regularity, comfort)

Concern	Proposed indicators	Proposed indicators for new research
2.6 Accessibility and quality of emergency services	% of living units totally destroyed by fire over one year	Av. delay between the demand for and delivery of an emergency service
2.7 Accessibility and safety of employment	% of total working population living more than X minutes from the work place (using normal means of transport at the normal time), e.g., X=10, 20, 30, 40 mins	Number of working days lost in one year as a result of industrial accidents, in relation to the total number of work days

3. *Surroundings and environmental nuisances*

3.1 Quality of air*	% of population living in areas where concentration *outside* the housing is over i) 60 μg/m^3 (annual av.) for *sulphur dioxide* and/or 200 μg/m^3 for 2 % of the observations (in 24 hours); ii) and/or 40 μg/m^3 (annual av.) for the *particles suspended in the air* and/or 120 μg/m^3 (in 24 hours) for 2 % of the observations	− % of total population exposed to concentrations of sulphur dioxide and substances suspended in the air above the specified levels for the periods given − % of total population exposed to concentrations of carbon monoxide above the determined levels in the specified period
3.2 Quality of water	− % of target population multiplied by the number of days in which the quality of the water provided has not conformed to the norms laid down: i) presence of Esch. coli in a 100 ml sample; ii) appearance of an unpleasant taste or colour − % of surface area (shoreline) per 100 inhabitants of the water plants managed for leisure in urban areas (or inside an area with a diameter double that of the urbanised area). The water quality should be sufficient i) to allow swimming, ii) for other water sports: fishing, rowing, iii) to improve the quality of the landscape	

Concern	Proposed indicators	Proposed indicators for new research
3.3 Exposure to noise*	– % of population living in areas where the *outside noise level*, expressed in Lec, is over: i) 75, ii) 65, iii) 55, iv) 45 dBA *between 6.00 and 22.00 hours* – % of population living in areas where the outside noise level, expressed in Lec, is over: 55, ii) 45, iii) 35 dBA *between 22.00 and 6.00 hours*	– % of total population exposed to noise levels which, expressed in Lec, are over: i) 75, ii) 65, iii) 55, iv) 45 dBA between 6.00 and 22.00 hours – % of total population exposed to noise levels which, expressed in Lec, are over: i) 55, ii) 45, iii) 35 dBA between 22.00 and 6.00 hours
3.4 Solid waste management*		(Indicator reflecting the occurrence in the environment of the disposal of solid waste and also the quality of the service, judged from the point of view of the inhabitants)
3.5 Exposure to natural dangers	Av. annual % of housing rendered definitively uninhabitable following natural disasters, such as: landslides, opening of chasms, floods, violent winds or earthquakes over the last 50 years	% of living units situated in an area recognised as exposed to a specific extent to a natural danger
3.6 Climatic conditions	– Annual number of i) hot days and ii) cold days – Av. monthly rainfall levels i) during the 6 months of the 'good' season, ii) during the 6 months of the 'bad' season, established over a 5-year period – Av. number of hours of sunshine i) during the 6 months of the 'good' season, ii) during the 6 months of the 'bad' season, over a 5-year period	(Indicator reflecting the temperature, wind and humidity, for example, as values corresponding to an 'index of comfort')
3.7 Quality of land and urban landscape	% of urban land area which is unoccupied, neglected or abandoned	% of total urban area occupied by i) conservation areas and protected buildings, ii) open air, non-abandoned spaces, iii) protected spaces

* All the figures in this table concerning the levels, thresholds, etc., are provided only for documentation reasons. They have been chosen specifically in the context of the towns of the member countries.

Source: OECD, 1978

Table 2.5
Possible list of urban environment indicators

Environment indicators	Environmental standards

Air quality

– % of population exposed to CO_2, HC, NOX, higher than determined levels	– Vehicle emission levels to be controlled
– Levels of SO	– Limits of SO_2 and control of fossil fuels
Lead levels	– Acceptable lead levels
– Acid rain levels	
– Radiation levels; incidence of illness connected to radiation	– Levels of 'harmless' radiation
– No. of incidents/reports of pollution	

Microclimate

– Heat degrees centigrade of the 'island' effect	
– Percentage of sunlight loss	
– No. of days with smog indicated	– Definition of smog

Water quality

– % levels of waterways/water bodies polluted	– Standard of chloroform for sanitary water
– % of population served by water treatment plants	– Standard of chloroform for drinking water
– % of population X no. of days supplied with sub-standard water	
– No. of incidents/reports of water pollution	

Noise

% of population exposed to noise external to the household environment higher than determined levels	– Daily and nightly dB(A) recommended, by area
	– Limits on new construction
	– Limits for different uses of the territory and requisites for sound proofing

Waste disposal

– Collection frequency	– Accessibility of collection
– % of population satisfied by the service	
– % of refuse collected recycled	
– % of destination to manure of reflux	– Acceptable agricultural use and dumping

Connection to sewage treatment plants

– % of population served by sewage treatment plants	– Admitted standards for sewage treatment plants
– % of surface area served by recycled waste water	

Environment indicators	Environmental standards

Green spaces and recreational areas

- Total % of green spaces — Level of public space/1000 inhabitants
- % of areas for water recreation
- % of areas occupied by public space
- Land destined for recreation per 100 children — Recommended standards for recreation space
  (under 14)
- Km of footpaths in the green spaces — Minimum size of parks
- % of sites protected for ecological value (flora, — Criteria
  fauna)
- % of wood forest cover
- % of protected trees — Criteria

Urban landscape

- % of unsuitable housing — Definition of unsuitability
- % of buildings that lack 'basic' comforts — Definition of 'basic' comfort
- % of buildings built before 1919, before 1939,
  and after 1939
- % of buildings occupied by conservation areas — Criteria
- No. of buildings registered and declared as — Criteria
  monuments
- General density of population
- % of empty and abandoned spaces

Traffic

- Percentage of urban area occupied by roads — Definition of standard road and of the relative
  speed of design
- Percentage of urban areas rendered pedestrian
  areas
- Percentage of population killed or injured on — Definition of residential urban road
  the roads
- Km of cycling tracks, in or outside roads
- Percentage of journeys to work made on foot,
  by bicycle, bus, metro, car
- Average speed in the rush hours

Exposure to risk

- Percentage of population exposed to floods — Standard frequency of the event
- Percentage of population exposed to earth — Standard frequency of the event
  movements, etc.
- Percentage of population exposed to industrial
  risks

Source: Planning Studies Centre, 1985

3 Centralities and peripheries:
A new strategy for the recovery of the urban environment

1 The city and its public spaces

The city has always been identified in its public spaces and vice versa. Public space has always constituted the fulcrum of 'centrality', or the city itself.

The hieroglyph of the city (a cross inside a circle) symbolised the focal point and the town's crucial role as a meeting point, that is as a public space. There have always been meeting points: the Greek agora, the Roman forum with its surrounding public buildings (temples and basilicas, theatres and arenas), and subsequently the town churches and cathedrals with their squares and the market places; then later the public gardens, the esplanades and paths, the main boulevards with their pavements, the railway stations, the shopping complexes and centres, the bars and cafes, and (alas today) the fast food restaurants and snack bars for youngsters. These have always been (public) places where people could meet in order to build up social, cultural and political contacts, to take part in common events, and to benefit from community life.

In short, they are places and spaces where everyone can enjoy the city, thus becoming 'civis', in other words 'citizen' and 'civil' at the same time.

So public space represents the town itself and produces the so-called 'city effect'.[1]

The city is what it is because of its centrality; and its centrality depends on its public spaces. A city which doesn't have sufficient public areas is not a proper city in the full sense of the word.

Bringing back the idea of public spaces simply means relaunching the overall concept of city.

91

2 The decline of public spaces and the disequilibrium of loads

In effect, we are faced by a problem of declining public spaces in our towns and cities.

Even though public spaces have always been given priority in the history of urban design and planning, nowadays they are undergoing a destructive influence, a mortal blow. Why is this happening?

It seems that the principal reason is to be found in the enormous expansion of urban population. This expansion is concentrated in the areas where the quality of urban surroundings is highest, thus creating an important new demand for centrality and public spaces. Faced by this demand (which was neither foreseen nor planned), it has been difficult to create a corresponding supply in the availability of centrality and public areas.[2]

The result of this lop-sided relationship between supply and demand for public spaces has been the 'overloading' of pre-existing areas, deforming them by overcrowding and by improper use.

This main cause - overpopulation in large cities with respect to the available space - goes hand in hand with two other factors: a) the persistence of the old-fashioned method of urban planning known as 'zoning'; and b) traffic engineering.

3 Two typical, inadequate responses: zoning and traffic engineering

3.1 The old-fashioned method of 'zoning'

The aim of the old-fashioned method of zoning was to ensure functional quality for the various areas of the city (administrative, residential, recreational, etc.).

Such a method is perfectly suitable for towns of a certain size and within the threshold limits of the city effect. But when these limits are exceeded, the zoning method increases the imbalance between supply and demand of public space because it tends to overload the traditional focal areas. At this point, it is important to create, through preventive and far-sighted planning, alternative focal points or centralities with relative public spaces.

The absence of such an approach on a large scale has forced the old urban centres (some more 'historic' than others) to become the only desirable location for all the functions and advanced services that effectively produce the city effect, while at the same time being too small to cater for the new level of demand.

The second factor, closely linked to the first, is the outcome of traffic planning. In the hands of the traffic engineers, and because of the overloading of the old urban centres, the main requirement or purpose has become that of 'fluidity'.

By adopting a sort of 'hydraulic' view of towns and cities, and with the aim of maximising access and minimising time, traffic engineering has created one-way systems, computer-controlled traffic lights, urban freeways with priority lanes where no stopping is allowed, link roads, underpasses, and a hotchpotch of other expedients which have reduced our urban streets to flyovers and race tracks (irrespective of the speed limits required by law, generally on the low side). And our squares and piazzas have become car parks. What sort of centrality, with its related social aspects, can one achieve under these conditions?

The inevitable degeneration of urban centres makes traditional public spaces obsolete - they are no longer places to go to, to strike up a conversation, maybe to learn something and to enjoy oneself. Furthermore, furnishing the streets and turning isolated areas into pedestrian precincts (although praiseworthy) would be disappointing and insufficient if not carried out hand in hand with the removal of the cause of the degeneration: overloading traditional urban centres and ignoring the balance between supply and demand of public spaces.

4   The loss of centrality in small and medium-sized towns

The decline of urban centres and public spaces is common not only to large cities but also to the other parts of the urban scene: the small and medium-sized towns.

Small and medium-sized towns, in spite of some pleasant features that improve the quality of life, have lost all meaningful centrality. Many of them have not achieved (or have lost) that critical level of development as modern, functional 'urbanity'.

In fact, when we talk about 'centrality'[3] we are referring to those major features of urban development which the average European citizen of today (and presumably tomorrow) looks for and expects in towns and cities. It is the centrality that the inhabitants potentially (if not always effectively) expect so much, so that if their expectations are not met they will leave the small town where they were born and grew up, thus impoverishing it still further.

5 Outlines of a new policy of recovery of the urban environment

5.1   Changes in centrality and the critical mass for city effect

In our present cities and towns the concept of centrality has changed considerably, as shown by indicators such as the effective quality of urban life. There is this parallel historical movement relating to the increased demographic intensity which has become stabilised around all major urban centres. This demographic element has always been considered as the 'critical mass' for achieving new centrality and city effect, together with other variables such as the increase in per capita income and consumption.[4]

One has to recognise that today (viewed for the first time against the historical background), the increase in per capita income and consumption (in each urban centre) has noticeably lowered the threshold level of population required for the 'critical mass' to achieve modern centrality and today's city effect.

Some twenty or thirty years ago, it was felt that in order to achieve such a city effect and sufficient centrality, one needed at least a million inhabitants as a 'market area' or 'catchment area' to enable the setting up and the continuing operation of those functions and advanced services that produce the 'city effect'; in other words, that quality of the urban environment which attracts and holds the population.[5]

Nowadays, half a million inhabitants (sometimes even less) may be able to create the necessary conditions for a high quality city effect.

But I don't believe that this 'critical mass' (whose level is certainly decreasing) will disappear altogether, either as a result of substituting physical accessibility by computer communications, or as a result of increasing personal contacts on a worldwide scale (otherwise known as the 'global village' effect).

To put it another way, I don't believe in the alleged 'post-urban society'. Consider these two categories: on the one hand, my jet-set friends (who represent a minute proportion of mankind, even though I wish them all the best for an increase in their number); on the other hand, the hundreds of millions of people who spend their days glued to the TV set (and soon to Internet). I don't believe that either category threatens to bring about the death of the city as we know it - that is, the place that satisfies the need for physical contact in public spaces - after at least twenty centuries of its existence.

I am sure that even jet-setters and TV (and Internet) addicts would not want to give up those physical and social contacts that urban public spaces ensure. If such a thing were conceivable, the demand for public spaces would already have declined in our towns and cities, as opposed to increasing everywhere (as has already happened) thus creating the real problem of the deterioration of the urban environment. And the city effect would have reduced, not increased, its requirements.

5.2   The 'depolarisation' of large cities and towns, and the integration of small and medium-sized towns into new poles

This is the reason why today's urban centres, historic or otherwise, that are a multiple of the minimum threshold level of the city effect, should plan and develop other focal points or centralities within their own boundaries, as alternatives to the traditional ones. I have called this a 'depolarisation policy'.

This is the reason also, at the same time, why those urban centres that still have populations below the critical threshold should combine into 'urban systems' which together would reach the required level, and together would achieve the city effect. The possible city configuration thus created would reverse the traditional gravitation towards the old town centre areas that have become overloaded and hypertrophic. I have called this the 'policy of integration and polarisation'.

In western countries, especially European ones, if we want to help large cities and metropolitan areas to lighten the heavy load of traditional centrality and to improve the quality of the urban environment, we must organise and bring into being new 'cities' - both within the bounds of the existing large cities, and between small and medium-sized towns (below the threshold required for modern urban quality).

In both cases (bearing in mind their very different points of departure) it is important not to violate the constraints that render the operation feasible: the achievement of threshold dimensions and the efficiency of urbanity.[6] Many of the usual steps taken here and there are aimed at improving a particular local situation without an overall policy relating to the urban framework described above. Such steps are often dispersive, costly, likely to be wasted in large measure, basically inappropriate and often counter-productive.

As an example, we might mention the scale of investments made in large cities to improve accessibility by means of vast traffic infrastructures and the creation of 'satellite' areas with low centrality. Or, in the case of small and medium-sized towns, the investments made in order to create 'monuments' of social welfare (such as universities and hospitals) without the necessary links to a sufficient catchment area.[7]

In this sense, a national urban policy (possibly supranational) is required to provide a 'framework of reference' of appropriate urban and territorial standards for the many projects and financial programmes carried out at the local level.[8]

6 The question of 'modernity' in urban planning

6.1 The proper way to request more public spaces

From what has been said so far, one can deduce the proper way to request public space for improving our urban environment.

We certainly have to insist on more public spaces, but directed towards the new centralities (not merely in order to beautify the old or new urban surroundings).

There is no question about restoring buildings, restructuring the visual surroundings, improving urban furnishings, checking the pollution of our urban atmosphere; these steps are so essential as to be self-evident.

In order to carry out and emphasise this aim effectively, we must be careful not to overlook some of the crucial points that affect the real improvement of cities and towns - both those that are overloaded and those that are losing their urban qualities.

The crucial point is that these enlarged public spaces must be used as strategic tools to create new opportunities for centralities.

On the other hand, I don't feel (like some people) that the development of new centralities (as alternatives to the 'historic' ones) in our cities and towns will impair the vitality of the existing downtown areas. In a period such as today, dominated by business services, leisure time, tourism and cultural research, our cities and town centres constitute a resource that is becoming scarcer and scarcer, but which is certainly not obsolete.

On the contrary, the only thing we have to fear and keep clear of is using our cities beyond a 'sustainable' dose, thus avoiding the risk of killing them by overdose.

And it would be foolish to imagine that 'gentrification' could be an overall solution to the problem. Gentrification is a useful tool for improving the urban appearance of certain old and abandoned areas of cities and towns, but it has nothing to do with the problem of creating new spaces for centrality, suitable for present-day requirements and levels of urban quality; in other words, focal areas that have the same attraction for the inhabitants, the same values and urban functions as those that are being challenged and substituted.[9]

6.2   The risk of an outmoded model for urban life

There is an element of risk inherent in the conventional approach to improving public spaces in cities and towns: that of seeing the answer as the revival of a previous way of life, against the modernisation of new urban living. This belief, this wishful thinking, can lead one to misunderstand and to underestimate the obvious requirements for a modern urban centre.

There is widespread nostalgia (or *laudatio temporis acti*) that harks back to the way of life in towns and cities when the population didn't exceed 50-100,000 people, composed mainly of noble and patrician families, bourgeois and artisans. The majority of the rest of the population lived and worked outside the town.

A correct sense of historical criticism (rare enough in conventional thinking) should lead us to compare our despised peripheries, not with the social life of our old urban centres, but with life in the countryside before the arrival of running water, sewers, electricity and other modern comforts. Europe's finest urban heritage comes from towns and cities of the size mentioned above. And a large part of the urban environment and setting, which as visitors we come across and admire so much, was more haphazard in its evolution than we really imagine. We have to beware of mistaking the warm mantle of time for inspired design and planning. In any case, that particular urban dimension is no longer recoverable, except in confined circumstances: such as special areas for tourism and recreation. And even circumscribed projects like these may suffer if, on the one hand, the problem of overloading and, on the other, that of city effect are not resolved.

Our past is a source of inspiration, but it also constrains us. If we don't want to destroy it forever, we must not lean too heavily on it by trying to invent an impossible 'modernisation' or by applying present-day criteria to our old cities and towns.[10]

We have already seen what this modernisation brings, through the slow adaptation of our old streets and piazzas and our old public spaces (conceived in their time for other uses and other users) to today's tangled mass of innumerable people and cars.

We are left with uncontrolled congestion of our public spaces, their deformation with respect to their original use, a serious problem of pollution (deriving from exhaust fumes, noise, visual perception), and a generalised move towards 'garagisation'.

6.3   A suitable approach to modernity

We have to satisfy the eternal demand for social life and public spaces in our cities and towns (bearing in mind its changed dimension) with new and updated tools, on the scale of the critical mass required for new urban values.

The following formula has been put forward: 'Restore downtown areas and monumentalise the suburbs'. I wholeheartedly accept this formula as long as 'monumentalisation' also means including other alternative focal areas and public spaces; and as long as steps are taken to stimulate and plan (outside the main urban centres) alternative integration between small and medium-sized towns with the aim of creating new functional units capable of providing the urban effect for all the inhabitants.

In my opinion, this is the main approach to be followed in order to resolve our problems of urban environment, included those connected with environmental pollution which, to a great extent, is caused in the last analysis by poor territorial distribution of built-up areas.[11]

Notes

1   On the role of public spaces in assuring the quality of the urban life, see Gehl (1993).

2   For some interesting considerations (but outside our angle of vision), see Warner Jr. (1978).

3   It is useless to say that we are continuing here to conceive centrality as that town-planning 'quid' which determines a critical threshold in the scale of urban services that produce the city effect (see what has already been said in Ch. 1 and more extensively will be said in Chs 5 and 6). Thus we do not mean 'centrality' as conceived in the regional analyses or in the theory of central places à la Christaller (1933) with the strand of extensive literature on regional sciences connected to it (for an up-to-date survey see, for example, Camagni [1992], in particular Ch. 4). Our opinion is that if this latter concept of centrality is assumed (which we will call approximately the 'descriptive-analytic' or 'positive' approach), the numerous critical objections which can be expressed are justified (and in fact in the literature they have been in part expressed: see for example, Bullinger [1986] and Boeventer and Hampe [1988]) on the

possibility of defining an 'optimal' centrality; whilst with the concept of centrality preferred by us (which we call 'policy-oriented' or - better still - 'planological'), the 'theoretical' formal objections desist, and strategic-design motives of maximum importance take over. We have already better explained this position in Ch. 1, paras 6, 7 and 8.

4   The concept of 'critical mass' would involve - on the theoretical plain - a vast examination and debate on the 'theory' of urban aggregations, which has always been a fertile ground for sophistry in regional and urban (neo-classical) economics. We are very careful about facing our subject from this angle, being satisfied with the observations that we inserted already in para. 6 in Ch. 1, on the relationship between the concept of centrality developed and sought by us, and that present in ordinary 'economic urban theory'. We are convinced, in fact, that this type of abstract analysis does not contribute anything on the operational plane, and luckily it stops at didactic and/or academic exercises. Nevertheless, for information and evaluation, we will indicate - among the very vast specialist literature of this type (for which the writings included in the manual by Mills [1987] can be a good survey) - that we have found a writing by Arnott (1979) and Ch. 5 ('Urban aggregates and city sizes') in the manual by Fujita (1989), two excellent scholastic readings concerning the theory of the 'urban dimension of equilibrium' and the 'optimal urban dimension'. For a general overview, reference can be made to an excellent and well-structured manual on 'Urban Economics' by R. Camagni (1992) which has been recalled several times.

5   We will return more extensively to this point in Ch. 5.

6   For a general discussion, although not conclusive, on urbanity, see Häussermann and Siebel (1992).

7   On this subject, see some other points of view in Murie (1994).

8   Further considerations in Sternlieb and Hughes (1975).

9   Further considerations in an interesting paper by Alpass and Agergaard (1978).

10   It is in this sense that the interesting proposals of modern architects must be adopted - but also carefully controlled - on the revitalisation of the old centralities. See, for example, the well known theses by Victor Gruen (1973). See also by the same author an older but very important text (1964) which anticipated many of the current questions on alternative centralities.

11 On the problem of peripheries, an important critical literature has developed. See an old work by Carver (1965), and the well-known and discussed work by Jacobs (1977), Ravetz (1978) and Herington (1984). See also a book edited by J. Gottmann (1975).

4 Urban planning and ecology:
What relationship?

Since environmentalism introduced - in the analysis of the dynamic equilibrium between development and available resources - the concept of 'sustainable' development,[1] the concept of 'sustainability' has begun to be applied to the 'urban' scale as well (in whatever way it is understood). This has coincided moreover with the reawakening, in the sphere of environmentalism (a movement born at the end of the 1960s mainly in the field of natural resource evaluation on a world scale) of new attention towards problems of the urban environment, which were first much neglected and which suddenly emerged only in the latter half of the 1980s (as already said in the Preface).

1 Urban planning and ecology: a promised marriage never consummated, or a case of hermaphroditism

Not that the problems of the cities, of their disordered development, their social and economic degradation, which is common - albeit with very different characteristics - to the great metropolitan agglomerations of the industrialised West and 'third world', of urban reclamation and renewal, have not long (if not always) been the subject of a vast scientific and popular literature. But the 'environmental' problems have had a 'political' life which is disconnected from 'urban' problems, and amongst which connections have been established which were no stronger than those established among all the categories of socio-economic problems.

The 'environmental' problems - politically - ended up becoming concentrated on the problems of pollution and the over-consumption of natural resources, such as water, atmosphere, the natural heritage, forests, the 'landscape',[2] etc., and on the factors which caused such problems: industry, energy consumption (and production), waste disposal, transport and its infrastructures, perhaps tourism, etc., and perhaps the actual physical expansion of the city (the 'concrete'). The city, if at all, was considered as a factor of damage with regard to the environment, not as an environmental problem in itself. And, if at all, it was considered one of the 'containers' of environmental degradation amongst other things, such as: the hydrographic basin, the 'region', the continent, the stretch of water (lake, bay, gulf, sea), the oceans, the polar caps, etc.

In short, the city has been considered one of the disturbing factors for an eco-system, by which has always been meant a 'natural' eco-system. But only with difficulty has the city been considered an eco-system in itself: because this would have implied the inclusion in (or the extension of) such a concept with respect to other 'not exactly naturalistic' components or variables.[3]

This does not exclude the fact that from the beginning (and perhaps even before) of the so-called environmentalist movement, large sectors of scientific awareness knew of the dangers of this optical distortion, of this sort of 'squint', on the part of environmentalism, concerning the city. And this does not exclude that a continuous and tenacious attempt to *integrate* the environmentalist outlook with the urbanist one has developed, above all from the point of view of planning and operational evaluation.[4] On the contrary, a retrospective look at the best town-planning literature of the past leads us to consider that the concerns, which today are called 'ecological', were central in the pioneering upholders of town-planning, up to the point of being able to define it as the ecology of its time. In short, we have been induced to claim that town-planning and urban ecology have always been the same thing (or at the most a case of 'hermaphroditism').

But the strength of mental fashions sometimes overwhelms the critical spirit - with notable cultural harm, which reverberates on the practical approach to political and administrative problems. And - as was said - only recently has attention turned again to the relationship between town-planning and environmentalist policy, and an explosion of attention has occurred concerning the theme of the relationship between land planning and the ecological equilibrium of the urban environment in the academic and political world.

We can only be happy about this situation. The convergence of the environmental problem with the urban one, which has always been felt and theorised by the more critical elements in planning, cannot but improve the performance of urban policy and of environmental policy.

Nevertheless a certain feeling remains that this convergence, arising from cultural and political pressure, has taken place with excessive attention being given to the object of the problem (the city and the environment) and with scarce attention to the method of conception or of approach to the problem, itself. In other words, much has been said about 'urban ecology', the 'ecological' city, the 'sustainable city' and a myriad of critical factors which are found at the junction of the two basic concepts (environment and city); but our opinion is that not enough work has been done on the basic concepts through which the action can be efficiently approached, and thus from which to begin for a good, scientifically suitable, treatment of the question.

Often these basic concepts are simple and elementary; sometimes their very simplicity is disturbing. But often they are overwhelmed by the quantity of 'aspects' and 'facets' in which the problem is broken down or seen. There is therefore the impression today that there is an abundance of a disordered description of the problems (which are not all new), and of their illustrating and cataloguing, which lacks a suitable 'taxonomy', to classify them and locate them in their correct place, in order to face them at the correct moment and with the correct instruments. In short, there is the impression that the listing and vast reporting of aspects, points of view, experiences, made in documents and conferences (of the type mentioned), is today over-abundant, and ends up constituting a sort of 'background noise' which prevents us from distinguishing the main clear and distinct melodic theme of a method for an appropriate approach to urban environmental planning.

In this chapter we intend to give an initial contribution to a conceptual and operational integration of the relationships, which have been widely discussed and illustrated in recent times,[5] between environmental quality and planning.

In conformity with the concerns recalled above, we will not go into an analysis of the various multiple aspects by which urban environment can be influenced, negatively or positively, with the development of anthropic activities,[6] but rather into how these multiple aspects can be conceptually and methodologically included in a process of planning, evaluation and decision.

To be coherent with this purpose we will concentrate on two essential aspects of a planning methodology for the urban environment:

1　The first concerns the assumption of some essential postulates, in which a good part of the discussion of the contents on urban environment and the ecological city risks losing its way.
2　The second aspect proposes the assumption of three instrumental components, considered essential, in fact prejudicial, for any type of urban environment planning procedure; components through which a good part

of the problems connected to environmental policy decision evaluation may find an appropriate placing.

The taxonomic and definitional postulates concern the concepts of land-use and environment as the objects of planning, in the framework of the current problems, and, at the same time, as an object of scientific analysis.

The essential, methodological approaches concern the treatment of the above-mentioned objects (land-use and environment), in terms of: 1) the appropriate spatial unit of evaluation and planning; 2) the analysis matrix of the land-use/environment; 3) the selection and definition of urban quality indicators (with the possible fixing of city effect and loading capacity parameters).

In the last paragraph, we will illustrate how the assumption of the methodology proposed - including the postulates - could be applied to the current state of discussion for an 'ecological' or 'sustainable' city, in Europe and in the western world.

2 Planning and ecology: some postulates

2.1 The exogenous nature of the conditions (technological, geomorphological, economic, etc.)

On the improvement of the urban environment and its factors, much has been said and much will be said (as mentioned above). However, for a correct organisation of the various problems which concern planning, evaluation and decision, we should separate the analyses and reflections about the factors which may influence the improvement of the urban environment, from those relative to the method and procedures of planning itself. Independently from however interesting, important and sometimes crucial they may be.

Let us give an example to aid comprehension. Nobody would say that the introduction of a new system of urban self-propulsion, such as the electric car, or a system for reducing industrial emissions, would not have a strong influence on pollution and on the quality of the urban environment. But these factors, like many others that we could list,[7] are considered by us to be outside our field of environmental planning analysis: which is limited to what planning (and only planning) can or must do (from the point of view of the methodological approach) in order to improve the management of the balance between land-use and urban environmental quality.

The quality of the urban environment (like that of the environment in general) constitutes - if understood in a very limited sense - only one of the objectives of city planning or management (both as analysis and as a decision-making procedure). If understood in a wider sense (inclusive of the social, economic, cultural, etc., environment) the quality of the urban environment represents *the* basic objective of planning.

In either case, planning finds itself faced with a conflict between objectives (in the first case external and in the second internal to the concept of the urban environment) which will have in some way to be composed, with a 'preference function' (as we call it in 'Planology').

To choose the preference function, it is necessary to know and evaluate the degree to which the objectives come into conflict. The more we examine the evaluation of the impact of alternative land-uses (which correspond to the same number of planning objectives) on the quality of the environment, the better will be the decision relating to the preference function.

The evaluation of impact of alternative land-uses will be made on the basis of given conditions, whether they be observed or programmed (or programmable); and among these conditions there will be all those to be considered 'exogenous' to the specific (mental) model that will be utilised as an instrument of evaluation, such as available technology, geomorphological conditions, economic resources, etc. All these can be called the 'technical conditions'.[8]

The preceding considerations represent thus a first postulate of the relationship between planning and ecology (and thus of our examination): planning and evaluation assume as 'given' the above-mentioned technical conditions.

In conformity with this postulate, planning and evaluation will leave aside the policies that aim to modify the said conditions; and deal only with maximising the effectiveness or minimising the costs of these conditions. In such a way, nevertheless, planning and evaluation provide data for the evaluation of the costs and benefits of the alternative presence or absence (through possible policy interventions) of these technical conditions.[9]

From the above postulate it derives that our examination too will leave aside the factors that may influence the said technical conditions, improving or worsening them, however important and crucial they may be.

2.2 The exogenous nature of the objectives that constitute the preference function

Analogously, an exogenous character to the method and model of planning to be used is required for the objectives. As with the conditions, the objectives as well are defined outside the method and planning model, even if they constitute its raison d'être. In fact they are the subject of the decision-makers, and not of the planners.

Exogenous are both the objectives of the first instance or starting objectives (which we will call goals or concerns) and the final or finishing objectives (which we will call targets).

The first are indispensable for the construction of indicators and measuring instruments. They are defined (exogenously) by the decision-maker at the beginning of the process. It is a serious error not to include the decision-maker at the beginning of the process of concerns definition, and not 'model' reality on them: the model loses the quality of a 'decision-oriented model', and assumes that of an indefinite 'positive model' whose variables are casual and not justified (not made explicit but assumed by use, by the intuition of the planner and often by past problems).

The second (the targets) are the final aim of planning and the planner. But their trade-off (or final combination), on the basis of a correct approach managed by the planner, is the task of the decision-maker; they are thus exogenous to the method, even if they are defined through the method and thanks to the method.

The first are not quantified. They must only permit the appraisal of the quantifiable indicators (variables) (see below para. 3.3). The second have no sense if they are not quantified, exogenously or endogenously to the model (see para. 3.1).

Therefore, a second postulate could be thus formulated: planning and evaluation assume as given the starting goals or concerns, and assume as exogenous constraints the final targets of the process.

This second postulate of the relationship between planning and ecology (which is a general postulate in any planning, in its relations with any ambit of community interests), should put some order into the subject, free the ground from misleading arguments and allow us to concentrate on the problems and issues that are typical of the planning of the ecological city.

3 The methodological prerequisites in the planning of the ecological city

As said in the premise, there are some approaches that we consider fundamental, in fact prejudicial, for the processes of ecological planning; fundamental in as much as they are prerequisites for the supplying of a correct framework for evaluation, and thus for decision.

3.1 *The appropriate spatial unit of evaluation and planning*

The first among these concerns that which we will call the 'appropriate territorial unit' of evaluation and planning. It constitutes a premise of validity for any other measurement and evaluation of environmental equilibrium. In fact, both an equilibrium in territorial and environmental resources, and the evaluation of indicators of urban quality cannot ignore spatial constraints; i.e., they acquire a meaning only within that territory whose scale is dictated by the nature of the demand on the territory and the territorial extent of its impact on the available supply and which constitutes the natural space for the enjoyment of that quality (urban in our case, but also other forms of well-being). Naturally the problem thus arises of the approach of the appropriate spatial unit of measurement of the equilibrium, and thus of evaluation, planning and decision-making.

In fact, it is known, that there is not a single appropriate ambit in which it is reasonable to manage ecological equilibrium in a rational way. Any anthropic activity, any demand on land-use, any factor of pressure on the environment, has its own impact area, and thus its appropriate ambit for evaluation and management. The most generally recognised ambits of impact are the 'planetary'[10] scale, the 'continental'[11] scale, the 'hydrographic' (basins) scale,[12] and finally the urban scale which is the specific object of our reflections.

But the majority of human activities, which produce pressure on the territory and environment, are connected to urban settlement, and of an 'urban' nature (albeit in the most complete sense which we will mention later), and have the city as their exclusive ambit of ecological impact. One could call it the 'urban basin'.[13]

If certain industrial and energy activities are excluded, and those linked to touristic consumption in areas exclusively dedicated to tourism, almost all the human activities are connected to the urban life of the citizens, which is a 'daily' life and functionally delimited within the arc of the day (in the ambit of that which Doxiadis and others have called the 'daily urban system').[14] Such an ambit corresponds analogously to the already expressed concept of the 'urban basin'.

The scale on which it is appropriate (i.e., reasonable and meaningful) to measure the relationship of equilibrium or disequilibrium between demand and availability of land-use (and construct the LURM mentioned in the following paragraph) is therefore this urban system or basin.[15]

And since we have assumed that urban ecological equilibrium is given by equilibrium between these demands and the availability of land-use, we may also call this system or urban basin the 'urban eco-system'.

In short, it seems obvious that the appropriate ambit for measuring, evaluating and managing any phenomena of impact on the city, is the same as that in which the human activities are performed which produce it.

It ensues that by urban ambit (system or basin) is not meant here only the physical phenomenon of the urban built-up area (even if it is within the built-up space that the major cases of activity intrusion and overloading occur), but rather the functions of the city, i.e., the functions that the citizens perform in the city.[16]

The space occupied by these functions is much more vast than that of the built-up continuum (one thinks of the development of commuting between the home and the place of access to many urban services and the place of work). But such a space has nevertheless a theoretical limit provided by the daily acceptability of access to urban services. Within the isochrone of this accessibility one can speak of an urban system (or basin).[17] Beyond this isochrone, a real urban effect is not produced, but rather a system of 'meta-urban' anthropic relations (holidays, journeys, tourism, national and international business, conferences, political life, etc.). And from the point of view of ecological impact, these activities constitute an occasional load, in the urban systems in which they are developed, which is perhaps in addition, but not organic or co-substantial to the system itself.

But even if more vast than the urban continuum, the appropriate space must nevertheless include a mass of residents, large enough to constitute an economic justification for the location of a set of social anthropic activities and 'superior' services which produce the city effect. Without this effect, in fact, that urban 'quality', which is at the basis of the modern process of urbanisation, which is the primary condition and *sine qua non* of any social well-being to which any family aspires, is not acquired. Any environmental planning (preventive and/or curative) applied in a territory which does not guarantee the catchment 'critical mass'[18] that is sufficient to create the city effect, is destined to fail, because the catchment load will tend to turn to those territories and situations in which such a city effect is realised and thus render useless and redundant the preceding interventions. In brief, the ecological equilibrium must be realised in those situations in which the socio-economic equilibrium is realised as well (and vice versa), with the control of the factors of overload in the territory, and in the bordering territories in which the overload tends to drift, with the risk of the failure of the actual policy of re-equilibrium.

The minimum limit of accessibility and the minimum limit of the critical catchment mass are the two contrasting constraints which dominate the choice of the planner of the Appropriate Spatial Unit of Evaluation and Planning.[19]

In short, in order to make sense, an analysis and evaluation of the loads and loading capacities (equilibrium between demand and supply of land-use) needs to legitimise in anticipation the spatial unit to which such an analysis is applied. For example: what sense is there in measuring the production per capita of refuse in a territory where people reside, if then these people leave their refuse in a territory where they spend the better part of their working day? or, what sense does it have to measure the relationship between public spending for urban services provided in an administrative area (municipality?), if the greater part of the consumption of such public services is made by citizens in a territory in which they do not pay taxes because these are paid only in the area where they reside? In brief, the appropriate spatial unit of reference is that which manages to embrace all the functions of supply and all the functions of demand of land-use.

A holistic approach, in this case, does not seem optional, but is rather required in order to give logical meaning to the evaluation. It is only in this sense that one can speak of an 'integrated' approach to planning.

If we mean by urban eco-system the system that collects the interdependencies of all the anthropic activities that produce a city effect, it is essential that the supply-demand balance is made only on the scale of that eco-system, otherwise a distorted and false balance will result.

The scale of that eco-system (i.e., the appropriate unit of analysis and evaluation for the balance demand-supply of land-use) is that for which the conditions of equilibrium of the said balance must (and can) be produced. That which (in terms of natural ecology) would mean that the tensions, pressures, impacts and eventual 'disequilibrium' which should be recorded in the balance, have the possibility of being absorbed, recycled, 'metabolised' by the same organism in question: the urban eco-system.[20]

If this equilibrium, or re-equilibrium, could not be realised (because the conditions of such an equilibrium would not take place), it would mean that it would be necessary to have recourse to an additional supply of spatial resources outside the unit of analysis in question; in other words, to put pressure (demand) and exercise an impact on another unit of analysis. It would mean, therefore, that the unit of the chosen analysis is neither an actual nor a potential urban eco-system;[21] and therefore as a unit of analysis and evaluation for planning and urban management it is not 'appropriate'.

Naturally the recommendation here to evaluate equilibrium between factors of land pressure and availability on the appropriate scale, does not mean - once the need for a balance on this scale is satisfied - that balances cannot be 'measured' for a zoning of more limited dimensions, if it may help to know better the 'overlaying' (or total and integrated load) of various pressures on a local basis, and allow for a more aware or wiser (positive or negative) locating, above all of industrial plants.[22]

3.2   The land-use matrix

The first is that relative to the analysis itself of the relationship between land-use and spatial or environmental resources.

Environmental malaise is always an imbalance between demand for environmental resources, from which arises the consumption of the same, and the supply of the same resources, which are - like all resources - by definition limited. The task of planning is aggravated, with respect to other socio-economic disequilibrium, by the fact that the greater part of the supply of environmental resources is constituted by resources that cannot be reproduced, and which represent absolute, and not relative (on places, times, cultures, productive capacity, etc.) constraints.

In the so-called 'urban' environment (we will see below the limited value of this concept) as well, environmental imbalance (whether it be from pollution, traffic congestion, the marring of the urban landscape, or the loss of social communication, etc.) is between the demand for the use of urban activities and the supply of environmental resources.

Thus the first analytical procedure required is that of listing:

− on the one hand, all the land-use demands, which satisfy activity needs (which satisfy in turn the citizens' needs); demands that are classified by type of activity or type of need to satisfy: housing, squares, roads, industrial zoning, spaces and public buildings for use, green areas to be used, zoning for pastimes and sport, shopping centres, and so on;
− and, on the other hand, all the available land resources (which constitute land-use supply), classified according to the intrinsic qualities of the territory and its 'vocations' of use, both from the natural point of view and from the point of view of anthropic pre-existencies (above all in the case of

city areas): e.g., historic buildings, the urban landscape, green conservation areas, land for agriculture, areas for public infrastructures.

The two lists may face each other as on a balance sheet.[23] But they may also constitute the vectors of a 'land-use and resources matrix' (LURM[24]), whose coefficients represent the transferral of existing resources into potential demand; or, vice versa, the transferral of the existing or policy-oriented demand into necessary resources (or spaces).

The construction of a land-use and resources matrix is not easy; but - albeit in different forms and approximations - it is an essential requirement for correct ecological planning of the city. The problems arise when the same land supply unit may at the same time satisfy several demands, and accept several uses, and thus be a demand for promiscuous use. We have classified such promiscuous uses as proper or improper,[25] if they are considered compatible or not among themselves, by nature or extent: by nature, when a use damages another in quality (e.g., a steel works in the same block as a concert hall, to use an extreme example); by extent, when a use, whilst not being incompatible with another (commercial activities with residential housing, for example), becomes so because of the overcrowding it creates.

The LURM constitutes a computational and evaluating model of the compatibilities and incompatibilities not only between alternative uses for a single unit of an available resource; but also of the compatibilities and incompatibilities of a demand for use - actual or policy-oriented - with the existing or potential available resources. The LURM, in short, constitutes an instrument for evaluating the opportunity cost of the use of a resource: i.e., of the advantage lost in terms of alternative uses.

And, in as much as it is an instrument of evaluation, it also constitutes the instrument offered by the planner to the decision-maker for its trade-offs between costs and benefits, for fixing its targets and for rationalising, finally, its plan decisions.

3.3   The definition of loading capacity indicators and parameters

The third issue that must be dealt with for a correct planning and evaluation of the urban environment is the construction of a system of indicators that is adequate for the decision model constructed. These indicators are, simply, the variables of the model. And, as said in para. 2.2, this is a 'decision model' if its variables (indicators) express in some way the problems or social goals or concerns of the decision-maker.

The first task of the planner is therefore that of translating the concern or goal into an indicator that is susceptible to having the role of a variable of the general model.[26] The indicator - obviously - is the instrument of measurement. And despite the obviousness, one does not understand how processes of urban planning and land-use - as almost always is the case - can be carried out without an adequate system of indicators. This is one of the factors that has made planning so unreliable: because it has disassociated it from the possibility of any control of performance and implementation.

Often a problem or social goal of the first instance is not translatable into a single and simple indicator. That problem or goal brings with it, besides the indicator that expresses it (which allows it to measure its state, or also the result), actions as well (and relative indicators) which allow for its implementation. The indicators of state or of result are accompanied also by indicators of action and achievement. To simplify things we will call all indicators which are conceived and used to identify actions and measure results programme indicators.

It is highly advisable that the list of social goals or concerns - which as said in para. 2.2 should constitute the starting point of the process of planning and evaluation - is organised hierarchically and 'structured' in a frame (which we have called the 'programme structure').[27] In it the horizontal list expresses the various typologies of goals (with their indicators) and their relationships; the vertical one expresses the interlinked relationship goals/means, for each of the pre-selected objectives and their relationships.

Each horizontal and vertical relationship produces indicators that can, fixed on certain values, constitute plan coefficients or parameters. The fixed values of the indicators may be supplied by the land-use matrix (LURM) (para. 3.2), if with the appropriate evaluations one arrived at determining an optimal programmatic loading capacity for each portion of the territory, for each typology of use or value threshold beyond which the unbalancing overload could be determined.[28]

With the evaluation of the optimum policy-oriented load one could arrive at the definition of a 'loading capacity standard', or 'holding capacity standard' as Chapin calls it, who makes it the basis for determining space requirements in plans.[29]

In the final analysis, the three issues that we have summarily indicated, ('Appropriate Spatial Unit of Evaluation'; 'Land-Use Matrix'; 'System of Indicators of Result, Achievement, and Loading Capacity') constitute three prerequisites to be combined together in order to render urban planning operational and efficient, intended as an integration of all the aspects or goals: social, economic and environmental.

4   Application to the case of a policy of urban 'sustainability'

What relevance may the postulates and methodological and instrumental prerequisites recommended above have for a policy of urban sustainability (above all on the European scale and with reference to the EU Urban Environment Group document mentioned above)?[30]

4.1   Implications of the use of assumable postulates

The first result of a clear assumption of the two postulates proposed would be that of separating cleanly (in the discussions which normally develop on the 'sustainable city') from the defence of the use of advanced technology, which is completely obvious and acceptable, with respect to the problems of management and planning.[31] This would avoid a great deal of confusion of language; and it would avoid being obliged - to escape such confusion - to make tiresome distinctions between the technical, geographical, cultural conditions, etc. To give an example, one can think of the different climactic conditions which can present variable decisive differentials and equally decisive cost comparisons in the implementation of environmental policies for the rationalisation of urban heating.

The second postulate, relative to the exogenous nature of the goals, induces likewise a clear separation of the reasoning of value judgements and on cultural preferences from balance assessments. The first ones deserve as much attention and analysis as possible, but do not merit being mixed - or worse 'smuggled' in - with 'technical' and economic compatibility arguments. Value judgements and absolute preferences (i.e., those that are not related to the trade-offs imposed by the conditions) must be dealt with for what they are, with a full awareness and notion of their significance, otherwise the general educational result would suffer greatly.

The defect of many international documents of a 'literary' nature is that of lumping everything in together: here a technical argument is developed, there a quality choice is introduced, and it is not clear whether we are faced with the opinions of experts or politicians, or the expert masquerading as politicians, or the politician who mimics the expert.

4.2   The effects of the adoption of the prejudicial instruments of analysis

But even more obvious would be the positive effects of the adoption of the methods of evaluation and of the prejudicial instruments of analysis suggested.

First of all they all aim at rendering the different situations comparable, if and when it is a question of making comparisons, in the evaluation of experts and decision-makers. To quantify the situations (for example, the impacts of anthropic actions on resources) it is necessary to have clear and homogenous units of measurement in the various situations.

Making a 'balance' of the supply and demand for territory implies the task of approximating a measurement of supply and demand which is conceptually valid, i.e., which refers to unitary concepts and comparable realities. If there is no common unit of measurement, each comparison risks being misleading or false. In this case as well, it is the absence of method which would create falsity in the data and thus also erroneousness in the opinions taken from these, whatever the attraction of the arguments. The lack of homogeneity in the indicators constitutes one of the most dangerous pitfalls in environmental planning.

The measurement of phenomena loses any sense if it is not applied to the appropriate territorial units of evaluation and planning. Many of the discussions on small, medium, big cities and their quality (of life, environment, etc.) are authentic *flatus vocis* if there is no guarantee beforehand of the sense and significance of the territorial, demographic, economic ambits to which they refer, and the thresholds (of accessibility, the 'critical mass' of services, the city effect) are not pre-established on which to be based, in order to give judgements. Throughout the world at debates on the 'sustainable city', I have not yet had the pleasure of coming across a premise or frame of reference, modest and numerical, in which a sort of conceptual 'glossary' was put first, also possibly with quantified parameters, of the words used (metropolitan area, congestion, and so on). The day when a serious (multidisciplinary and also multinational) work of research provides such parameters, the work of environmental planning which refers to it would lead to sure 'spontaneous' results. In the present conditions any intervention or policy is a lottery.

And in effect it is on the loading parameters (used however with the appropriate schemes of territory supply and demand equilibrium, and with the appropriate territorial ambits), which the efficiency of any environmental policy would be measured, which will always be nevertheless a trade-off between alternative uses of resources and a choice between alternative scenarios. Without appropriate goal and performance indicators and without reference parameters, any plan or any policy would just be a dream.

I do not think that such parameters and indicators (of goals, performance, load, etc.) will be able to reach a universal and absolute validity. They too are subject to temporal and cultural variables. But knowing the experience of others in measurable and comparable terms is the premise for a creative exchange of authentic experience and greater cohesion, if really desired.

Notes

1   A concept which was popularised above all in the Report of the World Commission on Environment and Development - The 'Brundtland' Report (WCED, 1987) but which had found a wide usage in some international study reports such as, for example, the study on 'Sustainable Development of the Biosphere', carried out by IIASA, Laxenburg, Vienna (see Clark and Munn [eds], 1986). Neither would it be right to ignore that, albeit with slightly different terms, the concept has had a much longer history, at least as concerns the first reports promoted by the 'Club of Rome'.

2   By 'environmental assets' at the most the 'landscape' was taken into consideration, indicating with such a term the countryside 'landscape' (marine, mountain, hilly, lake, etc.) rather than the 'urban' landscape proper.

3   It is not coincidental that the first phase of the environmentalist movement (let us say the first two decades from the mid-60s to the mid-80s) provoked a great amount of protagonism on the part of academics in the natural sciences (chemist, physicists, geologists, biologists, botanists, zoologists, etc.) whilst the experts on the city, the 'urbanists', found themselves somewhat marginalised. And it is not coincidental that it was taken for granted that 'ecology' only meant the ecology of natural life (and of man as a biological being), and not the 'human ecology' which had had a great development some decades previously (the 20s and 30s), above all with the so-called 'Chicago School' of Sociology, which amongst other things had given great importance to urban analysis, looking mainly at man as a 'social animal'.

It is worth noting that in a well-informed and extensive collection of essays on the theme of the relationship between planning and ecology (Roberts and Roberts, 1984), the 'naturalistic' meaning of ecology is taken for granted. Furthermore the editors of that work complain that - despite the fact that the 'progenitor of modern town planning' (Patrick Geddes, 1886,1904, 1915) was a biologist by training, justly considered as such, perhaps with some others) and that he was led 'to re-interpret the phenomena of urbanisation in ecological terms' (this too is true) - 'since the time of Geddes the place of ecology has declined in planning circles as other professions and considerations, initially public health and engineering, latterly economic and sociological, have become more central' (p. 1). But the authors (who are biologists as well) neglect to mention that Geddes in fact 'reinterpreted' the urban phenomenon as a *human* eco-systemic (and not only natural) phenomenon, and did not consider naturalistic ecology of any particular importance for urban analysis, apart from for methodology, considering the city, like any good biologist, as an 'organism'. Current attention on certain so-called ecological (natural) phenomena is important for planning, but has nothing to do with a systemic reinterpretation of the city itself as an object of planning. (On the role of Geddes in the history of urban thought, see Archibugi [1995] of which is forthcoming, a revised and augmented edition.)

4 Clear evidence of this among others is the work of the most important 'theorists' of planning, for example, that by Harvey Perloff. We must not forget that one of the most important contributions by Perloff (already mentioned repeatedly in the preceding chapters) as director of 'Resources for the Future' in the 1960s, was his focusing on environmental evaluation as the 'core' of town-planning; which was not difficult at all for him, a disciple of the 'Chicago School' already mentioned and which will have to be mentioned more often in the history of contemporary town-planning (see Perloff, 1957, 1969a and b, 1980; and some important collective works edited by the same: Perloff [ed.], 1961, 1968 [with Wingo], 1972, 1975). On the role of Perloff in the evolution of modern town-planning much more must be said: see for example the collection of writings edited by Burns and Friedmann (Perloff, 1985). For an in-depth examination of the role of the Chicago School in the development of the ecological conception in town planning see the Italian contribution by G. Giannotti (1966), with an introduction by F. Archibugi, in the research series published by the Planning Studies Centre.

5 A privileged reference will be made to a recent excellent report entitled 'European Sustainable Cities', produced in the ambit of the 'Urban Environment Experts of the European Union', constituted by the EC Commission in 1991 (and of which the author has been, incidentally, a member). This report was presented as a 'consultation draft' at the previously mentioned 'European Conference on Sustainable Cities and Towns', Aalborg, 24-27 May 1994 (EC Commission, 1994c).

6 This has been briefly done already in Ch. 2.

7   See in the report mentioned by the OECD (1990) a very well conceived list of possible actions, both as innovations to be introduced, and as policy guidelines for: urban area rehabilitation; better urban transport; and greater urban energy efficiency.

8   It would be helpful to open a separate chapter of analysis for each of these technical conditions, and give an ordered catalogue of all the factors for and against the urban environment, which those conditions - internally - represent. For example: a systematic analysis of all the available technologies and their efficacy on the reduction of environmental impact, in the various fields of anthropic activity; the analysis of the environmental effects of certain classes or categories of geographical factors (climatic, orographic, landscape, etc.) on living conditions. The analysis is less extensive on the economic constraints, which usually have a single parameter (the monetary one) to evaluate the opportunity costs of alternative plan solutions.

9   On the influence of technology in town-planning a vast 'polity' literature has developed which, in the opinion of the author, has not served a suitable development of the town-planning discipline. See, for example, amongst others, Castells (1985).

10   For example, many activities connected to the production and consumption of energy and chemicals (atmospheric emissions) or of wood products (deforestation), wherever in the world, have an impact on the planetary scale if these are over-sized; such effects are produced as global warming or the reduction and disintegration of the ozone layer. In these cases the measurements for evaluating and managing the equilibrium between the causes and effects of the phenomenon have their appropriate ambit on the planetary scale which would imply a decision-maker or a decisions system on that scale.

11   For example with 'acid rain'.

12   For example with the release into waterways of urban effluents.

13   Also because by now human settlement itself is becoming 'urbanised', i.e., requiring for the totality of the population easy access to urban forms of life. This means also that the crisis of the urban environment due to ecological disequilibrium is the most serious, both because today the majority of the population already - at least in western countries - lives in the city, and because - as mentioned - very soon the total population will live in the city, in urban living conditions. What will be the quality of these conditions is the very object of urban planning.

14   See above in Ch. 2, para. 5.

15 The concept of urban system or basin evokes a long and still not finished debate on the size of the 'planning area'. Despite the theoretical possibility of adjusting such an area to any planning intervention circumstances and context, for long-term land-use planning - above all in the USA - reference prevails to the 'metropolitan area' (see Chapin and Kaiser, 1985, p.115) on the subject: also because of the well known availability in the USA, from 1975, of a statistical unit of reference: the Standard Metropolitan Statistical Area (SMSA), which was created with criteria close to the needs of the planner, and with an abundance of available information. In Europe the debate has produced fewer results, both on the theoretical side and on that of the practical delimitation of statistical areas, apart from the case in Italy of the 'metropolitan systems' in 'Progetto 80' (a government study carried out in 1969 as a long-term perspective of a social and economic five-year plan 1971-75, which was then not followed up - see Centro di studi e piani economici [1971]): or the case, in Germany of the gebiet einheiten (basin units) of the 'Landesplanung programme' (agreed by the Federal Parliament in 1975, but which subsequent governments in practice shelved).

In conformity with the prevalence of the metropolitan area concept (neither adequately discussed or clarified anywhere) the concept of 'Sub-metropolitan Analysis Zones' has likewise been introduced and used (as they are called by Chapin and Kaiser [1985, pp. 118-120]). These zones, which are evidently more flexible for any problem of data collection and regarding any international comparison of situations, are also the most reliable with regard to the meaningfulness of the phenomena if they are examined in their interaction and systemic interdependence. They lend themselves therefore to many risks of bad interpretation. Their statistical usefulness however is important so long as they are firmly anchored to a clear methodological approach on the 'appropriate area of evaluation'.

16 The literature on the problems of the functional 'regionalisation' of the city is vast. We would recall and recommend the already mentioned (see Ch. 2, para. 6.1) work by Fox on 'Functional Economic Areas (FEA): Fox, 1973 and 1974 (Ch. XII), concerning the operationality of systems; and the work of Openshaw (1977), and Masser and Scheurwater (1980) on analytical modelisation. Concerning spatial analysis in general, see works by Berry (1966, 1972a); J. Friedmann and J. Miller (1965) and M.M. Fischer (1982). On regionalisation, understood as a search for an integrated basin of activities (work, mobility, etc.) more extensive references can be found in Chs 5 and 6.

17   For example, in the attempts proposed for territorial re-equilibrium in Italy (the above-mentioned 'Progetto 80', and the 'Quadroter', which will be discussed more at length in Chs 8 and 9), a minimum acceptable isochrone of 1-1.30 hours daily commuting time has been assumed (see Archibugi, 1983a, 1985b, 1987, 1993a).

18   For example, the 'critical catchment mass' for superior (metropolitan) urban services and for the city effect has been assessed (in the above-mentioned Italian projects for territorial re-equilibrium) between 500,000 and 1,000,000 inhabitants-users.

19   For further discussion on this point, see Chs. 5 and 6.

20   The metaphorical expression 'urban metabolism' has been long used (see for example Wolman, 1965). But the use that has been made of it concerns more the so-called 'material balance approach' - for which see much work by 'Resources for the Future' (Basta and Bower, 1982; Basta et al., 1978; Bower, 1977). But the concept that we use is applied to a set of urban functions which are much more extended than that for the flows of physical and natural materials.

21   The urban system as well - like any other system - is a complex of relations which are, in act or potential, in equilibrium; like a biological organism which is, or tends to be in equilibrium. Where such an equilibrium is not reached, the urban system not only enters into crisis (as in the cases in which it exists, but with overloading); but is also not realised, as in the cases when the desired processes of urbanisation fail to be activated, and certain centres, which may be urban as well, remain 'dependent' (for the rarer services) on the more important centres, which constitutes a factor in the greater overloading of the latter.

22   See the concept of 'Sub-metropolitan Analysis Zones' which is much discussed in Chapin and Kaiser (see para. 3.1). In my opinion the methodologies and experimentation implemented in Holland by the Ministry of Housing, Physical Planning and the Environment (VROM), with the institution of 'Integral Environmental Zoning' IEZ, are to be followed very closely and with interest (see De Roo, 1993). One might ask oneself if analogous methodologies could not be applied to a more 'integral' zoning, in which pressure factors are exercised that are not only those of noise, smells, toxicity, but also those belonging to a more complete conception of the environment such as: refuse output, urban traffic, urban landscape, social and cultural accessibility, etc.).

23   A balance of territorial needs, both as location requirements and as space requirements, is taken into consideration in any planning manual worthy

of the name. See the highly detailed manual by Chapin and Kaiser (1985) already mentioned, in particular Chs 11 and 12.

24 A more detailed explanation of the LURM is to be found in Ch. 7.

25 In the didactic work mentioned above (Archibugi, 1979, pp. 181-84), and see Ch. 7.

26 One can argue whether the choice, on the part of the planner, of the indicators for expressing the goals or problems of the decision-maker must not be subsequently agreed and approved by the actual decision-maker.

27 'Programme structuring' (concept, meaning, utilisation, etc.) has been the subject of many works by the author (Archibugi, 1973, 1986b, 1996), because I consider also that is an essential hinge of planning methodology. Programme structure may contain various levels of goals and actions for achieving them. If there are more than two levels, each level constitutes a goal for the lower level and a means for the upper level, in an interlinked system. Albeit at different levels of elaboration, 'programme structures' are to be considered the frame organisation of the social indicators elaborated by the OECD (OECD 1973, 1976, 1982), and other systems of objectives contained in 'national plans' (see references in the Preface). I consider the mentioned treatment by Harvey Perloff on 'the quality of the urban environment' to be a pioneering work (Perloff, 1969). See also a recent study carried out for the Italian Ministry of the Environment by the Planning Studies Centre (Centro di studi e piani economici, 1992). Certain environmental indicators are contained in a work by the Dutch Government, Ministry of Housing, Physical Planning and Environment (Nl, Government of the Netherlands, 1991).

28 As already said in para. 3.1, the optimal policy-oriented load, understood as the sum of loads due to the various load factors, may be evaluated, with regard to some 'effects', on the portions of territory that do not respond to what has been defined as the 'appropriate territorial unit of evaluation' (for example the IEZ indicated in para. 3.1 above). But whatever the overload is that occurs in a single area, it is necessary to know the load of all the bordering areas as well, to give an operational conclusion (of planning) to the measurement itself. It is not enough to know that we have reached an overload in some areas, if we are not able to spread it over other areas. And it is necessary to know even if a load factor (e.g., a single activity, hospital or industry) pertains or not to the overloaded area. If it does pertain, it will be thus necessary to evaluate

what disequilibria are created in other areas by the removal of the same. This is why the appropriate ambit of evaluation and measurement should coincide with the same ambit of planning and decision. Finally, it is not enough to know (and know how to know) the integral load of an area; one must also know at what moment of the planning process this knowledge must be used and for what purpose.

29   Chapin and Kaiser, 1985, pp. 405-481.
30   See para. 1. Obviously here we refer also to numerous programmes for the improvement of the urban environment which have been formulated in recent times on a national scale. Interesting perspectives may be found in the national plans for the environment of various countries (for example, the Dutch Government plan and those of the French, British, Canadian, and Japanese Governments, which we mentioned in the Preface).
31   On this point, see EC Commission (1994b).

5 The 'urban mobility integrated basin':
A prerequisite of rational planning

In the previous chapter, in our discussion of what we have called the 'methodological instrumental prerequisites of the ecological city' we identified three: the appropriate territorial unit, the territorial matrix, and the system of indicators (of urban effect and loading).

In this chapter (and in the following one) we will examine the appropriate territorial unit of evaluation and planning more in depth. And we will consider it, in this chapter, in the form of the 'urban mobility integrated basin' (UMIB), the concept and operationality of which will be discussed. In the following chapter we will examine the concept and operationality of the labour market basin.

We will refer rapidly also to the concept of 'policy-oriented mobility demand', which is another specific object of reflection (of a methodological and even epistemological nature), and which we must consider as an indispensable condition for the development of rational processes of mobility and (transport) planning (and consequent models), at various levels of the territorial approach. The concept and operationality of the UMIB presuppose in fact the adoption (and consequent research) of a 'policy-oriented demand', albeit limited - in this specific case - to 'urban' mobility (see para. 2 below).

1 The 'urban mobility integrated basin' (UMIB)

The concept and operationality of the UMIB has been the object of past analyses carried out in the ambit of the definition of a 'taxonomy' of transport demand,[1] and they have gone in step with the study of 'appropriate units of territorial urban planning', i.e., with the study of an 'urban systems' policy,[2] today called more appropriately 'urban eco-systems'[3] (we are linked directly therefore with what has already been said in Ch. 2, para. 2 and Ch. 4, para. 2.1).

The UMIB is defined as 'integrated' since it represents - as we will explain better and succinctly later - a multi-functional basin, which responds to the multiple requisites of an urban systems policy: it is as a basin for daily traffic, as it is for work,[4] health services, university activities, cultural and recreational activities and managerial activities,[5] etc.

The concept of UMIB has been developed in fact on the basis of a 'taxonomic' dichotomy between the 'daily' accessibility and 'non-daily' accessibility of people to territorial goods and services; and thus it has been placed at the basis of a definition and delimitation of the 'Urban Systems'.[6]

This is why the UMIB is to be considered thus the most appropriate ambit for the analysis and evaluation of a 'policy-oriented demand' for urban transport.

2 The policy-oriented demand for urban transport

The concept of mobility basin, and therefore of urban transportation, is not new in the literature.[7] Such a basin, however, has almost always been conceived as the result of 'current' measurements of various types: e.g., as the result of a function of maximum inclusion of flows that have an origin and destination which is external to the basin itself. In these approaches the evaluation of the demand for mobility is 'exogenous' to the procedure of the determining and identification of the basins.

More rare has been research aimed at linking explicitly and in 'policy-oriented' terms, the sequence:

land use territory
⇩
transportation network planning
⇩
demand evaluation

to a function of 'generalised minimum cost'.

Such research has not extended - moreover - the field of objectives to the (multidimensional) sector of social and environmental costs and benefits, which are linked in turn to an overall project of land-use; and which, furthermore, consider that the demand for mobility is strongly conditioned by accessibility.[8]

In mentioning research on the methods of determination of the UMIB, we have placed ourselves in a position that is overturned with respect to that indicated above: here, having considered as known and 'modelable' the causal and functional links between land-use choices and the generation of demand for movement and access, we have wished to look for a method of planning, the territorial distribution of those choices (not only concerning interventions for new settlements, but also those concerning the organisational distribution of old ones), in such a way that the necessity - and therefore the demand - for movement is minimal.

This means that the principal objective is - so to speak - 'shifted' from the satisfaction of the expressed demand to the satisfaction of needs that generate that demand.

In other terms, the mobility is no longer seen as a need, the satisfaction of which constitutes an objective of the plan; but rather it becomes a function of the cost which is to be contained at the indispensable minimum. Since the real objective is that of satisfying - in the best way - the demand for accessibility to services, the work place, etc., i.e., to a mix which we have defined as 'service-opportunity', and on which depends the city effect and urban living quality. In this sense we are talking about policy-oriented evaluation of demand, or more simply, 'policy-oriented demand'.[9]

3 General approach to the definition of urban planning objectives

Posed in these terms, the problem appears as that of defining a procedure of 'decision-making' relative to the delimitation of territorial spheres that are capable (in a long-term optic) of satisfying a multiplicity of objectives, which are not always compatible between themselves. Such ambits, which have been named for a while 'Urban Systems' and more recently 'Urban Eco-Systems', are those within which it is probable that a city effect can be produced, whose characteristics can be summarised thus:

1 Every individual must be able to have access - within a reasonable time - to various types of services, to those which constitute that 'urban living quality': to which everyone should have the right (and aspiration).
2 Every type of service has its optimal efficiency size, which is limited both at the higher and lower level: from this it derives that is there is not always a sufficient size population within the possible access isochrones, whilst in

other cases (of strong urban concentration) there is an 'excessive' population within the same isochrones, which determines a damaging 'giganticness' of the actual service structures (beyond the higher efficiency level).

3 The costs of commuting to work and services may contribute to the reduction of the quality of life.

4 The solutions for adaptation of the transportation system to the model of distribution of centres of demand (residences) and of the centres of supply (operational units), must be evaluated together with the impact that they have on the entire environmental and territorial system of which they are a part.

4 The UMIB accessibility system

Thus, at the basis of the system, one has the concept of accessibility. In fact, as a general prospect objective there has been proposed that of:

obtaining a repartition of the territory in 'ambits' (called 'Urban Systems') in which it is possible to guarantee for the whole population - with minimal adaptation costs - an acceptable access cost to that set of opportunities-services that can realise the city effect, or rather an elevated level of urban living quality.

On the subject of 'accessibility' we can distinguish three fundamental aspects:

1 Accessibility to what?
2 Accessibility for whom?
3 Accessibility with what costs?

If one accepts this division of the object of any analysis of accessibility into three aspects,[10] we can recognise also that in the first aspect is configured that which we will call *supply of accessibility*, i.e., the services to which one must or one desires to have access; in the second aspect is configured the *demand for accessibility*, i.e., the user of such services; in the third aspect is configured the *cost or price of accessibility*. The classic elements making up the market are thus present, albeit with all the institutional limitations that characterise it. Let us attempt now to analyse these three aspects in their contents.

Supply, from the point of view of spatial or territorial accessibility, is represented by the dislocation in the territory of those points (which we will call supply 'points' or 'centres') that are represented as the 'destinations' of movements.

The contents of these 'supply centres' - that are able to produce the city effect (since it is these alone that we are dealing with when we talk of 'Urban Systems') - in relation to the necessary user (population) thresholds, and in relation to acceptable access times, have already been analysed.

(In such works there has also been proposed the range of services that are susceptible to composing the 'opportunities-services' mix on which the concept of 'Urban System' has been constructed.)

In the analysis recalled concerning the quality of supply, the indicators have already been expressed by means of which the objectives are fixed; these were:

a   the minimum user threshold (linked to a 'frequency of use' indicator);
b   the maximum user threshold (linked to utilised technologies);
c   the temporal threshold of access (isochrone).

Wishing to further enrich the analysis of the contents of supply (for the purpose of enriching the articulated taxonomy of possible 'objectives' to be borne in mind) other indicators could be added, such as:

d   an indicator of the level of 'integrated functionality' of the preselected services;
e   an indicator of the level of 'collective utility' (attempting to express, in other words, the distinctions between indispensable, necessary, useful and superfluous);
f   an indicator of quality in relation to the urban agglomeration-effect (which in part is already contained in the indicator d, but which may also have a wider significance);
g   a specific indicator of the integrated presence 'services-job' (already present both in d and f, but which may have an autonomous and specific expression as well).

These analyses of possible objectives, to be linked to the 'qualification' of accessibility supply (by means of the indicators suggested above and others connected to new objectives), can be the objective of *ad hoc* research.

The demand, again from the point of view of spatial or territorial accessibility, is represented by the dislocation in the territory of those points (which we will call 'places' or 'centres' of demand) in which are placed the users of the opportunities-services. It is a question thus of the places of residence of the served population, which are represented as the 'origins' of the movements.

An analysis of the contents of the demand concerns thus in the first place the characteristics of the served population. But the classification of the population with regard to their access needs and therefore of movement towards the places or centres of supply (given the mix of opportunities-services considered suitable for the city effect) presents some particularly significant problems of approach.

In fact it is without doubt that from one merely analytical or descriptive point of view, the behaviour of the 'demand' aggregate should be analysed by single socio-demographic components of the demand itself: age, sex, professional condition, income, and perhaps cultural traditions and influences as well, etc.

But in modelling, one intends to identify and retain only those variables that are susceptible to receiving an objective (in as far as we are attempting only to model a system of objectives). The differences of 'present' behaviour between socio-demographic groups will be or will have to be probably annulled in the policy-oriented model which interests us now, and thus they can be neglected in this modelisation.

On the other hand, the 'spatial' nature as well of the model of accessibility that we are configuring renders less significant the analysis of demand by social-demographic groups. In fact a territorial 'specialisation' would be above all unrealistic of the places or centres of demand by socio-demographic groups; in other terms it is realistic to expect in general (except for specific exceptions) that the socio-demographic groups mentioned above distribute themselves 'presently' as well in a uniform way in the various places of residence on the scale that interests us, i.e., that of 'Urban Systems'. Thus, a specification of demand by socio-demographic groups, that could have importance for an overall evaluation of the needs for services in each urban system, has little or no effect on the system of spatial inter-relations (or of spatial accessibility) and thus does not solicit possible objectives *ad hoc*.

The diversity of approach between objective-oriented modelling with respect to one not objective-oriented, suggests on the other hand a further specification of demand, which normally is neglected in descriptive and analytical models.

In fact, given the 'policy-oriented' nature of the analysis proposed, it is implicit that the demand that we are dealing with is always a 'potential' or 'theoretical' demand, resulting from evaluations relative to acceptable standards of behaviour and need (rather than an 'effective' demand resulting from *ex post* empirical or statistical observations). In this logic one must bear in mind - negatively or positively, according to the circumstances - that demand which elsewhere we have defined as 'spurious': which can be defined both as an unexpressed demand (but which could or should be expressed, according to standards of satisfactory urban living quality), and as an expressed and satisfied demand, but with unacceptable access times and costs in principle (for example, with excessive commuter movement).

4.3   Costs (or prices) of accessibility

The aspect, access-costs (or prices), has in general been faced in economics of transportation studies from several points of view.

Costs for whom? Such costs may in fact be seen from the profile of the management of transportation units, from that of the interests of the users (families or firms), from that of the State, and other public bodies, in terms of costs for the infrastructures, public investments, environmental impact costs, etc.

In our attempt to model a system of objectives from which can be identified an opportune delimitation of territorial ambits appropriate for the spread of the city effect, we will attempt to get the most extended vision possible of such costs. In the first place the traditional factors of cost for the users will be borne in mind which are linked to the various types of journey (comparative costs), and, as well, to the various additional needs of investment for each type. But, at the same time, one will try to include in the model the consideration of less evident and less quantifiable factors as well, such as the comfort or pleasantness of the journeys, or the impact on environmental conditions (pollution, effects on the natural or urban landscape, etc.). There will not be excluded from the analysis also considerations on some factors of cost linked to the organisation and institutions in the territory: the border of an administrative region, of a service or consortium area; all this is considered one of the factors of 'attrition' that the demand must overcome or an impedance which any future policy-oriented arrangement must take into consideration.

Wherever possible, an attempt will be made to express the set of cost factors by means of 'proxy' indicators that can express them in general terms. An indicator on which there converges a common meaning both for the user, the operational units and for the State and the collectivity, is *access time* (which often synthesises the distance and cost of the modality in all its multiple aspects). But other indicators of costs that are not assimilable in that of access time, will be formulated and introduced in the modelling.

The cost factors in objective-oriented modelling, although multiple, are reduced to a single function: that of their minimisation.

4.4   The relations between the components of the accessibility system

The analysis of the components of the accessibility system (on the basis of which one intends to define the specific objectives of a method of delimitation of the UMIB) is completed with a reflection on the 'relations' that intervene between the three components of the system itself.

According to a 'classic' conception, the relation between supply and demand, in spatial or locational terms, is posed in terms of research into maximum reciprocal proximity.

Such research nevertheless is motivated in a very different way in two cases. The supply seeks proximity of demand with the objective of 'maximising the catchment area', leaving aside the induced costs for the users (apart from the extent to which these influence the market area). The demand seeks proximity of supply with the double objective of minimising the individual access costs, whilst at the same time maximising the number of 'opportunities' (or choice opportunities) available.

From the meeting-clash of the two systems of objectives (that correspond to those of the 'operator' or producer of the services and to those of the 'user' of the same), emerge the conditions to be studied and modelled for a process of decision-making of the type that we mean to formalise.

From the point of view of the operator, it is in fact indispensable to constrain oneself to a value of 'minimum threshold' of use, for each operational unit or 'place of supply' (no differently from how, in the economic theory of corporations, one speaks of minimum size of survival). For each 'centre of supply', therefore, this minimum threshold will result from the combined evaluation of the various (more or less integrated) 'opportunities-services' that are present.

From the point of view of the user, on the other hand, an availability must be formulated to support a certain movement (as acquisition cost) to go from the place of residence to the place of supply of the service.

The behaviour of the user is founded therefore on a simple spatial relation between 'distance' to be supported and acquired benefit; and this determines the 'complementary region' of the supply centre.[11] The behaviour of the operator has not only the 'spatial' component, in that the market area is no longer determined by the location of the centres of demand, but also by their demographic density.

The supply/demand relationships recalled above are strongly conditioned by the items of relative cost to access. In propositional terms, a reduction of access costs should have a positive influence on the reduction of trade-off in the supply/demand relationship, as we have outlined above.

The influence is different however according to the type of access costs reduction that is realised. In fact the reduction can have the effect of:

– strengthening the infrastructures
– relocating supply and demand
– a combined action of the two interventions.

In the first case, it is necessary also to bear in mind the fact that a strengthening of infrastructures may create an additional demand that is dependent on other causes, and thus that reduction of costs for the user may not respond to it, for which it had been promoted.

In the second case, two types of phenomena may be induced: that of the 'desertification' of the less favoured areas or that of a waste deriving from a policy of assistance for peripheral areas (in terms of services below the minimum threshold of use or in terms of under-used transportation).

In the third case a territorial operation is perhaps determined of the most suitable 'adaptation', the validity of which, however, is posed only in a long range viewpoint.

5 Operational specification of objectives: the use of multi-criteria decision-making analysis

The general objective proposed in the preceding sections may be reformulated in the following operational terms:

proposing aggregations of the places of origin of demand and of the places of supply in such a way that the generalised cost of access to the supply places of the opportunities-services is minimal, under opportune constraints.[12]

The search for 'maximum realism' that we have posed in the modelling of the process of choice in the delimitation of the UMIB, requires the introduction of further specifications that are relative to the cost items and to the demand/supply relationship.

For example, as already mentioned, among the user costs must be taken into consideration the cost linked to journey comfort and to the availability of facilities complementary to the origin and destination of the journey (e.g., nursery or crèche facilities or the ability to achieve various purposes with one journey).

For collective costs, one intends to take into consideration those connected to environmental damage, and to attrition of an administrative nature, etc.

As far as the user costs are concerned, it is by now common opinion that the choice of mode of commuting may result to a greater or lesser extent acceptable with regard to the better quality of life in work at the destination, of the quality of the means of transport, of the organisation of social services or of the facilities in the places of origin or destination.[13]

Although apparently the modelisation proposed could be led back to functions characteristic of mathematical programming, in reality - given the complexity of the characters that make them up - they lead to the preference of an approach of the type: 'multi-criteria analysis (MC) of preferences'.

This means, in general, transforming each of the functions proposed into a sort of 'target achievement indicator' - both of a quantitative and of a qualitative type - on the basis of which indicators could be organised the analysis of preferences, carried onto the various aggregative strategies.[14]

6 Concluding remarks

The methodology indicated is the fruit of research-lines which have been widely dealt with in the past in the framework of regional and spatial economics, and which would deserve further reflection and, above all, application to real planning processes.[15]

However, we have wished to represent an intervention in the field of research for regionalisation of a particular character: it fits into a special problematic of planning-oriented regionalisation. It is to the region-programme or region-plan, that the basic approach of this contribution looks.[16]

Naturally one must not ignore the fact that the problem was born as the delimitation of 'regions' for transportation planning. But - as already said - the first steps of our taxonomic research have arrived at the conclusion that

UMIB, Urban System and policy-oriented regionalisation have a reciprocal interest in being 'co-extensive'. For which reason here we have pursued the intention of viewing the delimitation of the UMIB (in as much region-programme for urban transportation) as a problem of multi-criteria decision-making.

There has been - in the literature - a certain amount of discussion about the opportuness of seeking 'fixed' ambits for urban transportation planning.[17] In fact some authors have challenged - not without reason - its usefulness.

The goal of 'regionalisation' may be posed in two ways:

1 As a research for a certain uniform set of criteria that may be used to split a country into a complex of exhaustive 'regions' which exclude each other reciprocally;
2 Or, as a research for a complex model of 'regions' that correspond to different needs and goals, the regions of which therefore may also intersect and be superimposed one on the other.

It is clear that the procedures suggested by us in this chapter fit into the first way of posing the goal of regionalisation (as was made clear besides in para 1 and 2). If the second way was chosen, we would be led (as Friedmann and Stuckey have indicated, for example[18]) to the question of how planning (and linked activities) could be 'spatially' organised so as to respond more efficiently to the needs of transport emerging in the various parts of the national territory. In this sense, the problem would not be that of designing a regionalisation useful for transportation planning, but rather that of conceiving a transportation planning that would satisfy regionalisation.

On the other hand, the arguments against fixed regionalisation must not be ignored. Regional transport, according to this way of seeing, is difficult to 'delimit'. It is essentially 'nodal', because of which it is relatively easy to identify a 'centre' or 'axis', but from this centre or axis it spreads out in space in such a way as to render any type of delimitation arbitrary. It moreover changes in time with the changes in technology and in the structure of the economy, so that any regionalisation may become obsolete after a short period of time.[19]

Nevertheless the advantages as well of a regionalisation for transportation are not to be neglected. Above all there is the advantage of providing a suitable framework of reference for co-ordinated policies of pluri-sectorial intervention in the territory; an intervention which - if singularly 'optimised' - could produce in some way an overall 'pessimisation'.[20]

The choice of an 'overall' and exhaustive regionalisation is in fact a 'plan' choice; and, as such, arbitrary. But it is for this exactly that we have wanted to point out, in this chapter, the need to use 'organised' 'decision-making' methods, but which are not 'mechanical': the methods that offer a greater flexibility and capacity of adaptation to the single concrete realities, and thus a greater 'realism' - even if they do not correspond to a total 'rationality' in the sense of a rigorous procedure of total optimisation.

The field choice - which is besides many years old for those who have advanced in Italy a policy of delimitation of 'urban' or 'metropolitan systems' as the foundation of an 'active' city policy and of the policy-oriented redistribution of the city effect[21] - may be summed up in a phrase by Karl Fox, who in other ways and in other contexts, likewise has taken for many years a stand for the exhaustive delimitation of 'functional economic areas'. He claimed that:

the fundamental community of 1970 in non-metropolitan areas is coextensive with the commuting field. It is delineated on the basis of the actual transportation behaviour of employed members of the labour force with respect to the journey to work. It is of great potential value as a general purpose social, economic, and political community, with capabilities for transportation planning and general urban-regional planning within its boundaries.[22]

In the Italian scientific experience we have tried in fact to enrich the Fox's 'Commuting field' and FEA with contents, with a system of planning goals, and by indicating a mixed mathematical and discretional delimitation procedure, which bore these goals in mind in a realistic and functional way. And as such we moved towards a general methodology of analysis and evaluation of mobility demand, based on the assumption that mobility demand may be the 'object' (and consequence) of an overall territorial planning process. And it is by means of the identification of the 'Urban Mobility Integrated Basins' that such an evaluation of mobility demand finds its correct application and forecast; and in the absence of which the errors and inefficiencies of all past and future urban transportation planning accumulate.

Notes

1   These analyses have been carried out in much research by the Planning Studies Centre aimed at the design of transport planning methodology (in

the framework of the National Research Council's Transportation Project): see in particular Archibugi (1984 and 1988a) and Archibugi and Las Casas (1985).

2   Urban systems policy, has distant origins, at least in Italy, since 'Progetto 80' (recalled in Ch. 2, para. 2.3). And it has been relaunched on several occasions in which the author has been to a greater or lesser extent involved; for example: Centro di studi e piani economici, 1971a and b; Ri, Ministero per il Mezzogiorno, 1983. See also Archibugi, 1966a and b, 1982, 1983a, 1987.

3   The urban eco-system, for which the recent Italian Ten-Year Plan for the Environment (Decamb), elaborated by the Ministero dell'Ambiente (Ministry of the Environment) (1992), represents the revisiting and perfecting of the 'Progetto 80' 'urban-metropolitan system'. See Archibugi (1992b) and Ch. 9 in this book.

4   We will come back to this point in Ch. 6.

5   I dealt with the same basic 'urban system' and linked 'urban mobility basin' approach, in two other SIEDS (Italian Society for Economics, Demography and Statistics) scientific meetings, with the problem of the determining of land needs for health services (report to the XXVII Scientific Meeting of the SIEDS, Selva di Fasano, Bari, 1981: Archibugi [1985b]) and with land needs for residential services (report to the XXVIII Meeting, Varese, 1983: Archibugi [1983b]).

6   For more elaborate information of the bases of such a taxonomy, see in particular the already mentioned essay by the author: *For a Taxonomy of Transportation Demand in the Ambit of Transportation Planning*, Archibugi, 1984.

7   We are referring to the studies linked to analyses of 'gravitational' models (of 'potentiality' or of 'spatial interaction') based on a concept of 'mass' and 'distance', and which for the latter accept in essence the 'journey time' as a more appropriate measuring instrument than others (see on the subject Ch. 11 of the work by Isard [1960], on the methods of regional analysis, and the contribution by Brown and Holmes [1971]). With particular reference to 'regionalisation' in transportation planning are to be pointed out the collection of contributions (already mentioned in Ch. 4, para. 3.1) presented to a Conference on 'Regional Transportation Planning' which took place at the Rand Corporation, Santa Monica (USA) in January 1971 (see J. DeSalvo [ed.], 1973). In this volume see in particular the contribution by Fox (1973) on the 'Delimitations of Regions for Transportation Planning', and that of

Friedmann and Stuckey (1973) on 'The Territorial Basis of National Transportation Planning'. As said, more recent analytical approaches - based however on the concept of 'functional distance' - are in Openshaw (1977), Masser and Scheurwater (1980) and M.M. Fischer (1982).

8   On this point, see Las Casas and Lombardo (1978).

9   Among the research referred to here, there is the work (to which we would refer for a more exhaustive discussion and application of the concept of 'policy-oriented demand' for mobility) carried out by the Planning Studies Centre a few years ago (in the framework of the CNR Transport Project). See references in Note 1.

10   On this point see Blancher, Jacquet-Lagrèze and Roy (1977).

11   The expression 'complementary region' is borrowed from the classic work of spatial economy of 1933 by Walter Christaller on 'central places' in southwest Germany (translated into English in 1965). With such an expression is meant the area within which the influence carries of a supply place of a certain 'level', in relation to the availability of the user to support the necessary access costs to reach this place.

12   For the formal expression of this objective, see again Archibugi and Las Casas (1985).

13   A recent survey by the *Institut de Recherche des Transports* in the Paris region has measured the influence of these factors on a wide sample of commuters resident around Paris (Davée and Marotel, 1983). The specification of goals, attentive to these 'cost' items may be made operational by means of formalisms of the type indicated in the aforementioned Archibugi and Las Casas (1985).

14   A longer explanation of the multi-criteria method and procedure as guide to the construction, selection and choice of solution can be found again in Archibugi and Las Casas (1985). The nomenclature is here very similar to that used by Hill (1973) and by Hill and Tzamir (1972), who call it in fact 'Goal Achievement Matrix'. In practice this phase of the procedure indicated could acquire the best of various methodologies, prepared by various authors, on the subject of 'Plan Evaluation'. See, for an overall panorama of the techniques of plan evaluation, Ch. 29 of the general work, already cited, on the principles of regional planning, Archibugi (1979); and also Lichfield et al. (1975). On the procedures of multi-criteria or multi-objective evaluation, there is a good critical panorama in Nijkamp and Voogd (1983), which contains an interesting bibliography.

15 The literature on 'regionalisation' is very vast. Bibliographical reviews are those of C. Harris (1965), Macka (1967) and Berry, Goheen and Goldstein (1969). The contributions of Vining (1953), Duncan et al. (1960), Friedmann and Miller (1965) may be considered classics on the subject. See also Dziewonski (1964). More recently operational methods have been introduced which are illustrated in the already mentioned Brown and Holmes (1971), Masser and Scheurwater (1980) and Fischer (1982).

16 As was indicated by the author a long time ago in a work on the 'delimitation of planning areas': L'analisi ecologica per la delimitazione di aree di programmazione ('Ecological Analysis for a Delimitation of Planning Areas') (Archibugi, 1966a). See also, among the works of the geographers, those by Muscarà (1968) and Vallega (1976).

17 See above all the contributions in the already cited 1971 conference at the Rand Corporation (DeSalvo [ed.], 1973).

18 See Friedmann and Stuckey, 1973.

19 A contribution by Alonso dwells on these aspects (1973), in the already cited Rand Conference of 1971.

20 The contribution of N. Wengert (1973) to the 1971 Rand Conference commits itself very favourably on the political and administrative aspects in favour of a delimitation of 'regional transport'.

21 On this point see the literature recalled above in Ch. 2, para. 2.3.

22 Karl A. Fox (1973) in his previously cited contribution to the 1971 Rand Conference on 'regional transportation planning' (p. 95). K.A. Fox is among the authors who have worked hardest in upholding the necessity for a delimitation of functional territorial areas: among the many works dedicated to this theme (for which see the works already quoted in Ch. 2, para. 6.1 and in Ch. 4, para. 3.1: and section 8.2.3, Decentralisation or Regionalisation in National Economic Policies, in a volume with J.K. Sengupta and Fox [1969]). Recently the most important contributions by Karl Fox to regional economics have been collected in a volume edited by Prescott et al. (1994).

6 The urban labour basin:
Misleading formulations

That which, in Ch. 4, was defined as an 'appropriate territorial unit of evaluation and planning' which, in Ch. 5 we analysed in the form of the 'integrated basin of urban mobility', we will now look at in the specific form of the 'labour market basin'. As will be seen, whilst there are various different starting points, the reflection will lead us to the same conclusions: the integrated urban eco-system. The route, *per se*, may give us however some interesting autonomous views.

To the extent and within the limits of the development of an 'active labour policy', in all western countries the concept has become widespread of a 'labour market basin' (or more simply 'labour basin') as a territorial ambit of reference for the application of a labour policy in all its aspects: management, information, education, training courses, re-adaptation, protection, evaluation, forecasting, etc.

On such a concept, however, there is no uniformity of views. It would not be pointless to widen the discussion starting from an analysis of what can be meant and should be meant by labour market basin.

1 An interpretative definition of the labour market basin

Let us begin from what may be meant by labour basin, and in particular from the less controversial questions. The actual use of the word 'basin' (*bassin*, *gebiet*, *bacino*), with its undoubted hydrographical references, leads to understand that one is referring to a territorial space in which a certain confluence or collecting is realised of the substance concerned, in our case labour. In the concept of basin there seems therefore to be implicit that of

137

'movement' and inter-relation between the various points of the same space that are linked by the movement and flow, in our case, of labour. It results that the affinity of the concept of 'basin' with that of 'market', i.e., the territorial ambit in which goods flow together to be exchanged, to the greater satisfaction of those who supply them and those who demand them.

The basin or market, understood in this sense, implies that the goods in order to be consumed must be transported from their place of existence or production to their place of consumption. These two places (production and consumption) may be the same, but usually they are not. The basin or market are, therefore - whatever the points of origin of production and consumption - where the goods flow together in a single place, which is in fact the basin or the market. The basin or market are therefore that territorial ambit that includes both the place of production (or supply) and the place of consumption (or demand) of the goods exchanged.

For many tangible goods (minerals, cereals, today milk as well, eggs and almost all foodstuffs, cotton, wool, products of manufacturing industry, books, caravans - but not houses yet - and many others) the 'basin' or market of the flowing together of production and consumption is now much more so the whole world, rather than more limited geographical areas. Transport, preservation of food and other products, and information have unified basins and markets of production and consumption. Mass production has stimulated mass consumption and vice versa. And this has 'widened' the markets, and destroyed the old physical concept of 'place' of exchange, from which the basin and market took their origin. For personal services, which have not been influenced by electronics or telematics (for example, housework, hair care, the maintenance of objects, the hairdresser, medical assistance, any type of non-computerised school, not-reproduced artistic work) a user basin survives still with a corresponding 'market'.

But in particular a basin exists, which corresponds to a 'market' in the case of the peculiar good or service which is *labour*. In the case of labour, the place of production-supply of the good is the place of residence of the worker, and the place of consumption-demand is the place where - given the present productive technology - is located the worker's job (field, factory, office, shop, studio, etc.). At the most, if the places of residence coincided with the places of work (in other words if everybody worked at home) - let us suppose because all households were economically self-sufficient, or because their work could only be tele-transmitted - the transport of the labour-good would not happen, and the concept of labour basin would not even exist (or it would coincide, like that of the market, with the place of residence of the family, or with the whole world).[1]

138

To the extent to which labour needs to be provided in determined places of production which are not the place of residence - and we know that in modern industrial society this is the case for the great majority of jobs, and there is little probability of the situation changing in the short term - the territory is articulated in a set of places, each of which realise a relationship (or flow): residence-job, with another place, which is more intense than with other places. The set of the places, between which the most intense relationships are determined, defines the ambit of the labour basin. In this way, the labour basin constitutes a typically 'gravitational' area.[2]

Such a definition of the work basin presupposes as given the places of supply (the residences) and the places of demand for labour (the factories, offices, etc.). And it is logically indifferent to the choices that on the part of the workers or, on the part of the entrepreneurs (including the state) may be made with regard to location both of the residences and places of work. The labour basin will adapt itself permanently to all the innovations and changes with regard to locational choices both of residences and places of work, and it will permanently change its borders that will ensue only from the identification and selection of the most intense relationships between home and work, at a given instant.

To the extent to which the location choices of labour demand (or of the production installations) depend on the location of residences,[3] we will have continuous transfers of factories towards residences and the existing human settlements; and, vice versa, to the extent to which residences depend on the location of factories and job places,[4] we will have continuos transfers of residences towards the factories and developing activities. Economic history is full of cases in which one or the other movement has prevailed: which has permanently modified the confines of the respective labour basins and created to a greater or lesser extent intense relationships between the same, even if necessarily of a transitory nature, in the expectation of achieving a new equilibrium.

However, the reciprocal dependence between the location choices of residence and work place is not the only factor that modifies the confines of the basins. Such confines tend to 'widen' and 'narrow' in relation to professional mobility or work substitution; i.e., in relation to the rhythm at which the firms (for reasons of technological change) and the workers (for economic or social preferences, which are always changing or in motion) are inclined to change work force or jobs. If the rhythm of substitution is more intense, the number of places, between which the relationship residence-job is realised most intensely, becomes usually greater because of the wider opportunities that are sought or realised. Given the relative rigidity of what is pre-existent (homes and factories) this tends to widen the commuting field and the times of transport, rather than the transfers. With this the territorial ambit of the basins tends to increase.[5]

2 An operational definition of the labour market basin

At this point one must ask: is this 'analytical' and interpretative notion of the labour market basin usable for operational purposes in the ambit of an active labour market policy?

It has already been said that the above-mentioned definition presupposes as given the places of work and residence. In reality, it has been said also, they are in motion, under a reciprocal influence. Perhaps it is best to examine the conditions of such motion with respect to the expectations and objectives of the two decision-makers about the two locations: the entrepreneur and the worker. In principle the objective-functions of both are not in conflict: both tend to maximise the opportunities offered by the market.

For the former, the entrepreneur, the wider the market, the better the chance of finding the qualifications that he needs, without mentioning the advantage, in a large market, of avoiding a possible 'local' shrinking of the work force, with its effect on the 'cost' of labour, and of obtaining in general - despite and versus the existence of the trade unions - greater competition from the side of supply (albeit together with greater competition from the side of demand) of labour.

For the latter, the worker, likewise, the larger the market, the better the chance of finding preferred work or that which is more promising from the point of view of his or her professional aspirations, and there will be more chance of finding other employment if a job is lost.

For both, entrepreneur and worker alike, the maximisation of opportunities has a constraint: the vaster the market (understood, therefore, as a basin and thus as a relationship, in motion, between the place of residence and the place of work), the greater will be the sum (and the average) of the distances between place of residence and place of work, and lesser therefore the accessibility to the work place from the residence. Such lesser accessibility - as is known - means greater transport costs, in the unit of time that, for biological reasons, conditions the provision of labour, i.e., the living day. This greater cost of 'daily' transport is expressed both in economic terms (i.e., in terms of material resources used for the provision of the transportation service) and in terms of non-economic welfare (in terms of the time wasted by the worker[6]).

Accessibility, therefore, exercises the function of constraint on the objective-functions of both subjects, in proportion to how much each subject supports of the costs themselves, whether economic or not, of transport.

The subject that supports the greatest costs of transport seems definitely to be the worker, in all senses. This does not mean that the entrepreneur as well may not have to undergo such transport costs, both when he assumes, in part and wholly, the financial burden (the economic burden cannot but have an effect moreover on the real labour cost) and when he undergoes the burdens in terms of lesser productivity and greater absenteeism.

On the whole, nevertheless, one can be sure that the cost of transport constitutes a greater constraint to the objective-function of the worker than it does to that of the entrepreneur: and this is demonstrated by the more marked tendency - in parity with other economic conditions - of entrepreneurs to widen the confines of the labour market, with respect to the workers.

In conclusion, it can be claimed that the objective-function both of the entrepreneur and the worker is that of maximising the opportunities by the labour market and minimising the costs of accessibility. And that as a consequence the 'optimal' labour basin, as territorial ambit of the optimal labour market, will be that whose territorial confines allow to the best degree the realisation of that objective-function.

At this point it would be a question of choosing how to express the opportunities and how to measure them; and, at the same time, how to express and measure accessibility. It is a question in short of quantifying the objective-function.

Let us suppose that one chooses as indicator or measurer of opportunities (indifferently both for the entrepreneurs and for the workers) total employment (possibly bound to a mix); and as indicator or measurer of accessibility, the time (isochrone) of transportation. And let us suppose that of each of the indicators the value (or field of values) is chosen which, in trade-off, are considered appropriate or preferred. Thus doing, we would have determined also the confines of a labour basin that is usable for operational purposes.

3 A definition of the labour basin on the basis of an integrated approach

But such a conclusion would only be partial. Since the definition of the objective-function on which it rests is partial.

In reality, that objective-function concerns the locational choice made by the worker with respect to the place of residence, on the one hand, and by the entrepreneur to the place of work (factory), on the other, just as they influence each other reciprocally (see above para. 1). But such choices undergo the influence of *other* factors that are not their reciprocity, which is expressed in the labour market alone. For which reason it is not just the relationship 'employment opportunities-accessibility' that can determine the optimal labour basin.

The worker, in his or her choice of residence, bears in mind, on the one hand, to a great extent employment opportunities and the distance from the place of work, but, on the other, also opportunities for housing, education for his or herself and, above all, for the other members of the family, the vicinity to relations and friends, satisfactory recreational facilities, respect for certain habits or social status, environmental amenity, etc., in short all the factors that may be considered as conducive to social well-being and the 'quality of life'.

And the entrepreneur, likewise, bears in mind greatly availability of manpower in necessary quantities and quality, but he or she is obliged to bear in mind many other factors, such as: the raw materials market, the outlet markets, the transportation and technology to be respected: in sum, all the factors that constitute the entrepreneurial 'combination' of productive factors.

If the set of these factors influence the locational choices of the residence and work places, and if a definition in operational terms of the labour basin derives from the formulation of a (constrained) objective-function that is valid for those locational choices, it would be necessary to incorporate all these other factors in the formulation of the objective-function on which can be determined the optimal labour basin. An optimisation founded on a partial objective-function would not only be illusory for the purposes of the determination (or explanation) of the labour basin (as resulting from empirical analysis), but also harmful, in as far as it could become a 'sub-optimisation' (which has become frequently a maximisation of the worst) with respect to an integrated objective-function.

4 The measurement of the integrated objective-function

Anchoring the notion of the labour basin to a definition of integrated objective-function of social well-being is without doubt difficult and complex. We think however that the characteristics may be simplified without too much risk or harm.

It is a question of anchoring the operational empirical definition of the labour basin not only to the relationship 'employment opportunities/

accessibility to the work place', but also to the more general relationship 'all the opportunities-accessibility to all the places' and to the relationship 'opportunity-accessibility' *tout court*.

The problem is therefore that of synthesising the expression of each of the two terms (by means of significant indicators-measurers and values considered preferable) and construct thus concretely an 'integrated' objective-function.

4.1 *The opportunities*

In an analysis of all the factors that constitute social well-being (and which can be the object of a function of social well-being), one can observe that they are all determined by means of the availability of goods and services and of a certain environmental quality.[7]

The availability of goods and services, spatially understood, is reduced furthermore to those goods and services that cannot be transported in the place of consumption, because in this case a locational indifference is determined with respect to their availability. One is referring thus to those goods and services in which the place of production and place of consumption coincide: i.e., the natural goods (those that, in another way, contribute to a great extent to 'environmental quality') and the services properly called of every type.

For the purposes of our analysis into the concept of 'opportunities' (in the integrated sense) that are available to be maximised, 'manufactured' goods (including agricultural products) are excluded that can be accessible in an indifferent way to the location of the places of residence. The opportunities that the citizen wishes to maximise by means of the choice of residence are, therefore, those of services, of those activities that are called 'tertiary', of all types, that are in fact non-transportable activities for which the place of production and consumption coincide.[8]

The services (public or private, divisible or indivisible, marketed or non-marketed, etc.) are therefore the best proxy and indicator of the 'general opportunities' that are part of the objective-function of social well-being (in parity with the capacity of income acquisition).

The service opportunities thus represent very well the set that characterises the factors of social well-being, present in an overall objective-function, if the natural opportunities are added to them (that can be 'produced' by the services); but since the service opportunities are also those in which the labour factor (with respect to the 'primary' and 'secondary' activities, i.e., agriculture and industry) is preponderant in the combination of productive factors - and thus the employment induced by these service activities will become the employment which is more and more important out of total employment in practice (apart from the fringes of industrial and agricultural employment that can be possibly evaluated separately); it follows from this that the service opportunities represent also the most important indicator for employment opportunities. They are in effect one of the two terms of reference, on the basis of which is determined the optimum location of residences (whence the housing demand) and of the work places (as centres of supply of the services).

In such a case, 'general opportunities' of well-being and 'partial opportunities' of employment largely coincide, at least in as much as it is useful that these latter are also indicative of the former (and not vice versa), in the evaluation stage of the choices with regard to residences. As far as natural goods are concerned, that influence well-being independently from the service opportunities, it is necessary to evaluate them in themselves and ensure their presence, in the proportions and standards that are considered opportune, at the stage of the identification of the territories that constitute the ambit of the locational choices of the residences.

4.2   Accessibility

For the other term of reference on which is constructed an 'integrated' objective-function of social well-being, i.e., accessibility to all places (and not only those for work) - which is the travelling time as a variable/constraint to be minimised - the identification between the indicator of general accessibility and that of the partial one (to the work places), is even more direct and persuasive: it always stays the same travelling time. In fact, even if the access needs are differentiated noticeably according to the type of service required and its 'frequency', they have a maximum threshold for all the services to which one has access from residence, which is that which is acceptable in the space of a day. The maximum acceptable travelling time for the citizen for access to any service in the day, does not differ from that which is acceptable for access to the work place. The indicator is the same (travelling time); and there is no reason for the standard which one wants to fix on them to differ, both whether it is a case of home-work commuting, or that of home-school, or home-place of amusement, etc.

5 The optimal dimension of the labour basin

The conclusion of the preceding reflections is the following:

1 That the prerequisite of a labour basin is that of ensuring an optimal relationship residence-workplace, in the sense of maximising the work opportunities to the minimum travelling time;
2 That, nevertheless, the optimal relationship residence-work place must be integrated - in order to be effective - also with an optimal relationship residence-supply centres of the services in general, otherwise the labour basin will not function;
3 That, luckily, the relationship residence-service centres may avail itself of the same indicators and measurers of the relationship residences-places of work (approximately), and therefore the empirically determinable optimal ambit for a relation is valid also for the other one.

Proceeding now to a further approximation to the contents of an optimal relationship 'opportunity-accessibility' (that determines how we have deduced also the optimal labour basin), it is a question of how to define what types of services maximise the opportunities and what distance or travelling time constitute the access constraint.

5.1   The services that maximise opportunities

The services that maximise opportunities are the more 'rare' urban services i.e., those that - whilst not being able to be used apart from in the space of a day - have a rarer frequency of use for the user.

Naturally the average frequency of use of such services depends on the average income of the users. But whatever their frequency of use, the services have to exist in order to constitute an opportunity of use.

As is known, every service needs, for its provision, to reach its own dimensional threshold. A theatre, a newspaper, a university, a specialist clinic, etc., need a certain critical user mass to exist as an operational unit. The overall usage, in turn, is a proportion of the total population, and such a population varies in respect of the individual frequency of use. In order to exist, albeit with a very low frequency level, a concert hall will need a minimum population threshold to serve, in which to 'attract' the clientele of music lovers. If the rate of frequency were to increase, obviously the minimum population threshold would diminish. At a given rate of frequency, every service will have its required minimum population threshold; it is the services whose minimum population threshold is higher which constitute, together the condition of maximum opportunity.[9]

It is clear that if the frequency of use hypothesised was to be considered not very high, for example, in respect of the evolution of the average income per inhabitant, then the fixed threshold should be consequently lowered (given the technical parameter of users per utilised installation). If then the technical conditions change as well, the population threshold may change for reasons that are different from the frequency of use).

In this sense, therefore the population threshold may be an indicator of the maximum of services that can be instituted, that is to say the maximum of opportunities to offer to the citizens.

5.2 The distance (travelling time) that constitutes the accessibility constraint

It is necessary that the objective of maximum services to be instituted in a given territory in order to have a city effect represented by a minimum population threshold, is compatible with the standard value assigned to accessibility, expressed by the distance or travelling time for access to those services (by an isochrone).[10]

Such an isochrone has a relationship with the kilometric distance, a relationship that is determined by the technical parameter of the available systems of transportation.

The territorial surface interested by this ambit is that which should contain the minimum population threshold, in order that the opportunities of supplied services are at a maximum.

If this minimum threshold is distributed over a surface that is superior to that given by the above-mentioned access standard, it is necessary:

- either to diminish the service opportunities (reducing the population threshold);
- or to increase the average acceptable travelling times (and the consequent costs of transportation).

If the minimum population threshold can be placed in a surface that is inferior to that given by the access standard, then the access standards can be simply increased, i.e., the average planned travelling times diminished.

Those opportunities to be maximised in the relationship opportunity-accessibility (which determine - we repeat - the urban system and also the optimum labour basin) may be expressed in terms of urban services and their qualification: but as requisites they include also that of a certain environmental quality, and those requisites, that are particularly important for the identification of a suitable labour basin, of a polyvalency of work opportunities for the work force.

This last requisite is largely satisfied, as said, by the sought maximisation of service opportunities (to the extent to which the presence of all the services ensures also the presence of almost all the work opportunities). On the outside remain the opportunities for agricultural and industrial work. And yet, such opportunities will have to be verified for their presence in the planned territorial ambits, case by case, by means of a policy of installation redistribution and of investment in the territory, which will have to respond both to criteria of maximum efficiency for each activity category; and to an equal distribution of the new installations with regard to the labour supply to be satisfied and to the need to ensure an acceptable mix in each territorial ambit thus conceived.

The relevant aspect to be emphasised at this point, is that, among the requisites for a labour basin, there is that of satisfying the need for the maximum of diversified work opportunities, and that is allowed by the complexity of the activities that are realised at a high population level. The same 'management' of the labour basin is rendered more efficient if the basin itself presents those requisites and thus those dimensions.

The other one among the requisites indicated, that of environmental quality (not produced by service activities), will be ensured, if in the concrete analysis of natural environmental resources, there is assigned with discretion to each urban system (or also labour basin, in the identity that we have argued) a quantity of natural goods (areas for free time, forests, parks, etc.) that is sufficient to satisfy - on the basis of predetermined standards - the needs of the given population.

6   The 'urban' labour basin functional to labour management

We have thus arrived, in our opinion, at an operational conception of the labour market basin: that which is identified in a territorial ambit in which can be evaluated and measured an integrated function-objective of social well-being.

In this sense, the labour basin is identified in an integrated basin of urban and social services and in a traffic basin. The labour basin is identified in an 'urban' labour basin. And this latter is identified *tout court* in an 'urban basin'.

By deduction, the invalidity ensues of any other territorial ambit gathered from the partial optimisation of residence-work place relationships, or worse still, by the mere registration of pre-existent residence-work place gravitation, empirically collected.

It is a matter now of taking rapidly into consideration the functionality of an urban labour basin conceived in such a way with respect to an 'active' policy or management of the labour market.

We have already mentioned how the foundation of such a policy or management of the labour market is the possibility of ensuring a more effective functioning of the labour market. That which means ensuring (like any functioning market should) the best encounter between the demand and supply of labour: whence to avoid in some cases a surplus of unsatisfied supply in the presence of a demand that is likewise unsatisfied. If, as said, this can happen when the most numerous labour opportunities are supplied with the constraint of a standard of accessibility, it is evident that only by identifying the 'proper' ambit or territorial level, in which surplus or deficit can be measured with a minimum of meaningfulness (i.e., the cases in which the equilibrium has the theoretical potential to be realised), will one be able to maximise the capacity of encounter between demand and supply and minimise the cases of missed encounters.

Certainly the identification of the appropriate territorial ambit in which to evaluate the encounter between demand and supply of labour is not *per se* the only operation necessary; it is the premise to the application of policies of 'adaptation' and of assistance to placing (information, professional training, etc.) without which an active labour market policy does not exist. Nevertheless, a condition for its efficient operation is that which is placed or applied to a correct and proper territorial ambit.

Below the threshold of activities and opportunity ensured by the correct and proper territorial ambit, that policy - whatever the quantitative result reached - does not maximise the opportunities offered to the labour market operators (workers and companies), and the encounter between demand and supply is not realised in optimal conditions.

Notes

1   If - as we have observed before - the concepts of 'basin' and 'market' coincide, the expression 'labour market basin', even if backed up by customs, becomes somewhat pleonastic. This is why we would tend to change the expression 'labour market basin' into 'labour basin', for joint reasons of logic and simplicity. A further sophistication could emphasise the fact that one thing is the place where the relationship place of residence/place of work is realised (which we have placed at the base of the concept of labour 'basin') and another thing is the place where the labour is 'traded' (supplied and demanded), which could also be different from that mentioned above. In this case the distinction would be recovered as legitimate between labour basin and labour market (which we have proposed as pleonastic). But in this case, a very restrictive meaning would be given to 'labour market', and which - to a large extent - goes beyond the conceptualisation that has by now become normal usage both in economics literature and common language.

2   Some classic and unexcelled treatises on spatial interaction are by C. Ponsard (1954, restructured in 1988) and J.R. Boudeville (1964, 1968).

3   This is the well known case of investments in regions with a high potential of work-force that is easily adaptable to the production processes referred to.

4   This is the likewise well-known case of migrations of potential workers, and their families, to places with a high demand for labour.

5   In these cases it would be worth bearing in mind the distinction - which we have considered sophisticated in Note 2 - between the labour basin (the place of the performance of the work) and the labour market (the place where the labour is traded). In this case, however, the labour basin increases its coefficient of 'spatial' significance; and this meaning restricts itself also to the exercise of a home-work commuting, which can only be 'daily'; the same commuting which we have placed as a foundation of the interpretation of the city, and of the 'urban' phenomenon. In this case - for the sake of brevity - the 'labour basin' coincides with the 'urban labour basin', which is the point on which our attention is concentrated in this chapter.

6   Time wasted or time 'freed', which today is increasingly evaluated 'economically' in the most recent systems of economic accounting.

7   This latter is evidenced by itself only to the extent to which it is not the result of activities of production of goods and services, but of natural

data that are not reproducible and if anything are only to be conserved, because otherwise it too would be reduced to an availability of goods and services.

8   It is not by chance that some traditional service activities, when organised on a large scale as mass production (and transportable), have been called, even in layman's English, 'industries': the credit industry, the show-business industry, the culture industry. On the dynamic concept of tertiary activities, see a work by the author (Archibugi, 1977).

9   This reasoning was at the basis of an empirical evaluation that was carried out some years ago in Italy in an official project of the national territory (known as 'Progetto 80', as already mentioned [Ri, Ministero del Bilancio, 1971]). Wishing to divide the national territory into territorial ambits in each of which the presence of all the 'rarer' urban services might be realised, and given the average hypothesisable frequency on the basis of certain standards, for these services, 'Progetto 80' claimed that a territorial ambit which would serve that purpose (it was called the 'metropolitan system', 'superior urban system' or 'territorial system') could not have less than a million inhabitants. After twenty years, because of the effect of the average increase in the frequency of rare consumption (which in turn was a function of the increased income conditions), the threshold was reduced - by another study that came in the wake of the first - to half a million inhabitants.

10   Utilising still the example of 'Progetto 80', this decided to fix a standard of accessibility to superior services (that could be assumed also as a standard of access to all work places) in a maximum travelling time (isochrone) of 60-90 minutes.

7 The land-use/resources matrix:
An instrument for environmental planning

We should remember again that, founded on some basic postulates concerning the particularity of the methodological approach of planning to the evaluation of environmental policies (discussed already in Ch. 4, para. 1), an appropriate methodology consists in using instruments of analysis and evaluation which are identified as:

- the identification of the 'appropriate territorial unit of evaluation';
- a 'land-use/resources matrix' (LURM), and
- the definition of indicators and parameters of city effect and of loading capacity.

In this chapter, we will focus further on the second of these instruments: the land-use/resources matrix (LURM) illustrating in particular its possible use in evaluation and planning processes. We have also said that the availability and use of such an instrument seem essential prerequisites for correct planning, and a means to avoid possible and dangerous errors of evaluation.[1]

1 Why a land-use/resources matrix (LURM)?

To this method of the construction and utilisation of a land-use/resources matrix (LURM) - actual and programmatic - we should arrive, by means of a co-ordinated series of technical-economic enquiries and political evaluations of the land resources available.

The aim is to provide 'parametric values' for the said physical resources - with regard to their availability (supply) and gauged social demand. It is a case, in other words, of ensuring a conventional 'value', of national interest, for the territorial and environmental consumption of resources as a result of the development of human activities: this for the purpose of evaluating the overall social costs and benefits of such consumption.

After a brief examination of the nature and characteristics of the LURM, we will look here at the possible utilisation, to then proceed to the evaluation of programmes and territorial projects, in the context of the organic[2] processes of territorial or environmental planning.

In this, however, we will not leave aside the examination of the various methods of evaluation discussed today and applied to plans and projects, with respect to which the LURM may constitute, certainly not an alternative, but simply a support. By not entering into the merit of the discussion of such methods, we will avoid examining towards which of these methods the LURM may be - so to speak - more akin, or rather towards which it shows greater or lesser disposition to lend such support.

2 Nature and characteristics of the land-use/resources matrix

The LURM is not different, in its basic purpose, from other 'matrices' that in the literature have been proposed in order to facilitate instrumentally the analysis and evaluation of socio-economic projects with regard to their environmental impact.[3]

Nevertheless in our description we will above all try to rigorously adhere to a twofold 'vector', corresponding to a twofold way of looking at the 'territory':

– at the 'territory' as the availability of a resource, having a multiplicity of original 'qualifications';
– at the 'territory' as an object of anthropic use, according to a taxonomy of use that is appropriate for the purposes of planning.

In other words, we shall look at the territory as a resource 'supply' and as a resource 'demand'.

This particular way of constructing a land-use matrix deserves some justification.

As has already been said in Ch. 4, para. 3.2 (dedicated expressly to anticipate and summarise what LURM is as an instrument of land use planning), environmental malaise is always an imbalance between demand for environmental resources, from which arises the consumption of the same, and the supply of the same resources, which are - like all resources - by definition limited. The task of planning is to ensure a balance of such resources. The environmental imbalance is aggravated, with respect to other socio-economic disequilibria, by the fact that the greater part of the supply of environmental resources is constituted by resources that cannot be reproduced, and which represent absolute, and not relative, constraints (on places, times, cultures, productive capacity, etc.).

As we have already said, in the so-called urban environment as well, environmental imbalance (whether it be from pollution, traffic congestion, the marring of the urban landscape, or the loss of social communication, etc.) is between the demand for the use of urban activities and the supply of environmental resources.

Thus, it is opportune to emphasise that the first analytical procedure required is that of listing:

– on the one hand, all the land-use demands, which satisfy activity needs (which satisfy in turn the citizens' needs); demands that are classified by type of activity or type of need to satisfy: e.g., housing, squares, roads, industrial zoning, spaces and public buildings for use, green areas to be used, zoning for pastimes and sport, shopping centres;
– and, on the other hand, all the available land resources (which constitute land-use supply), classified according to the intrinsic qualities of the territory and its 'vocations' of use, both from the natural point of view and from the point of view of anthropic pre-existencies (above all in the case of city areas): e.g., historic buildings, the urban landscape, green areas allocated for conservation, land for agriculture, areas for public infrastructures.

The two lists may face each other as on a balance sheet.[4] But they may also constitute the vectors of a land-use/resources matrix (LURM),[5] whose coefficients represent the transferral of existing resources into potential demand; or, vice versa, the transferral of the existing or policy-oriented demand into necessary resources (or spaces).

The construction of a LURM is not easy; but - albeit in different forms and approximations - it is an essential requirement for correct ecological planning of the 'city' and region. The problems arise when the same land supply unit may at the same time satisfy several demands, and accept several uses, and thus be a demand for promiscuous use. We have classified such promiscuous uses as proper or improper,[6] if they are considered compatible or not among themselves, by nature or extent. By nature, when a use damages another in quality (e.g., a steel works in the same block as a concert hall, to use an extreme example). By extent, when a use whilst not being incompatible with another (commercial activities with residential housing, for example) becomes so because of the overcrowding it creates.

The LURM constitutes a computational and evaluating model of the compatibilities and incompatibilities, not only between alternative uses for a single unit of an available resource; but also of the compatibilities and incompatibilities of a demand for use - actual or policy-oriented - with the existing or potential available resources. The LURM, in short, constitutes an instrument for evaluating the opportunity cost of the use of a resource: i.e., of the advantage lost in terms of alternative uses.

And, in as much as it is an instrument of evaluation, it constitutes also the instrument offered by the planner to the decision-maker for its trade-off between costs and benefits, for fixing its targets and for rationalising, finally, its plan decisions.

The layout of the matrix hinges therefore on the confrontation and resulting impact of these two conceptual entities: that are obviously to be further defined, analysed, measured and evaluated.[7]

On the other hand, we consider such a lay out as conforming with the appropriate approach to the process of physical planning (and even general planning tout court) seen as the impact of objectives and programmes of action (demand) with respect to the means, instruments and resources available (supply).[8]

In the LURM, therefore, are placed on one side the data relative to available territory or 'supplied' for the various uses made of it, and which we need. On the other side are placed data relative to the territory requested or 'demanded' for the existent activities, or for the activities that the planning process would want to develop.

The confrontation or the impact between territory demand and supply is realised by means of a territory balance, that represents the verification of compatibility - in the territorial and urban field - between required resources and available resources, between programmes and means.

3 The territory balance

The territory balance may be conceived as a transformation of a territory supply vector (understood as input) in a territory use vector (understood as output). Naturally the inputs must be classified according to a qualitative typology inherent in the territory itself (independently from the current uses, unless such uses have compromised the territory to such an extent as to render impossible its 'requalification': in such a case these uses become an organic part of the quality offered). The outputs, on the other hand, are classified, as said, according to the various typologies of use inherent in the present or future activity programmes in question.

The crossing of the two classifications, accompanied by the appropriate measurements, gives rise to a table of territorial inputs and outputs, in which the inputs represent the qualifications of the territory and the outputs its use destination. We have called this table 'Table of territory supply and demand' (see a summary and aggregated version in Table 7.1 extracted from Archibugi [1982]).

The table can be constructed with factual surveys at a 'given' time. It constitutes a 'statistic' survey that can be expressed by numbers, even without a geographic/cartographic point of reference, with suitable units of measurement that are to be studied case by case. Or it can be expressed, on the other hand 'cartographically' (assigning, for example, a colour to the territory qualifications, and a 'net' qualifications, and a 'net' to the uses of the same).

The table may also be 'projectual' or 'programmatic': if it refers to a future time $(t + x)$ and if it expresses policy intents.

In both cases there are numeric and/or graphic representations of a 'static' type: whether 'present' or 'future' state.

The territory balance can also be expressed in 'dynamic' terms. It is a matter of finding a form of expression of the 'variations' that intervene between the present state and the future state.

Before giving form to the future state of the table, one passes through the 'balancing' operation between the territory programmatic demand and the available supply.

If in the representation of the 'present state', the equilibrium between territory supply and demand is guaranteed by the accounting equation of the territories actually available and actually used, in the representation of the future state an imbalance could occur between territory 'supply' and 'demand': an imbalance that must be evaluated, measured and eventually eliminated in the planning process, if the plan wants to ensure its fundamental requisite of coherence, compatibility, and therefore feasibility.

The 'future state' table of supply and demand, or the 'programmatic table of territory use', becomes thus the tool of control and monitoring for the consistency and, therefore, feasibility of the plans.

Table 7.1
Territorial (or Environmental) Supply and Demand

Environmental Resources (Supply)	Environment Conservation (and its characteristics)	Residential Centres (and their typologies)	Spatial Uses (Demand)			
			Free Time (and its qualifications)	Agriculture (and its possible sub-utilisations)	Industrial Locations (and Mining)	Transport and Service Infrastructure

A. *High Mountainous Areas*
  1. Bi-seasonal Mountainous Areas
  2. Seasonal Mountainous Areas
B. *Sub-Mountainous Areas*
C. *Hilly Areas*
  1. Steep Slopes
  2. Medium Slopes and Variable Morphology
  3. Light slopes, Uniform and Plateau Land
D. *Watery and irrigatable Plainland Areas*
E. *Coastal Areas*
  1. Beach Area
  2. Rocky Area
F. *Mainly Wooded Areas, Forests and Woodland in Special Locations*
G. *Areas with Specialised Cultivation*
F. *Areas with Historic Centres*

N.B. For each relationship there should be considered the disaggregation of the data in: *proper uses*: promiscuous, non-promiscuous; *improper uses*: promiscuous, non-promiscuous. Obviously the classification of environmental resources in rows and that of the use of territory in columns given here only represents a summary. In effect, it would be much more disaggregated according to the special requirements of each plan and the special characteristics of each territory

Source: Archibugi, 1982

The confrontation between a present state and a future state, and the measurement of the changes that ensue (or would ensue in the projectual hypothesis), the confrontation in other words between the 'actual' table and a 'programmatic' or policy-oriented table, gives rise - as said - to a dynamic evaluation of the territory balance itself. In fact the confrontation is expressed by means of a change (of numbers and spaces): with fewer or more numbers and spaces.

The table of more and less, i.e., of 'variations', generates a dynamic territory matrix: an entry of territorial quotations from a typology to a different use from the preceding one; an exit from a preceding use to a new typology.

The 'dynamic' matrix, the sums of which equal each other, obliges us to consider not only the overall availability, but also to evaluate the impact that any possible plan process intends to exercise on the territory and on the transformation and requalification of the same. Moreover, if in numeric terms the 'dynamic' matrix - that is of the diachronic and 'policy-oriented' changes - obliges us to verify quantitative consistency at every stage of advancement of the decision-making process, in spatial (cartographic) terms, such a matrix forces even more complex analyses of coherence and rationality: in as much as they are linked to the rational and 'appropriate' use of locations and to the topological 'direction' of the change and development.

4 The 'economic' evaluation of territory

The LURM thus described may moreover constitute a valid tool of plan and project 'evaluation'.

In fact the evaluation of plans, that has had some methodological developments in the last decades, has suffered right from the start from scarce reference to the 'national interest'. The methodologies worked out for plan evaluation, not unlike those created for the evaluation of single projects (from the cost-benefit analysis approach applied to plans and projects), have adapted the analyses to an objective situation in which there is an absence of significant national planning, from which can be drawn valid criteria and references in order to compare the single evaluations of plans, programmes or projects.

This has happened for 'cost benefit analyses', that despite recognised demand, have not generally obtained from the competent authorities and from the appropriate planning processes, the necessary 'national parameters' of reference. This is happening because of the multiple procedures of 'environmental impact analysis' that, beyond their undoubted descriptive and cognitive value, have difficulty in becoming instruments of evaluation (and thus of decision) exactly because they are not performed through territorial evaluation 'parameters', as they can be formulated only from one national and overall point of view.[9]

This happens also, at least judging from the albeit limited but important experience had, for the methodologies of plan evaluation that have recently been introduced, whose reference parameters are inductive and arbitrary, and in any case, elaborated by plan formulators and evaluators case by case, with a low level of information and a high degree of superficiality.

To be complete (even if it is a bit marginal to the subject being dealt with), we will mention that in the case of territorial plans, the reference parameters are obviously not the 'shadow-values' of a monetary type, commonly considered necessary for a cost-benefit analysis (shadow-wage, investment shadow price, social discount rate, etc.), but rather non-monetary criteria, and some 'weights' given to such criteria, or to objective indicators that are necessary in order to render comparable the single plan or project analyses. In the case of the territorial plans, a fundamental reference parameter will be moreover the design of a territorial framework of reference that will select and suggest the appropriate use of each part of the national territory and fix use priorities according to needs and to that which is urgent.[10]

The 'physical' balance of the territory, extrapolated from the LURM in the above-mentioned ways, may give rise to an 'economic' balance of the territory if we assign a monetary price/value to its physical portions.

It is information that, however collected, would significantly enrich the knowledge of the available territorial resources and of the territorial costs of the plan operations.

Above all, a 'market' price can be given to each portion of matrix territory. The methods of 'estimating' such a price are long established and systematically taken into consideration in the disciplines of real estate evaluation.

The so-called market prices reflect the exchange values of the territory units with regard to the existent supply and demand, and in consideration of the personal and individual convenience of the users.

This convenience is translated into the relative appreciation of such units to which must be added the deriving surcharge, when necessary, from the control (monopoly) that, from the side of the supply, is exercised by the 'owners' and is to be understood as the generator of a 'position rent' (as is known such a control is relatively diffuse in the real estate sector, in the sense that when a territorial asset has overcome the level of purely agricultural use, it becomes almost always a rare and irreplaceable asset, when in fact it is not as well irreproducible).

But the 'collective' convenience in the use of these portions of territory is almost never reflected in the market prices. Since the collective demand is almost always a public demand, and since the public body at every level is a very poor buyer, the market price is almost always determined by the private market, which is then used for transaction by the public bodies, if other forms of acquisition do not intervene that, however, do not in any way decide the price (e.g., requisitions, expropriation, with or without indemnity).

The price or value of public interest of the various portions of territory, even if practically unexplored, apart from some rare exceptions, should not be difficult or impossible to determine. It could be estimated with criteria not dissimilar from those with which the 'market price' is estimated: i.e., as a meeting point of the curves of supply and demand; the only difference is that such curves would be extrapolated from the 'plan' rather than from the 'market'; and the thus decided price, rather than the denomination 'market price' would deserve that of the 'planning price'.

Such a price would be assigned by the public authority, based on indications of the plan evaluations, with reference to the scarcity that the LURM would reveal of various portions of territory supply with respect to the needs (and the resulting demand) of the corresponding territory, that the plan itself would express (naturally for appropriate uses).

It is a question of an 'assigned price', a sort of shadow price or 'planning price' - as one prefers - extrapolated from the territory supply and demand 'curves' for the given typologies of qualification and appropriate use, arising from the plan hypotheses (for all those that we would want to formulate in the planning process).

5 The utilisation of the LURM

The existence of an 'assigned' price, or price of reference, allows for the calculation of the 'economic' effects, expressed in money, positive and/or negative, i.e., in terms of gains and benefits and losses or costs, of alternative land-uses, that correspond to alternative types of 'consumption' of environmental-land resources: this in all those cases in which there is determined competition of use for a given territory (or territory typology); and it would allow also for the monetary expression of the costs of all the 'improper' uses of the same territory.

The LURM in its 'monetary' reference form could constitute the 'reference parameters' or indicators that are indispensable in order to give concreteness, reliability and systematicity to the single evaluations of projects and programmes that involve the territory and the environment.

In fact having a 'price' for various areas with regard to the reasonable use that can be made of them in an overall planning framework, and with regard to the relative 'scarcity' of such areas, constitutes not only a factor of knowledge and learning for the evaluation of the most convenient uses of an area, but also a method for the evaluation of projects and programmes that include alternative uses of such areas. After all, this is spoken of when in the language one refers both to the possible 'impacts' (usually negative) of the projects on the environment, and to the projects of utilisation of areas and territorial resources.[11]

Certainly the assigned price is assigned also with regard to the plans and programmes - as said - and to the territorial 'load' that provide (as territory 'demand'); whilst the evaluation of plans and programmes would be carried out also with regard to the assigned prices. Without doubt we are in the presence of a 'circular' type of problem (in this case as in many others in planning procedures). But if we bear in mind the iterative sequence of a planning and evaluation process the cognitive and heuristic nature will be grasped.[12]

6 Other instruments of evaluation interlinked with the LURM

The idea of a LURM must naturally be accompanied by a series of concrete decisions that have to highlight, on the one hand, the feasibility of construction and, on the other, the feasibility of utilisation.

Above all the idea of a LURM must be accompanied by other equally essential instruments which constitute, as said at the beginning of this chapter, essential requisites for authentic land-planning. We repeat again that these other instruments are:

–   the identification of the appropriate territorial units of evaluation and planning;
–   the definition of indicators and parameters of land loading capacity.

The LURM, in fact, must be constructed for an appropriate territorial unit of reference, if it is going to have any validity. If the unit is inappropriate, i.e., it does not have the requisites to permit a significant evaluation of the land demand and supply, the application of the LURM has no sense.[13]

Moreover, the LURM, once constructed, may function if the quantifications which are inserted in it, are based on standard and parametric values which render its relations meaningful. Without these standards and parameters the use of the LURM becomes a waste of time.[14]

Notes

1   See what was said in Ch. 4.

2   By 'organic' here we mean procedures (and relative plans and projects) which are not detached one from another, but which are inter-related, effectively and potentially, both vertically (hierarchy) and horizontally (interdependence), like any obvious theory of planning suggests.

3   We are referring, for example, to the 'Environmental Impact Matrix' developed by Edmunds and Letey (1973), or to other forms of environmental quality matrices such as Nijkamp's 'Environmental Quality Profile Matrix' or the 'Environmental Quality Matrix for Various Uses' (Nijkamp, 1977).

4   A balance of territorial needs, both as location requirements and as space requirements is taken into consideration in any planning manual worthy of the name. See the already mentioned highly detailed manual by Chapin (Chapin and Kaiser, 1985), in particular Chs 11 and 12.

5   A more detailed explanation of the LURM is to be found in the author's manual (Archibugi, 1979). Further technical considerations also in Archibugi (1988b, 1990a).

6   In the didactic work mentioned above (Archibugi, 1982, pp. 181-84).

7   The definition of the territorial typologies with which to articulate the two vectors indicated is in fact the first task of the above-mentioned research, and already there are some important problems. The problems of the classification of territorial resources (that we will consider as 'supply') have long been dealt with and debated. It is useful to recall amongst the best treatments of the subject the classic work by Chapin (1965) that is notably improved in the 3rd edition (Chapin and Kaiser, 3rd edition, 1985)

8   On the conception of planning there is obviously ample specific literature, under the nomenclature of 'planning theory' (Chadwick, 1971; Faludi, 1973a and b; McConnell, 1981; Alexander, 1986). See also the papers given at the First Worldwide Conference on Planning Science

(Palermo, 8-11 Sept. 1992). A selection has been published (in Italian), edited by F. Archibugi and P. Bisogno in Per una teoria della pianificazione ('Towards a Theory of Planning'), Prometheus 16/17, 1994.

9   A critique of the experience of Environmental Impact Evaluation applied to plans and projects from a methodological angle of the type illustrated here, is in an essay by the author included in the volume of essays edited together with P. Nijkamp entitled 'Economy and Ecology' (Archibugi, 1989b).

10   This in effect was the case with the 'Quadroter' research experience had in Italy, which aimed essentially at constructing a National Territorial Frame of Reference. Greater details can be found in Chs 8 and 9.

11   It is obvious that the availability of 'national' parameters, of 'shadow-prices' of the territory, could give meaning both to cost-benefit analysis applied to territorial projects (especially in the 'Planning Balance Sheet' version proposed by Lichfield and colleagues [1975]) and in the procedures of 'Environmental Impact Assessment' in their various versions. See on this last point the general comments contained in Archibugi (1989b).

12   The iterative sequences in the planning and evaluation processes are widely treated in all the writings concerning 'planning theory' mentioned in Note 8.

13   The concept and modality of identification in the appropriate territorial unit of analysis, evaluation and planning have been developed in Chs 5 and 6.

14   For the definition of environment indicators and parameters, see the work carried out by the Planning Studies Centre on behalf of the Ministry of the Environment (Ri, Ministero dell'Ambiente - Consiglio Nazionale delle Ricerche, 1991a and b).

8 Ecological equilibrium and territorial planning:
The Italian case

We will now continue to examine, from different points of view as well, the bases of the ecological equilibrium which is, for us, the pre-condition for the ecological city.

We will try and summarise again therefore:

- the scientific premises of territorial planning which are also the foundations of an ecological equilibrium between human activities and the territory or natural environment;
- the guidelines of an urban policy inspired by the above-mentioned foundations of ecological equilibrium;

and then subsequently we will give:

- the exemplification of these guidelines through their application to an actual territory (Italy), as the result of the first work of an Italian research project (Quadroter).[1]

Finally, we will:

- illustrate a possible way of using the results of the research, when assumed officially for the configuration of a framework of reference for territorial planning.[2]

1 The foundations of ecological equilibrium between anthropic activities and territory

It is commonplace today to affirm that a serious policy of environmental safeguards must aim to prevent environmental damage *ex ante* rather than intervening *ex post* when the damage has already taken place. In order to pass from a strategy of cure to one of prevention it is necessary to make sure that the pressures and impacts on the territory and the environment occur according to modalities, positions and conditions that are 'preventive', i.e., planned *ex ante* so as to control their effects and hoped-for absorption. This 'environmental' planning of interventions (of any type of intervention) on the territory must permit the simulation of the overall territorial and environmental impacts and keep the possible effects under control.

This type of planning, in order to serve its purpose, must have in the first place an appropriate timeframe; i.e., it must be long term (in the majority of cases).[3]

In the second place, rather than seeking, case by case, the conformity and environmental impact of each type of intervention, it should establish *a priori* a series of guidelines and territorial and environmental constraints for all types of intervention, in such a way that, from its very conception, we know how and where an intervention can take place without environmental damage (or with 'sustainable' damage); and, at any rate, in such conditions that it is assured that the pressure is rationally managed or absorbed ('metabolised').

The strategic land-use destination of the territory, understood not as an abstract system of constraints, but as implemented by the plans in consideration of real emerging land-use needs, is the most efficient way of exercising environmental control over a territory. All this on condition (as we have said previously, and in particular in Ch. 5, 6 and 7) that 'appropriate' territorial ambits are identified and defined in order to manage the equilibrium (inevitably quantitative) between territory demand (usage needs) and supply (geophysical characteristics, pre-existences, etc.).

If the container (the territory or the environment) is overloaded with contents (activities), the resulting disequilibrium can be compensated for by a spill-over of the surplus. But in order that this spill-over happens in a non-chaotic way, it is necessary to predetermine the ways in which it can and must be channelled; and we must also predetermine the ways in which this chaos can be avoided, directing the activities within ambits (containers) that have sufficient capacity to sustain the activities in equilibrium.

This is the true essence of feasible, rational territorial planning: the maintenance of equilibrium in the best possible way between the supply and demand of the territory in the medium and long term.[4]

It is not the case that the overloading of activities occurs throughout the territory: there are some parts that are largely unused and others that are in danger of degradation out of neglect. What is lacking is an opportune and rational 'territory organisation', which represents the essential condition for the prior avoidance of overloading, and thus of environmental harm.

But what is the 'appropriate', optimal ambit for the evaluation of the anthropic/eco-systemic relationship: activity/environment, or demand/supply of territory? In what ambit can one manage this relationship entirely from the inside, without unloading externally possible disequilibria and without throwing out of balance other equilibria?

As already said (Ch. 4, para. 2.2), it is common knowledge that there is not one single appropriate ambit in which one can rationally manage an ecological equilibrium. Any activity and any pressure on the territory has its particular impact area, and thus its particular appropriate ambit for evaluation and management.

For example, many activities that are linked to the production and consumption of energy or chemical products (atmospheric emissions) or of wood products (deforestation), wherever they take place on the earth have an impact on a planetary scale; they produce effects such as the earth's warming or the reduction or breaking up of the ozone layer. In these cases the decisions necessary in order to evaluate, measure and manage the equilibrium between the causes and the effects of the phenomenon have their appropriate ambit on a world scale and management is inconceivable without a certain degree of co-operation and authority on this scale.

Likewise, other world-scale phenomena of pressure and pollution have reduced impact areas, only continental (the case, for example, of acid rain), or only for water basins (in the case of the release of urban effluents into rivers and streams). In such cases co-operation and/or authority have the continent or the water basins as their 'appropriate' ambit.

But the majority of human activities that produce pressure on the territory and environment are linked to urban settlements, are of an 'urban' nature, and have the city as their exclusive ambit of ecological impact (we could call it the 'urban basin').

Apart from some energy-producing and industrial activities and apart from those activities connected to touristic land consumption, almost all human activities are connected to the urban life of the citizens which is 'daily' and functionally limited to the daytime. They take place in the 'urban basin'.

In such a case, the 'appropriate ambit' for the measurement, evaluation, and management of the impact phenomena is the same as that of the urban activities: it is the urban basin.[5]

Obviously, by city impact area or urban basin and by 'urban' activities, we mean that which is connected not to the simple physical delimitation of the urban fabric (even if the occupation of such a space has a very important role in determining the ecological disequilibrium of the sort mentioned above) but rather to the city functions, i.e., to the functions that the citizens carry out in the city. The space occupied by these functions is much more vast than that of the continuous fabric (consider the development of commuting between the place of residence and the place of access for many urban services and jobs). But such a space has however a theoretical limit: that given by the daily acceptability of the commuter activity, which is expressed in a given temporal (or isochronic) access distance.

This 'system of urban functions' - or more simply urban system - which is a system of relations, constitutes the 'appropriate' sought-for space for the measurement, evaluation, and management of the demand for (or the pressures on) the territory and environment deriving from urban activities. In fact, it constitutes the natural ambit of impact of these activities. The search for equilibrium in urban functions is identified with that for the equilibrium between territory supply and demand. The urban system is identified in an 'ecological' urban system - an 'urban eco-system'. Consequently the best organisation of the urban systems on the territorial scale constitutes the best way of preventing ecological disequilibria.

Thus, so-called territorial planning is identified in so-called environmental planning and vice versa. If one is different from the other, it means that the other one is lacking; and is therefore bad planning. The first without the second does not grasp one of the most important 'effects' of bad management of the territory; the second without the first does not grasp one of the most important 'causes' of environmental disequilibrium (pollution and degradation).

2 The urban system as a more appropriate place of eco-systemic measurement, evaluation and management

The urban environment crisis due to ecological disequilibrium, i.e., to the disequilibrium between territory supply and demand, is of the utmost seriousness, both for the fact that today the vast majority of the population lives and works - at least in the West - in cities, and for the fact that it is

166

presumable (and indeed to be hoped for, in a political conception of equality of social and economic conditions for citizens)[6] that soon the entire population (again, at least in western countries) will live in towns or cities, i.e., in an 'urban' living condition.

It is true, however, that as the urban living condition becomes hegemonic, the dualism of urban/non-urban life will be changed; the concept of the city will be transferred to include use of the non-urbanised territory (on the part of the urban users). In other words the geographic and conceptual 'confines' of the city[7] will change and the conception of the urban system or (the same but more precisely) the 'urban eco-system' will be put forward.

If this happens, clearly the concept of urban environment will have the opportunity for a new and more functional natural-anthropic integration; with only the distinction remaining to characterise the various effects of the obviously anthropic action on the elements of nature and on the socio-economic conditions.

With the concept of the 'urban eco-system', therefore, I prefer to indicate a system that in general incorporates the effects and conditions of the anthropic action on the environment; and this concept has been used as a reference scheme for the measurement, evaluation, and management of the anthropic impacts on the natural environment as well but originating from urban activities.

We have assumed as the definition of the urban eco-system (as already proposed elsewhere[8]) that of a complex of functional relationships of a determined community that develop in the territory in relation to the daily residence of the citizens. Since it is with regard to such residence that people today manifest the greater part of their consumption and activity needs, it is in relation to this residence that the parameters of the requisites of urban living and of the well-being or malaise that may derive from urban living are established.

On the other hand - as for any system - the 'urban system' as well is a complex of relations that are in fact or potentially in equilibrium; like an organism that is, or tends to be, in equilibrium. Where such an equilibrium is not achieved or cannot be achieved, the urban system not only enters into crisis (as in the cases when it existed but is overloaded), but also is not produced (as in the cases when desired urbanisation processes are not activated).

If we identify in the equilibrium, the optimal relationship of the conditions of urban life, we can say that the achievement of the equilibrium, i.e., the structuring of the urban system is a condition for the creation of a satisfactory system of urban conditions.

Without the realisation of a 'prescriptive' urban eco-system, or the insertion of whatever condition of human settlement in an urban eco-system, the postulated conditions of urban well-being are not achieved; the essential equilibrium between the complex of relations mentioned is not produced.

There are many factors that may determine urban well-being: social relations, physical accessibility (transport) and economic accessibility (levels of income), to determined urban services and satisfactory working conditions, the variety of work opportunities, recreation, culture, etc., physical-environmental conditions (quality of the air, of the daily landscape, etc.). It is therefore the correct mix of these factors that produce urban well-being, which is to a large extent environmental well-being, since humanity for the most part aspires to live in urban conditions.

In fact it is in the city that the various imaginable objective factors of personal and social well-being are thrown into the melting pot; since ways of living different from the urban type are non-existent or undesirable, or simply marginal.

By 'correct mix' is meant, therefore, an optimal synthesis of such factors, in such a way that the presence of one does not damage that of another; in brief the various factors of well-being should co-exist and be compatible.

The reciprocal 'incompatibility' between the various well-being factors manifests itself in various ways. Amongst the most evident and most felt today there is that (above-mentioned) of the relationship between demand for space or territory, that is essential for user accessibility to certain services and uses, and the scarcity of such territory. For example, making access easy to urban services implies the maximum diffusion of the individual car; but this well-being factor is incompatible with the scarcity of spaces and territory (streets, car-parks, etc.) available to accommodate the necessary number of cars. Obviously some superior urban services can only be concentrated in the territory and this makes the availability of space particularly scarce. Nevertheless, still by way of example, the location of services can be adapted to respect the efficiency constraints of these services with the needs of accessibility that demands as well that certain constraints are respected (for example, not exceeding certain access times or certain thresholds of atmospheric or traffic pollution). The task of planning (in this case of territorial planning) is to find a technically possible trade-off between the two constrained objectives.

But in order to establish the optimal requisites for the urban system it is necessary above all to identify its dimensions: of surface, users (population), activities.

168

For example, at a particular level of the development of habits, consumption, available income, a certain 'critical mass' of users, a certain 'catchment area' (limited by access constraints), and a certain urban scale are indispensable for the existence of the services that produce the so-called 'city effect'.

Below such a user critical mass, every effort to produce a city effectis destined to fail. Probably in such cases (below the urban effect) the best conditions from the environmental point of view are produced. According to a survey carried out by Censis (a well-known Italian survey institution) it seems that in Italy the most 'liveable' city from the ecological and social viewpoint is Macerata (a medium-sized city and provincial capital of central Italy of around 50,000 inhabitants): but without the city effect - which may bring with it some environmental imbalance but is nevertheless sought for by the citizens (perhaps the youngest or most demanding) in their settlement - the level of 'liveability' in Macerata is completely irrelevant; the town will lose its 'brains' and opportunities in favour of the agglomerations that are more attractive from the point of view of the urban services offered.

In Italy, if one casts a glance at the conditions of urban values and their hierarchies - despite the proclaimed 'crisis' of the metropolitan areas; despite the would-be 'de-urbanisation' (based on the loss of inhabitants on the part of the largest municipalities in favour of the smaller ones which are in any case close to the large metropolitan centres); despite the marvels of 'diffuse' development and the information technology that sustains it; despite the undoubted positive effect of regional administrative decentralisation which should have developed the urban effect in many regional capitals, etc., (phenomena about which many learned territory analysts have held forth) - there is still the impression that 'urban values' are even more concentrated than they were in the past, and that the image of many cities that were once the centres of important urban activities (culture, theatre, publishing, finance, entrepreneurship, international relations, etc.) is fading because of the loss of functionality and dimension.

An 'alleviation' of the environmental pressure caused by the overloading of the more intensely urbanised areas, includes the possibility of developing alternative centralities that reach, nevertheless, the 'critical mass' conditions for the development of the urban effect outside the areas that are to be alleviated.[9] If these size constraints are not respected in areas that are losing urban values, these areas will not be able to constitute valid alternatives to the 'metropolitan' areas, and any attempt to resist in time (with a suitable programme of land-use orientation) the negative effects of overloading will be wasted.

Any intervention would be healing and curative and to a great extent ephemeral as opposed to being preventive; it would not correspond to the foundations of ecological equilibrium (as argued in the preceding paragraph).

3 A reorganisation by 'urban eco-systems' of the Italian territory: the 'Quadroter' research project

Adopting these foundations for ecological equilibrium, a special research project carried out in Italy and called 'Quadroter' proceeds to a reading of the Italian territory and its present disequilibria.[10]

The main object of this reading was the actual distribution of urban settlements and their relative density, that which is also called the urban framework; this same distribution, as mentioned, constitutes the principal factor in the overloading and degradation of the environment.

The territorial distribution of the 'superior' urban services is then evaluated, those which produce the city effect; the services that are in fact the principal factor in the future evolution of urban settlements. The general strategy adopted has been to design a reorganisation - for the future - of urban settlements in order to avoid further concentration in the already overloaded urban areas (the 'metropolitan' areas); and this in order to realise a feasible reorganisation of the presence in the territory of the superior urban services, that are, as mentioned, the principal factor in the evolution of the urban settlements.

The 'feasibility' of such a reorganisation consists in the fact that these services cannot be distributed 'diffusely' in the territory without any sort of constraints. But rather they need in order to be economically justified (and not create - as is the case of the public services - a serious waste of resources) a certain critical mass, and a certain user threshold, that is often in inverse relation to another aim constraint that territorial planning must bear in mind: the temporal access constraint for the same critical mass or user threshold.

For the overloaded, commonly called 'metropolitan', areas, the strategy consists of creating alternative polarisations to those of the (monocentric) historic centre, to the predetermined user critical threshold (the 'access' constraint in these cases is in reality more than respected, and certainly improved with the improvement of traffic congestion factors that could diminish travelling times and thus access to the superior urban services). The critical user threshold constraint means that, in order to be really alternative these polarisations must be at least as important as the monocentric one they would oppose; and avoid the risk of dispersion in 'decentralisations' that do not have sufficient strength to constitute a real alternative, and would create a further 'peripherisation' that would be costly and chaotic.

For the areas of diffuse settlements (in particular for the medium-sized urban centres), the strategy consists of creating polarisations that are able to hold in check - by reaching the necessary user thresholds - the persistent attraction of the metropolitan areas. In this case, the problem is often posed of the best trade-off between the critical user threshold constraint and that of access time.

For some areas (that are in fact very numerous in Italy) of particular environmental and historical-cultural interest, which are affected by metropolitan and urban development, marginally but still with devastating results, the strategy consists of designing a 'special' development, based on particular *ad hoc* functions, of a conservative and protective nature, and keeping them away from a generic and destructive development.

On the basis of these strategic criteria, born out of reading of present urban settlements and the territorial distribution of the superior urban services together with the series of 'strategic' aims of urban policy (included in the elaboration of the 'Ten Year Plan for the Environment' [Decamb] produced by the Ministry of the Environment at the same time - 1992), the following aims have been assumed in common as for an Urban Environment Policy:

1   The design of alternative centres to the single historic centre for the metropolitan areas (and this in appropriate size and number to each identified metropolitan system);
2   Design aimed at the requalification of the metropolitan peripheries (an aim that is a corollary of the preceding one);
3   The planning and management of urban transport as regards the depolarisation strategy of the historic centres of the metropolitan areas (this too is a corollary of the first aim);
4   The recovery and restoration of the 'historic' centres in the metropolitan areas (as units for recovery in special urban contexts);
5   The design of new 'systems of cities' for areas with diffuse or low urbanisation (in order to achieve suitable polarisations for the sought for city effect);
6   The restoration of the historic centres of the intermediate cities and in the new systems of cities;
7   The qualification of non-urban areas, as 'territorial units of historical-cultural and environmental recovery' ('UTRAS' in Italian).

On the basis of these aims, the Quadroter project has proceeded to design a reorganisation of the urban framework for the medium and long term, whilst obviously bearing in mind the constraints represented by the present urban settlement that cannot be easily ignored.[11]

The Quadroter project has also outlined a reorganisation of the national system of transport (both of passengers and goods) that is coherent with that, above-mentioned, for urban settlements: it is fundamentally aimed at a functional separation between 'inter-systemic' transport[12] and 'infra-systemic' transport.[13]

Map 1 (found in Ch. 9) delineates, cartographically, and very summarily, the design of this reorganisation desired by the urban framework, as has emerged in the first instance from the Quadroter project; and also the design of pluri-modal and inter-systemic 'corridors' as deduced by the General Plan for Transport (the Quadroter has not yet verified the coherence of the Transport Plan with the design of the new urban framework).

On the scale of each urban system, the Quadroter project, as mentioned, has arrived at proposing a reorganisation of the territory, bearing in mind the present settlements, the problems of overloading (or of 'underloading') that it noted, and the need to ensure future development aimed at the re-equilibrium of territorial loads.

For each of the seven aims indicated in the preceding paragraph the Quadroter has developed some guidelines which are described in the next chapter.

4 The nature and limits of the Quadroter project as an instrument of territorial and environmental policy

Having illustrated the research for a construction of a 'Territorial Framework of Reference for Environmental Policy' (Quadroter) and its ecological foundations, we will conclude with some notes about the functionality of the Quadroter as an instrument of the policy of the territory and of the city.

The Quadroter was conceived, in fact, as an instrument of 'programmatic orientation' for any type of operation of land utilisation that at various levels of responsibility - sectorial or spatial - authorities and public bodies and also private bodies will want or will have to undertake in the future (plans, programmes, projects, etc.).

As such, the Quadroter is - from the institutional point of view - an instrument of dialogue, of further study and negotiation between various institutional actors: ministers, public bodies, regions and other local bodies with their plans and projects. Thus the Quadroter is also an instrument subjected to a permanent action of verification, updating and modification.

The Quadroter has assumed an eco-systemic reading of the Italian territory, oriented towards programming, i.e., aimed at conceiving and proposing alternative ways of territory organisation, with respect to present and predicted evolution. The way in which the minimum cost and maximum social benefit may be realised; and the ways that are feasible, i.e., essentially 'compatible' with the overall needs and inevitable development of social and economic activity. Feasibility and rationality become in this sense synonymous.

The Quadroter, from the methodological aspect, is not very innovative with respect to the research developed for the territorial projections of 'Progetto 80' (1969), which laid the foundations of one of the four 'social projects' of Project 80 itself: that dedicated to the 'Environment'.[14] It is very innovative, however, from the aspect both of the available information and evaluations and of the programmatic contents (for example, the growth of economic availability and income per capita, by increasing the frequency of use of the superior urban services and in general the catchment area, has lowered the minimum thresholds of use, expressed in user units, that are indispensable for their existence).

But it is without doubt that the Quadroter, in its guidelines on the future use of the territory, will be able to be subjected to periodic revision, with respect also to the way in which the operators have followed (or not followed) it in mind.

In a document prepared in 1989 for the Ministry of the Environment, in which the construction of the 'Quadroter' was advocated, it was said that:

the role of the Quadroter is essentially that of expressing the use objectives of the territory (and therefore of the environmental resources) so that the socio-economic activities (the actions, interventions, projects, works, of private or public origin) that concern it always conform to these objectives; and so that their importance is evaluated and their results predicted - in terms of environmental damage or even benefit - having as a permanent point of reference those objectives.[15]

The acceptance of the strategic guidelines of the Quadroter would render therefore more coherent amongst themselves, and more co-ordinated to their purpose, the multiple lines of intervention that emerge from the national, regional or local initiatives of public and private bodies. This is why the conformity or not to those strategic lines would be the means for the evaluation of the efficiency of the instruments that put into effect with respect to the objectives of environmental protection and ecological equilibrium that have been assumed. The function of the Quadroter would be therefore that of an instrument of indicative and 'cognitive' planning available to all the decision-makers in the exercise of their prerogatives, and not lastly to central government that has many instruments of intervention for the orientation of the choices of the other decision-makers, whether public or private, towards solutions that are as much as possible rational and co-ordinated.

Notes

1   The 'Quadroter' project is a 'strategic' project sponsored by the CNR in collaboration with the Ministry of the Environment, which aims at constructing a 'Territorial Framework of Reference for Environmental Policy' relative to the whole Italian territory. This research - for which the author is scientific co-ordinator - has been used for the preparation by the Italian Government (Ministry of the Environment) of a Ten-Year Plan for the Environment (Decamb). Further information on Decamb can be found in Ch. 9.

2   Actually used in the design of the Ten-Year Plan for the Environment, proposed by the Minister for the Environment in 1992 (Ri, Ministero dell'Ambiente, 1992).

3   This obviously does not mean that 'preventive action' may not have a short-term horizon, or that single short-term policies may not have a preventive effect, as well as a 'curative' one. What one wishes to emphasise is that a large part of the damaging effects and risks for the environment come from a certain distance in time, and cannot be managed in a way that is compatible with other needs or objectives unless sufficiently extended time scales are employed. Short-term policies serve only to resolve emergencies, and sometimes involve very high lateral costs that equal the costs avoided. Whilst it is only with long-term policies that one can bring about a convergence of actions that minimise costs and maximise benefits from all the points of view and objectives concerned.

4   See other works on this subject by the author summarised in Ch. 7.

5   This is the basin in which the environment is under most stress because of atmospheric pollution (the emission of toxic substances, smells, as well as noise).

6   In fact 'total' urbanisation may become an aim of public policy.

7   On this subject it is symptomatic to observe that some considerations made on the concept of the city earlier in the century by Wirth (1938) are still valid. These were updated by me some time ago in a paper on the 'idea of the city' (Archibugi, 1966c).

8   On the concept of the 'urban system', a wide treatment may be found in the author's work on 'urban systems policy' (Archibugi, 1986a), which will be included in the forthcoming Theory of Urbanistics (1995); for its adaptation to the concept of the 'eco-system', see what has been said in Ch. 2, para. 2. For the analytical appraisal of the 'urban system', see the already recommended collection of essays edited by Bertuglia, Clarke and Wilson (1994).

9   On this point see Ch. 3.

10   The research was published in an internal National Research Council publication (Archibugi, 1994c). It is currently in the course of publication.

11   This reorganisation is illustrated in the next chapter describing the Urban Environment Programme of the Italian ten-year plan for the environment. Essentially it is based on:

a   the reorganisation of 10 'metropolitan' cities, with as many 'plans' of territorial and environmental recovery ('eco-plans'), that propose, for each city, alternative centre strategies that are, we repeat, in ratio to the size and problems present in each. For example: for Rome there has been suggested the creation of 4-5 alternative centres to the historic centre, to which will go parts of the catchment areas of the Roman and metropolitan population; for Naples, besides two other alternative centres, integration has been proposed with a third centre (that of the city and district of Caserta); for Bologna, the creation of a single alternative centre; and so on;

b   the organisation of another 27 'systems of cities' throughout the national territory, in which will be grouped and integrated - with an appropriate transport strategy and distribution of superior urban services - a great number of medium-sized and small towns and cities, that by themselves would not reach the necessary urban effect and that - despite their apparent revitalisation - represent a constant risk of persistent gravitation to the metropolitan areas, and certainly not a factor of alleviation of the same in the growth of urbanisation. Some, influenced by the relative territorial diffusion of settlements and by levels of economic activity, believed that they could or had to 'theorise' a certain growth by 'network' or by 'directrices'; it is a question of an interpretative reading that is 'pedestrian', and therefore a bit trite, of that which is taking place under one's eyes (as in other cases that have happened in the past, when the phenomenon of metropolitanisation has been over-rated, the evidence of vast built-up areas called 'megalopolises'). As regards the significance of the phenomenon it is a superficial reading. The network or diffuse distribution or that by 'directrices' does not change the need for 'centrality' in the urban phenomenon; and it is from this 'centrality' (from its public spaces, its superior urban services, and its social and 'image' quality) that the 'urban effect' is born; and not from the sum of physical facts that create only environmental damage without creating the city;

c   finally, the organisation of a large number of 'territorial units of historical-cultural and environmental recovery' (UTRAS, in Italian) distributed through all the territory (and belonging - for the superior urban services - to the eco-systems mentioned above; some of which cross over between the said systems, the regions, etc.). On a first reading, the Quadroter has identified over 270.

12   By means of the identification and organisation of 'pluri-modal' corridors on a national scale (in accordance with the 'General Plan for Transport' already devised and brought up to date by Cipet - the International Committee for the Economic Planning of Transport).

13   Those aimed at serving specifically each urban eco-system, in the above-outlined strategic characteristics (of 'depolarisation' or 'polarisation').

14   See Ri, Ministero del Bilancio e della Programmazione Economica (1969) and the Centro di studi e piani economici (1971).

15   Ri, Ministero dell'Ambiente, 1989, p. 41.

9 The 'Urban Environment Programme' of the Italian Government Ten-Year Plan for the Environment (Decamb)

In this final chapter we intend to summarise the illustration of the 'Urban Environment Programme',[1] as worked out and featured in the Ten-Year Plan for the Environment (Decamb) presented by the Italian Minister of the Environment in a preliminary document in March 1992.[2]

The illustration of said programme will be preceded by:

1 A brief recap of the Ten-Year Plan for the Environment (Decamb), going through its general attributes and essential content;
2 Brief mention of a few of the scientific premises which have guided the development of the 'Urban Environment Programme' (and which are not found in the official text of the document).

1   The Ten-Year Plan for the Environment (Decamb) of the Italian Ministry of the Environment (1992)

The initiative of the Italian Minister of the Environment[3] to work out a long-term plan for the environment was developed alongside analogous sets of documents worked out by other European and non-European governments.[4] The intention was to construct a systematic guideline for governmental actions for at least the following decade, since many of the actions cannot but be considered in such a long-term perspective if one wants to evaluate their effects. In an 'added note' to the State of the Environment Message of 1989, the then Minister of the Environment Giorgio Ruffolo confirmed that:

> an action with which one wants to affect the character of the direction of productive development structurally, to intervene in the organisation of the

territory for its use in a way which does not bring about the depletion of environmental resources and to contribute to the modification of consumer orientations, then this cannot but be expressed in a long-term framework.[5]

Following this logic Decamb was conceived as an instrument[6] for:

1 'Establishing credible and measurable goals';
2 'Evaluating the problems of equilibrium and reciprocal congruity of various promoted and selected actions in a global manner';
3 'Establishing priority scales for needs to be satisfied';
4 'Organising the instruments and their mode of intervention, starting from the concrete evaluation of the functions which they must perform, with respect to the initiative and the programme to be realised'.

Decamb is thus articulated as a series of 'Action Programmes', for each of which a 'programme structure' is laid down, consisting of three separate operational levels. For each programme these are defined as: 1) Objectives, 2) Action Programmes, and 3) Actions.

Decamb has fifteen programmes (in the first preliminary draft of the document it presented):

1 The 'Urban Environment' Programme
2 The 'Conservation of Nature' Programme
3 The 'Atmosphere' Programme
4 The 'Water' Programme
5 The 'Land Conservation' Programme
6 The 'Waste Disposal' Programme
7 The 'Forests' Programme
8 The 'Coastlines' Programme
9 The 'Industrial Risks' Programme
10 The 'Agricultural' Programme
11 The 'Chemical Industries' Programme
12 The 'Transport' Programme
13 The 'Energy' Programme
14 The 'Environmental Education' Programme
15 The 'Environmental Information' Programme

The programmes listed above, which Decamb has expressly declared subject to further extension and integration, have been classified in three general categories:

- 'Environmental' Programmes: those which aim at having a direct effect on the environmental conditions, and fall under the responsibility of the environment administration (no. 1 to 8 in the list);
- 'Environmental Compatibility' Programmes: those which aim at constraining programmes which have goals that differ from the environmental ones, ensuring compatibility with environmental requirements (no. 9 to 13);
- 'Support' Programmes: those which aim at supplying optimal operational conditions for all the other programmes (no. 14 and 15).

As can be seen, the Decamb places first in its list of programmes of action, a programme for the urban environment.[7] Moreover the Decamb has articulated its programmes on the basis of indications that emerged with certain welcome recommendations from international bodies to which Italy belongs. In particular, the 'Regional Strategy for Environmental Protection and the Rational Use of Natural Resources in EEC Member Countries Covering the Period up to the Year 2000 and beyond' (UN-ECE, 1988), elaborated by the European Economic Commission of the United Nations, a body that has dedicated with varying fortune much attention to the prospect of a medium- or long-term environmental policy.

The articulation of the Decamb programmes admits inevitable overlaps between one programme and another. In certain cases recourse has to be made to the conventional attribution of responsibility between the individual programmes. In particular this has happened in the case of the 'Urban Environment' Programme, which cuts across other programmes with regard to conditions and quality factors, such as the atmosphere, water, waste, transport, energy, in as much as these are dealt with in other programmes as well.

However, the Urban Environment Programme is distinguished as regards one particular factor: that of the urban and territorial order, a factor that is considered more decisive than others for a recovery of urban environmental quality in the medium and long term. This means that the sectorial treatment of environmental pollution problems, such as urban heating, waste disposal, motor traffic and its emissions, noise, the distribution of drinking water, and effluent treatment, have been reserved for the single programmes and are not found in the discussed Urban Environment Programme.

The marked orientation of the Decamb towards a policy of long-term urban environmental re-equilibrium and development control on a national scale arises from a vision of a territorial policy that has been extant in Italy for several decades, and which has not always found an adequate response as far as government action and the general political consciousness are concerned.[8]

The environmental and territorial policy premises that underpin the elaboration of the Decamb Urban Environment Programme deserve to be quickly recounted.

2 The cultural and scientific premises of the Decamb 'Urban Environment Programme'

2.1 Identity of the environmental policy and the land-use policy

The basic premise is that the best environmental policy always coincides with the most appropriate land-use policy. And that important policies for the protection of the environment (air, water, coasts, forests, biotopes, landscape, etc.) should converge with production policies (energy, agriculture, industry, transport, etc.) in a 'territorial framework' of compatibilities that will act as a point of reference for all types of decisions, from general programmes to individual projects.

The urban environment, i.e., that in which we for the most part act and work and in which we find in our daily life the most important factors of our environmental well-being, is also that in which we can best create an equilibrium between the demands of land-use provoked by our activities and the actual protection of the environment.

Nevertheless, this ambit, that represents the most appropriate territorial unit for the realisation of an analysis of the ecological balance between activities and environmental conservation, must be conceived in a different manner from the physical urban continuum that characterises, especially in Europe, the idea of the 'city'. It must be conceived as a 'system' of functions - with none excluded - that take place in daily life, and that produce what may be called the city effect. Therefore a large part of nature and of natural values, which constitute a function of the urban well-being of the citizen, are included in the concept - and in the physical delimitation - of the 'urban system'.

Since the population realises (multi-functional) integrated environmental socio-economic well-being essentially in 'urban living' - including the built environment and nature - the ambit of the eco-systemic equilibrium coincides with the same ambits that constitute an appropriate territorial level for socio-economic planning aimed at the well-being of the population. The 'urban systems' - of the 'ideal-type' sort - become 'Urban Eco-Systems'. This is why

180

a real city effect is only produced in a balanced ecological ambit; and, vice versa, why a real effect of environmental well-being is only produced in an urban context.

The identification in the territory of such ambits and of such suitable territorial units of potential urban-natural ecological equilibrium between human pressure and environmental protection constitutes the fundamental premise of a correct and lasting environmental policy.

It is with this vision that the Decamb Environment Programme has again taken up the hypotheses and proposals already put forward in the country (from 'Progetto 80' onwards) for a reorganisation of urbanisation and of the urban fabric; and thus ultimately - as mentioned - to realise that complete equilibrium of urban-environmental values, by means of the delimitation of territorial entities (the above-mentioned urban systems or eco-systems) to which in the past were given a variety of names (city-region, city-territory, urban basin, systems of cities, functional urban regions, etc.) that represent real anthropic environmental eco-systems.[9]

2.2 An analysis of urban decay in Italy

The Decamb 'Urban Environment Programme' has taken its cue from the realisation that economic development, by provoking an uncontrolled and chaotic development of cities, is destroying their environmental quality.

It is destroying above all the environmental quality of those cities that are suffering a function overload, whether through the uncontrolled increase in the metropolitan conurbation and in the anonymous urban peripheries or through an excessive and disfiguring pressure on the 'historic centres', which tends to alter and destroy functionality and transform these centres into anonymous areas given up to traffic and pollution (from traffic, rubbish, noise, etc.).

Economic development is also destroying in Italy - in the view of Decamb - the environmental quality of some 'intermediate' centres, medium- or small-sized, that were once in Italy the hub of important urban activities and were rich in urban values. These intermediate centres - even though they are still not influenced by the decay of the overloaded metropolitan areas, and even though they are still quite 'liveable' (going by various specific physical and social indicators) - are losing nevertheless any real attraction as centres of 'superior' tertiary activities (which we will call 'superior' urban services), and therefore as the accepted residence for the more culturally and socially advanced strata of the community.

The fact that some medium-sized towns have replaced certain large metropolitan centres as the destination place for immigration from rural and peripheral areas of the country (within the context of an overall decrease in demographic and migratory pressure) does not in any way mean that these towns are improving in relative terms the quality of their overall urban environment. In fact these towns in Italy are in a worse position with respect to the past: this is probably because user thresholds for superior urban services, the presence of which engages the city effect, have risen historically. Urban quality (not seen only in terms of pollution and the stress caused by traffic) is becoming more and more concentrated, in Italy, in a few metropolitan areas, despite - as mentioned - their undoubted environmental decay.

All this is occurring without taking into consideration that these 'intermediate'-sized towns, with their uncontrolled and unexpected growth, are about to be hit by environmental degradation (from pollution and traffic) without thereby gaining the urban effect and quality that they deserve.

In short, environmental decay is advancing nationally - for one reason or another - on all fronts, whilst at the same time urban life is involving the vast majority of the population.

It may be said therefore that development is eating away dangerously and beyond measure at the peculiar resource that are cities; a resource that - above all in Europe and in particular in Italy - has achieved an irreplaceable historical and heritage value. Its destruction renders - above all from the point of view of the city - development unsustainable.

The Decamb Plan aims to block this tendency towards decay in the Italian urban environment and bring it back in the long term to a sustainable development level.

This is the reason why the Decamb Plan includes this specific programme for the improvement of the quality of the urban environment, in response to an urgent historic need that has been present for a long time, and in response also to the commitment assumed by the European Community (in relation to the above-mentioned Council of Environment Ministers Resolution, December 1990).

This programme (like, and perhaps more so than various other of the Decamb) intersects with goals and programmes of action expressed in other programmes.

In particular, the quality of air and drinking water in the cities, the decrease of pollution caused by motor traffic, noise reduction, climate improvement, waste management, etc., are important objectives, and therefore the object of action programmes, in the other Decamb programmes mentioned above such as: the 'Air Quality', 'Transport', 'Land Conservation', 'Forestry' and 'Waste Management' programmes.

Therefore with regard to the aspects that relate to the safeguarding and improvement of the quality of the urban environment in the above-mentioned sense, the specific Decamb 'Urban Environment Programme' is linked to actions planned by the other respective programmes.

However, the 'Urban Environment Programme' intended to develop in the direction of the qualification and requalification of the urban environment, not in its single physical/environmental aspects (air, waste, noise, etc.), but rather in its overall urban values, which are fundamental to the so-called city effect.

These values (which are certainly changeable in the course of time) guarantee - within certain time periods and community feelings - an overall level of socio-environmental well-being; a well-being that is not only measurable with physical indicators, and is - amongst other things - decisive in the residential choices both of families and of the more important productive activities of the 'superior' tertiary sector and of the 'quaternary sector' (as some call it).

It is to this type of 'eco-systemic' well-being, of the socio-environmental sort, that this programme makes specific reference. Obviously this type of well-being is also influenced by physical-environmental conditions (above all to the extent that transport technology development on the one hand, and telematics on the other, 'reduce distances' and access costs); but not in a prevailing and certainly not in a decisive manner. It is above all influenced by an 'urban' life condition, that is made up by the presence of 'superior' urban values (in essence certain 'superior' urban services), that are in this case decisive for the perception and evaluation of urban quality.

Vice versa, the actual success of environmental programmes (air, waste, noise, etc.) is largely influenced - in the long term and with the 'preventive-type' - by the success of the 'Urban Environment Programme'.

In fact, the greater part of the pressure that urban development has exercised and continues to exercise on the physical city environment depends on the 'overloading' of activities and residential settlements, and in the long run on the overloading of the land-use of the actual cities.

These settlements are due to the search on the part of those settled - who are the consumers (families) and the producers (providers of services, entrepreneurs) - for 'urban quality'. A better distribution of urban quality in the territory (the specific aim of the programme in question) determines a better distribution of the 'load' and of the pressure on the territory and the environment itself: that is if this better distribution aims at progressive elimination of the overload.

This therefore represents an indispensable factor in the recuperation of the balance between such pressures and the environment, and in the reduction of urban pollution (from motor traffic, waste, heating, etc.) by attacking the source and not the end manifestation.

The territorial units (or basins) that have an optimal balance between human settlement and urban quality (in the above sense) are also those in which the search for and the evaluation of a balance between the various pressures and the environment, between pollution and its absorption, is made easier, less costly and more efficient.

This is why an urban quality policy represents an important preliminary for the lasting success of a policy aimed at safeguarding the environment.

3 The Decamb 'Urban Environment Programme'

3.1 General objectives

Bearing in mind the general limits of the 'Urban Environment Programme', as expressed above, the general objectives of the programme are the following:

A the urban environmental requalification of highly urbanised areas (metropolitan areas);
B the urban environmental requalification of areas and cities 'losing urban values' (medium-sized cities);
C the urban environmental qualification of 'non-urban areas'.

These three objectives correspond to three different territorial directions of the same general objective: the improvement of the urban environment (above all from the point of view of the citizen, or rather of the user of the city, wherever he or she is residentially located).

Indeed, the general objective presupposes the maximum utilisation of the residences already existent in the country, and the minimum development of additional residences, unless they are essential and indispensable for the improvement of the living and residential conditions of the above-mentioned citizens.

The three objectives may be further described as follows.

With regard to Objective A, that which is relative to the 'urban environmental requalification of highly urbanised areas (metropolitan areas)', it presupposes that the decay of the urban environment in metropolitan areas is due mainly to an 'overloading' of functions on the part of a generally limited territory (the 'historic centres' of the principal cities), in respect to the

184

huge increase in the demand for superior urban services which is linked to the increase in population and to the relative increase in productive activities.

This produces hyper-congestion (of the traffic as of excessive settlements with respect to functions) of the (more or less historic) traditional 'centres'.

At the same time, the above causes the creation and expansion of vast peripheral areas that gravitate around the centre. These peripheries alienate urban functions in favour of the centre ('centralities' and public spaces), and thus end up bleak and anonymous. This goes both for the peripheries near to historic centres (adjacent in a built-up urban continuum) and for those further away made up of small and medium-sized centres (once relatively autonomous) that today gravitate for the superior urban services around the historic centre that acts as a 'metropolitan' centre.

Regarding Objective B, i.e., that concerning 'the urban environmental requalification of the areas and cities "losing urban values"', the Decamb 'Urban Environment Programme' points out that Italy (and perhaps the whole of Europe) is full of 'intermediate' cities, once rich in urban values, and that today - notwithstanding an environmental physical quality that is not degraded to the extent of those of the metropolitan areas - are 'losing' their urban values.

These cities and towns are an important environmental and urban inheritance. They represent a precious, rare and irreplaceable resource (on the world scale as on the national one). This resource risks being degraded with time because of the abandonment of centralities and superior urban services, and because of the absence of a national policy with regard to the cities on a national scale (today desirable also on a European scale).

Although the clogging up of the metropolitan areas has been relatively halted (not however the territorial extension of the same which spreads, like the proverbial oil spill, swallowing up small new centres in the relative conurbations), and although some are showing a certain increase in population with respect to non-urban areas (with an ever-declining population), the intermediate cities are nevertheless showing a marked loss in urban values with respect to the metropolitan areas, a loss that is not compensated by any indications of greater 'liveability'.[10]

What is lacking in the 'intermediate' cities (albeit with many differences from city to city with regard to individual services) are the superior urban services: high-culture activities, economic business centres, specialisation in health services, etc. This provokes an exodus on the part of the more qualified families, of the young in search of better opportunities and of the highly intelligent, thus an erosion of the once relatively rich cultural and social humus takes place.

Not much is necessary in order to fully recover this type of urban quality: it is sufficient that these intermediate cities organise themselves within reciprocally accessible radii that are acceptable to the day by day functioning in new 'systems of cities', that they attempt to avoid (for those near to the attractive influence of large metropolitan centres) further dependency on these centres, and that they try to reach with their organisation the 'critical' catchment area thresholds that are capable of developing and nurturing within the new territory to which they belong the urban conditions and the superior urban services, that are producers of the city effect.

Finally, as far as Objective C is concerned, that regarding the 'urban qualification of non-urban areas', it deserves a precise and careful definition, in terms of what is understood here by 'urban qualification'.

In fact, even in many areas of the country that have never historically achieved up until now urban quality, in that they have not developed urban centres worthy of being defined as 'cities', there still subsists a population (in small centres) that cannot be excluded from acquiring in the future an 'urban' condition of life.

If there is a spontaneous migration towards the large centres and, desirably, towards the centres of new 'systems of cities' - that are organised between the intermediate cities like some new polycentric cities - we will be able to accept the consequences. But if this spontaneous migration does not occur it will be necessary to retrieve for urban life these small centres as well, ensuring thus the protection of an important part of the environmental assets, for which these centres represent a kind of depository, and an important part of the historical-cultural heritage that these centres again represent.

We will be able to ensure urban quality for this type of area, which has never known it before, if these areas are 'functionally' integrated in the urban eco-systems or systems of cities that are the object of the preceding general objectives.

By functional integration is meant 'role' not 'dependency'. These areas, in other words, should perform within the new urban eco-systems or city systems, the role that is not performed by any of the territories of the same system: that of 'free' areas of environmental and historical-cultural recovery. If one has used the concept of 'recovery' it is because such areas (that however have never known urban quality) have suffered or are suffering, or risk suffering serious environmental degradation or the degradation of their historical-cultural heritage because of their marginalisation from centralised urban development. This degradation on the one hand has caused certain environmental safeguards to be lost and on the other has degraded a not insignificant monumental and architectural heritage.

Today many of these areas risk a secondary environmental degradation - particularly those that are near to metropolitan centres or those with intense tourist activity - if they are subject to a confused invasion of non-specialised activity (to the role that should be assigned to them in the general economy of the urban system to which they belong).

Their recovery would ensure them a functional integration of urban values, and not generic compensatory help, in the quality of 'internal areas' without a specific urban function; moreover it would give the local, regional and national urban collective the chance to safeguard an environmental and historical-cultural heritage of the utmost importance.

3.2 The action programmes

The Urban Environment Programme therefore, which is aimed at the qualification and requalification of urban life, in the way indicated above, and which is developed in the three indicated general objectives, is articulated in a series of 'Programmes of Action' (grouped in the same three directions).

The programmes relative to Objective A - 'Requalification of the metropolitan areas' - are:

A.1 'A programme of actions aimed at the design of alternative centres to the single historic centre of the area';
A.2 'A programme of actions aimed at the requalification of the urban peripheral zones of the metropolitan areas';
A.3 'A programme of actions aimed at traffic planning with regard to the depolarisation strategy of the metropolitan areas';
A.4 'A programme of actions aimed at the urban restoration of the historic centres of the metropolitan areas'.

The programmes relative to Objective B - 'Urban requalification of areas losing urban values (intermediate cities)' - are:

B.1 'A programme of actions aimed at the creation of new "systems of cities" as "Urban Eco-Systems"';
B.2 'A programme of actions aimed at the restoration of the historic centres of the intermediate cities and in the new systems of cities'.

The programme relative to Objective C - 'Urban qualification of non-urban areas' - is:

C.1 'A programme of actions aimed at the setting up and design of "Territorial Units of Environmental and Historical-Cultural Recovery" (UTRAS, in Italian) within the Urban Eco-Systems'.

The programme articulation would assume the 'programme-structure' of the attached Figure 9.1.

A characteristic of the programmes of actions is that the majority of the 'actions' referring to each programme are made up of 'territorial projects' and are, therefore, as many as will be needed according to the objective's line of direction, from which the programme of actions receives its inspiration.

This does not rule out that for some programmes, actions may arise on an administrative and managerial level that are independent of the territories and the relative projects.

As far as the 'territorial project actions' are concerned, their nature will obviously differ according to the respective plans.

For example if a programme of actions aimed at the urban requalification of highly urbanised and conurbated areas consists of 'equilibrating the superior urban services' burden by means of the creation of alternative centres', then (in Italy's case) an obvious action would be 'to design alternative centres in Rome's metropolitan system'; the actions will be as numerous as the metropolitan areas in need of such an intervention or action.

Again, by way of example, if a programme aimed at the urban requalification of cities losing urban values (intermediate cities) consists of 'equilibrating the superior urban services' burden by means of the organisation of systems of cities that reach the threshold of the "catchment areas for such services"', then an 'action' of the said programme would be 'to design a system of cities, i.e., an Urban Eco-System for the cities of west Tuscany (Pisa, Lucca, Livorno, Massa)'. The actions will be as many as there are the 'systems' designed among intermediate cities that have to be included in the programme of urban requalification.

In the following paragraphs, for each programme of actions, instead of a general 'action' category relating to that programme, a list of concrete projects for the Italian territory will be provided that should be carried out in order to ensure the accomplishment of each of the programmes of action. These are 10 programmes of 'depolarisation' for overloaded areas; and 27 programmes of 'polarisation' of intermediate cities lacking in urban values (with starting situations, however, completely different; and with prospective achievement of a sufficient city effect within different time frames).

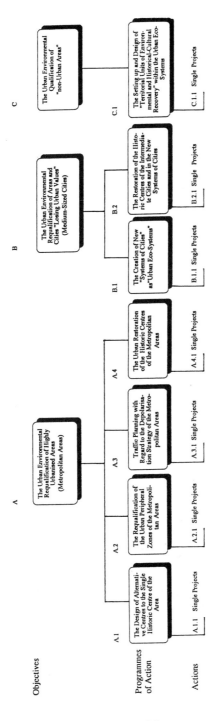

Objectives

Programmes
of Action

Actions

(from: Italian Ministry of Environment, 1992)

Figure 1   Urban environment programme: programme structure

189

4 A short description of the action programmes

4.1 The design of alternative centres to the single historic centre of the area

The only strategy possible in order to oppose hyper-congestion, to depolarise the function of the historic centre, and to reduce the overload is that of designing alternative centres that absorb a part of the centrality functions and public space functions reserved for the traditional centre.

However, these alternative centres must have certain dimensional requisites and they must represent an integrated functional whole with the same force of attraction as that of the historic centre, and, at least, have requisites that respect the 'physiological' thresholds of use necessary for the economic development of the superior urban services in question. Decentralisation that does not have the polarising capacity of the historic centre is destined to fail and to thus constitute a waste. Alternative centrality in other words should respect the dimensional constraints of use that are considered sufficient for the functional economic development (not forced or protected) of the superior urban services on which it is based and centred.

To obtain this it is necessary to design and promote the guided positioning (on the part of urban and territorial plans on a suitable scale) of superior tertiary activities (starting from public activities) in central locations chosen somewhere in the peripheral areas to be recovered and requalified. The amount of the alternative centralities of this type depends on the size of the (user) population that presently gravitates to the hyper-congested centre, and on the size standard of the catchment area considered the minimum for the functioning of alternative centralities.

Excessive diffusion produces the opposite result to the one sought for: further reinforcement of the traditional centre with an increase in the confused and chaotic peripheral settlements, a great waste of new resources and the continuation of the decay of urban quality.

In brief, the fundamental constraint that inspires the design of new 'central places' is that of the redistribution of the functional 'burdens' in a catchment area that constitutes, however, a sufficient 'critical mass' for the superior urban services provided previously (and perhaps redundantly) by the historic centres that are to be decongested.

The design of these new central places constitutes the 'actions' of the programme.

The Italian metropolitan areas in which we have to put into effect these 'actions' with this strategy, and which therefore need as many alternative centre projects are:

1 Rome, where there are catchment areas in the metropolitan area that suggest at least four or five alternative centres;
2 Milan, the catchment area of which is such that at least three alternative centres are justified, plus an alternative centre dependent on the strengthening of Pavia's historic centre, in a single urban system;
3 Naples, the catchment area of which justifies at least two alternative centres, besides the strengthening of Caserta's centre in a single urban system;
4 Genoa, the catchment area of which justifies the strengthening of Savona in a single urban system;
5 Turin, the catchment area of which justifies the design of an alternative centre within the metropolitan area;
6 Bologna, the catchment area of which justifies the design of an alternative centre within the metropolitan area;
7 Florence, the catchment area of which justifies the alternative strengthening of Pistoia in a single urban system;
8 Palermo, the catchment area of which justifies another alternative centre within the metropolitan area, and the alternative strengthening of Trapani and its territory, within the confines of the same urban system;
9 Catania, the catchment area of which justifies the alternative strengthening of Syracuse in a single urban system;
10 Bari, the catchment area of which justifies another alternative centre within the same metropolitan area.

For each of the 'alternative centre projects' to be promoted in the above metropolitan areas, there will have to be drawn up - in agreement with the regional, provincial and local governments concerned - various 'eco-plans', i.e., environmental 'master plans', that will be in part indicative and in part normative.

These ten metropolitan cities to be reorganised for the improvement of environmental quality are exhibited in Map 1.

Map 1   Italy: general map of the urban eco-systems

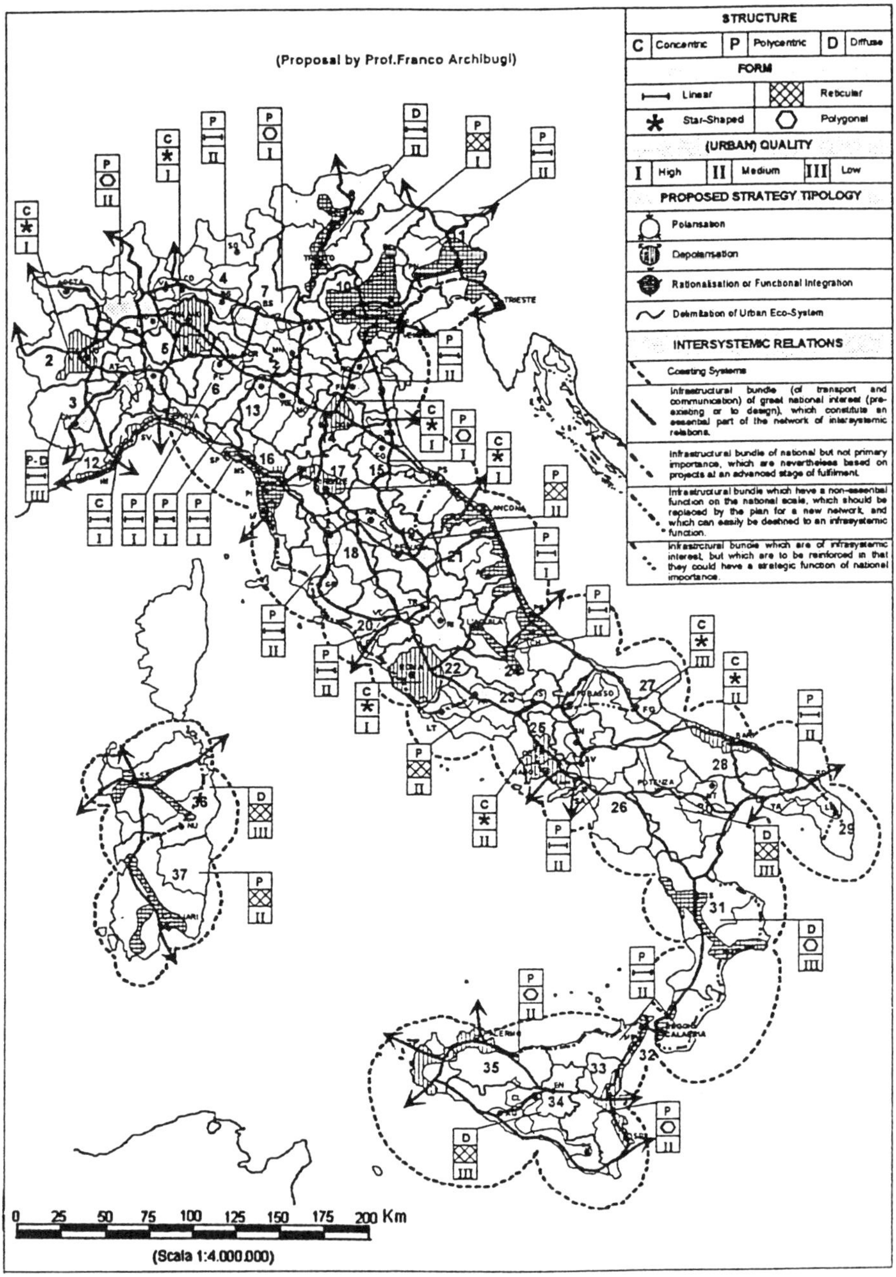

(from: Italian Ministry of Environment, 1992)

4.2   Design aimed at the requalification of the metropolitan peripheral areas

Action for the design of alternative centres in the metropolitan areas coincides largely with another action linked to this programme of actions for the requalification of the metropolitan areas: that aimed at the requalification of the metropolitan peripheral areas.

In fact, the eventual alternative centres would be securely placed within these peripheral areas, in a strategic position, and in locations that would maximise the recovery of urban quality in the peripheral areas. It would mean the concentration of public spaces, (modern) monumental buildings, meeting places on the scale required by the prescribed catchment areas in the pre-chosen locations, which would be more efficient and direct with respect to the previous overburdening of the historic centres. The restoration of equilibrium between the supply and demand for central areas, squares, and public spaces, surely means initiating a process of recovery and requalification of today's 'peripheral' areas and zones (besides better management of the balance between the pressures and the available territorial and environmental resources).

The design of the new centres in the peripheral metropolitan areas should give rise to a vast movement of ideas and proposals from the wealth of opportune ideas arising from the competitions that will be in keeping with the strict initial terms of reference.

The design of the new centres in the metropolitan peripheral areas would constitute the 'actions' of this programme (as already mentioned).

4.3   The planning and management of urban transport with respect to the depolarisation strategy of the 'historic' centres in the metropolitan areas

An action simultaneous with the two preceding ones, and aimed at the same objectives of the programme of actions, consists of the tight linking together of the planning and management of the urban transport systems in the metropolitan areas in question with the pre-chosen strategies of the two preceding designs, in the same integrated design.

The management of automobile traffic should be such as to promote the development of the new alternative centralities and to 'free' as well the traditional centre from the overburdening of traffic, as another factor of further depolarisation.

Planned transport development (supply of transport) should not continue to respond uncritically to the development of the demand for transport as this appears nowadays, but rather should respond to transport demand as it is 'programmatically' simulated and determined by the territorial plan within an overall conception of 'land-use /transport'.

With this approach, the historic centres should be destined and geared more and more for cultural and tourist activities, for which they perform an irreplaceable function, which is moreover always expanding in terms of the relative dimensions of the activities. Transport demand for which investments in infrastructures and services are made should be calculated with respect to this 'different' land-use and this different territory destination. We will see what implications this can have for real traffic needs (for example, the fact that tourists and those benefiting from their 'spare time' are more favourable towards pedestrian accessibility than to other types of accessibility).

At the same time accessibility to new alternative centralities, and the connected investments in infrastructures and services, should be calculated and designed, not with respect to the 'actual' traffic demand, which could be modest and limited, but rather with respect to the (simulated) demand generated by the new land-use destination. In order to help the new centralities to grow, the strategic weapon could be above all the creation of metropolitan railway systems that conform to territorial strategies, and are not merely in line with a present demand for transport in the absence of any strategy.

The various projects referring to this programme of actions would constitute the 'actions' of this same programme.

4.4 The urban recovery and restoration of the 'historic' centres in the metropolitan areas

In connection with the other actions aimed at the requalification of the metropolitan areas contained in the programmes already indicated (design of new centralities, recovery of peripheral areas, urban transport planning) the picture can be completed with a programme relating specifically to the restoration of the historical centres that make up the metropolitan areas.

The relief granted by the other actions will allow the historic centres to be restructured with the aim of a recovery of their age-old function, and of a specific adaptation to their new functions (touristic, cultural, etc.), to which they can be oriented without over-burdening their building or urban structure.

A good urban 'restoration' is, in short, essential for their renewal within the modified context of environmental pressure.

The historical centres of the metropolitan areas that deserve the most attention within the framework of an integrated policy of environmental renewal, and thus suggest as many 'actions' for recovery and restoration, and special project elaboration, are those of Rome, Naples, Venice, Milan, Florence, Genoa, Palermo and Bologna.

Each of the projects in question would constitute an action for this programme.

4.5   The design of new 'systems of cities' in the non-metropolitan areas ('urban eco-systems')

The accomplished actions of this programme coincide with the territorial projects to which they should make way, i.e., the 'functional integration' territorial projects between various intermediate- and medium-sized cities that are able to provide for the new 'urban eco-systems' the critical catchment mass in order to achieve the city effect (the superior urban services). These territorial projects will be distributed strategically throughout the eco-system's whole intensive and polycentric territory and will be able to create an alternative polarisation for these cities that gravitate towards the present metropolitan areas.

The projects that the study group of the 'Quadroter' elaborated - based on numerous past proposals[11] - concern the projects that we will list below:[12]

1   A 'Pre-Alpine Piedmontese City', based on the functional integration of Novara-Vercelli-Biella-Ivrea and adjacent territory (including Valle d'Aosta). The potential catchment area for the 'superior urban services' (SUS) would consist of 1,100,000 inhabitants that today gravitate towards Milan and Turin with serious social and environmental costs.

2   A 'City of the Tanaro', based on the functional integration of Alessandria, Asti and Cuneo and their territories; the catchment area for the SUS would be of 1,200,000 inhabitants that today gravitate towards Milan and Turin with serious social and environmental costs.

3   A 'City of the Lakes', based on the functional integration of Varese-Como-Lecco-Bergamo and their territories; the catchment area for the SUS would be of 2,500,000 inhabitants that today gravitate almost totally on Milan, with very serious social and environmental costs.

4   A 'City of the Po', based on the functional integration of two very near cities (but which ignore each other) Piacenza and Cremona (plus the territory of Codogno); with a catchment area for the SUS of about

700,000 inhabitants that today mainly gravitate towards Milan with serious social and environmental costs.

5   A 'City of the Adige', based on the functional integration of Trento and Bolzano and their territories, with a catchment area for the SUS of about 800,000 inhabitants who are today marginalised from the SUS.

6   A 'City of the Garda', based on the functional integration of Brescia-Mantua-Verona and their territories, with a catchment area of about 2,200,000 inhabitants that today continue to gravitate for the SUS towards Milan and the Venetian area.

7   A 'City of the Veneto', which represents a good example of functional polycentrism between Venice-Padua-Mestre-Vicenza-Treviso (and also Belluno), that has to be better infrastructured and equipped. The catchment area is of 3,300,000 inhabitants, and perhaps there are the bases for a division into two complete systemic units: Venice-Treviso-Mestre-Belluno on the one hand, and Padua-Vicenza on the other.

8   A 'City of the Delta', based on the functional integration of Ferrara and Rovigo and linked territories, with 600,000 inhabitants as a catchment area for the SUS.

9   A 'Julian City', based on the functional integration of Trieste-Udine-Gorizia, which is moreover sanctioned by a special region status, with a catchment area of 1,200,000 inhabitants, and many urban values inherited from the past, but with a parochial mentality that creates marginalisation.

10 An 'Emilian City', based on the functional integration, already partly existent and in part to be reinforced, of Parma-Reggio Emilia-Modena, with an overall catchment area for the SUS of 1,400,000 inhabitants that still gravitate towards Milan and Bologna.

11 A 'City of Romagna', based on the functional integration of Ravenna-Forli'-Cesena-Rimini and their territories, with a catchment area of about 1,000,000 inhabitants that are included only in part in a urban system of life and gravitate anyway towards Bologna.

12 A 'Tuscan-Tyrrhenian City', already largely in existence with Pisa-Lucca-Viareggio and Massa that need to be better integrated functionally, with a catchment area today of about 1,600,000 inhabitants with poor urban quality, even with the rich values inherited from the past.

13 A 'Sienese-Maremman City', based on the functional integration between Siena and Grosseto and their vast territories, with about 500,000 catchment area inhabitants with a strong vocation for development, and who gravitate for the SUS towards Florence and Rome.

14 An 'Umbro-Aretine City', based on the functional integration of Arezzo-Perugia, with a potential urban catchment area of about 1,000,000

inhabitants, today varying in quality and gravitating towards Florence and Rome.

15 A 'City of the Marches' or 'Picene City', based on the functional integration of Ancona-Pesaro-Ascoli and Macerata (i.e., the Marche Region), with a catchment area of about 1,500,000 inhabitants with a very low urban quality and ready to split into two urban systems as soon as conditions allow (Pesaro-Ancona on the one hand, Macerata-Ascoli on the other).

16 A 'City of the Tuscia', based on the functional integration of Terni, Viterbo, Rieti and Civitavecchia, with a potential 700,000 inhabitant users that today gravitate towards Rome with serious social and environmental damage.

17 A 'Latin City' or 'City of Lower Latium', based on the functional integration of Latina and Frosinone and their territories (with the addition of Isernia), that reaches 1,100,000 potential users who enjoy a limited level of urban quality and gravitate when they can towards Rome.

18 A 'City of the Abruzzi', that is finding it difficult to maintain urban values with a potential catchment area of 1,200,000 inhabitants (the entire region) who gravitate almost exclusively towards Rome.

19 A 'City of Central Campania', based on the territorial integration of Salerno, Avellino and Campobasso, that have very low urban values, despite the noteworthy development of the Salerno area, with a catchment area of 1,500,000 inhabitants that continue to gravitate towards Naples, with very serious consequences for the Neapolitan urban environment.

20 A 'City of the Daunia', made up of the integration of the cities of the Molise (Campobasso, Termoli) with Foggia and the other centres of the province, which with their territory reach a potential of almost 500,000 inhabitants, with a very weak urban structure, diffused and without special centralities.

21 A 'City of the Salento', based on the functional integration of Brindisi-Taranto-Lecce, with a potential catchment area of 1,700,000 inhabitants including their territories, who today make do with low urban quality that is mitigated by constant gravitation towards Bari.

22 A 'Lucan City', based on the functional integration of Potenza and Matera, two non-existent urban entities, that together with the whole of Basilicata constitute a catchment area of just about 600,000 inhabitants who today gravitate for the little they ask towards Bari and Naples.

23 A 'City of the Sila', including the territories of the provinces of Catanzaro and Cosenza, with extremely low urban quality, and very

difficult functional integration, but with a catchment area of 1,500,000 inhabitants.

24 A 'City of the Straits', based on the functional integration of Messina and Reggio Calabria, and on the prospect of a more stable crossing of the Straits, with modest urban quality but that amounts to an urban catchment area of 1,200,000 inhabitants.

25 A system of small towns in central or southern Sicily, made up of the agglomeration of various small centres of the provinces of Agrigento, Enna, Caltanisetta and Ragusa, that are hard to polarise and are with difficulty functionally integrated and polycentric, but which represent a potential catchment area of 1,200,000 inhabitants.

26 Finally the 'system of cities' of southern Sardinia, polarised on Cagliari, with about 1,000,000 inhabitants, with low urban quality and which are to be reinforced in a concentrated and polarising way.

27 And that of northern Sardinia, polarised on Sassari, with a potential catchment area of about 600,000 inhabitants and urban quality still a long way off in the future.

The 27 'systems of cities' proposed above are to be realised in different ways and with different lengths of time. But they have potential requisites in common: within the territorial space in question and within the minimum catchment area.

They involve about 80 'intermediate cities' that represent a very important part of the urban population, which have not achieved modern levels of urban quality and which in relative terms are losing urban quality in comparison to the 'metropolitan areas'.

Without a policy of creation and design of the aforementioned 'systems of cities', the urban environment of these intermediate cities, although it will improve in physical terms, will tend to worsen in social and cultural terms. Moreover many of these cities will become 'peripheries' of the metropolitan areas (for many rare services they are already thus, and for others for which they are not, it is at the cost of having given these up).

The absence of such a policy moreover will compromise any policy in support of the metropolitan areas aimed at their decongestion. In fact without the 'polarisation' of the intermediate cities formed autonomously, no 'depolarisation' will be able to take place in the metropolitan areas and any environmental policy in the one or the other Italian urban context will be destined to failure.

Therefore the success of the programmes of actions A.1 and B.1 are closely inter-related.

The 27 new 'systems of cities' of the more than 80 'intermediate cities' may be classified and distinguished internally according to their degree of income development, the level of which may to a greater or lesser extent facilitate the take-off of urban quality and the city effect sought for, and according to their level of urban values that, although in decline, to a greater or lesser extent facilitates recovery.

For each of the 'new systems of cities' (like for the new 'alternative centres' of the metropolitan areas, see Programme A.1), 'eco-plans' will have to be elaborated - in agreement with the regions, provinces and other interested local bodies - i.e., environmental 'master plans' that are in part indicative and in part normative.

4.6 The restoration of the historic centres of the intermediate cities and in the new systems of cities

If the need was felt in the case of the larger metropolitan areas for a specific programme dedicated to their historical centres (see para. 4.4 above), even in the case of the non-metropolitan areas, the need was felt for a similar specific programme because of the large quantity of historical centres that are also in the SMCs that are designated to constitute the networks of the 27 systems of cities. This programme has as its object to recover, restore and revalorise the historical-cultural heritage of buildings, monuments, institutions, etc., which have to be safeguarded more carefully, to not let them fall short of the development selected.

These recovery projects in part will follow methodological and design lines that are similar to those concerning all the existing 'historic centres', independently from their belonging to metropolitan areas or not. In part, on the other hand, they will present problems that are different from those of the metropolitan areas. The Decamb has taken this into consideration in two separate 'programmes of action' in relation to this diversity. The historical centres of the metropolitan areas must be 'conserved' in order to 'save them' from the contamination of urban development; those of the areas where the Decamb intends to institute 'new city system' networks in order to strengthen the city effect, probably the historic centres will be able to give a direct and important contribution to the 'polarisation' of these networks to be implemented; and thus their projects will be more oriented towards a controlled development rather than to a simple conservation.

Italy is rich in territorial areas (often defined as 'internal' areas) that, because of their geomorphological nature (mountainous or hilly, reduced or conditioned accessibility, peripheral or isolated, etc.), have not been involved in the industrial economic development, and therefore residential expansion characteristic of the stronger areas.

This has resulted in their environmental decay. A decay that is marked by the abandonment of these areas by the adult population, the lack of activity opportunities, and above all by the decline in agricultural activities. Numerous programmes of economic and financial assistance have not halted the above-mentioned abandonment.

The environmental decay of these areas is today at risk of finding itself reproposed in new ways: through a disordered 'return' of second homes, the locating of rubbish dumps, the construction of warehouses in need of space, i.e., by the regurgitation of the areas that have reached their maximum capacity and are overburdened.

Today these areas are in danger of being doubly penalised - from the environmental point of view - by an uncontrolled and unregulated territorial development. A first analysis has pointed out 270 of these areas throughout the whole country (see Map 2).

The environmental recovery of these areas merits being the object of a programme of actions.

This programme of actions consists of the following actions:

1 The precise legislative definition of the requisites of such areas to be defined as 'Territorial Units of Historical-Cultural and Environmental Recovery' (Utras).

In fact such areas must be officially defined for their characteristics and functions if they are to benefit from certain assistance conditions. We must never ignore their integration function in the urban systems to which they belong which in turn allows for their qualification.

2 The promotion of consortiums between local bodies, with special programme agreements (with the presence of the central government authority).

(from: Italian Ministry of Environment, 1992)

The Quadroter, has already identified over the whole national territory the areas that deserve attention as 'territorial units of historical-cultural and environmental recovery'. It is a matter of ascertaining and negotiating with the respective regional and local authorities the Quadroter proposals, the confines of such areas, etc. It will be possible to do this with special programme agreements under the promotion of the national government for a unified design of the Utras.

3   Elaboration of 'eco-plans' for each Utras that is in concordance with the preceding actions.

As with Programmes A.1 and B.1, the eco-plans are environmental master plans that are in part normative and in part indicative.

5   Conclusions

The Urban Environment Programme of the Ten-Year Plan for the Environment, made known by the Government in 1992, as yet has not had practical implementation. But this, and the reasons behind this, are not the subject of our examination here (and are the not reason why we have illustrated its characteristics here). This will be the task of historians and theoreticians of political science, if they believe it worthwhile.

This programme has been recalled here because it represents a further exemplification of the directions of national city policy, which meant to bear in mind criteria, concepts, and reflections developed in the course of this book; as well as from the methodological point of view and technical-scientific requirements which condition the validity of the eventual choices of that policy.

It is an exemplification which must serve to make clearer the general theories which have been developed in this book, which are not meant to be based only on Italian experience, although the latter may be coherent with them.

Notes

1   For which the author was co-ordinator.
2   The Italian Ministry of the Environment, the Ten-Year Plan for the Environment (Decamb), Rome, March 1992.

3   The Minister from 1988 to 1992 was Senator Giorgio Ruffolo.
4   In particular we refer to the official documents on long-term planning of the Japanese, Dutch, British, French and Canadian governments. (See Note 2 of Introduction and relative references to the bibliography.)
5   Ri, Ministero dell'Ambiente, 1989a, Added Note by the Minister, Giorgio Ruffolo, Rome, 1989, p. 38.
6   Ri, Ministero dell'Ambiente, 1992, p.1.
7   This represents (as already noted in the introduction to this work) a clear novelty, both with respect to other long-term plans worked out in the other states referred to (Japan, Holland, Canada, France, the UK, etc.), and with respect to the usual division of the 'subjects' of environmental policy, as resulting from the 'grey' literature of existing national and international organisations (the UN, EC and OECD families, etc.). In a way not different from what has been happening in the EC environment - where attention to the problems of the urban environment, which is effectively the natural environment of the vast majority of European citizens, came about with a certain time-lag with respect to the initial development of environmentalist culture (or more precisely the 'Green Paper on the Urban Environment' and the Council of Ministers' ruling in December 1990, which are the first documents on the issue). In Italy as well it has taken time to get attention to the problems of the urban environment as such introduced into the environmentalist movement, despite the numerous efforts at the cultural and scientific level on the part of scholars and professionals to draw the attention of the public and politicians to this issue.
8   This goes back to the end of the sixties, when the Ministry of Budget and Economic Planning worked out a document on medium- and long-term prospects (called in short 'Progetto 80' - 'Project 80'), which should have inspired the preparation of five-year plans of development in the eighties (plans which never saw the light of day during the seventies, nor subsequently, due to the general crisis of all medium-term planning in Italy). One of the four 'social projects' of 'Progetto 80' concerns just the 'environment'; and the territorial projections on which the project (worked put by the Centro di studi e piani economici - the Planning Studies Centre - under the present author's direction) was based provided for a national territorial re-equilibrium of 'pressure' on the environment, based on the creation of 'urban systems' which represented alternatives to the great metropolitan areas which featured on the national scale. The official publication of the Ministry of Budget and

Economic Planning was dated 1971 (Ri, Ministero del Bilancio e della Programmazione Economica, 1971).

9   The Decamb 'Urban Environment Programme', as indeed the entire Decamb, was advanced through the Ministry of the Environment by the works of a special 'group for reflection on the guidelines of medium- and long-term environmental policy', set up in 1988 by the Minister of the Environment, Giorgio Ruffolo (and of which the present author was the co-ordinator). In this group's 'Report to the Minister' (Ri, Ministero dell'Ambiente, 1989b) an extensive illustration of the scientific and intellectual premises which were later used in Decamb can be found. The demarcations of the various urban eco-systems proposed for the entire national level (37 in total) were indicated as early as in this document, as was the still provisional identification of the Utras (about 270 in total).

10   For example, Macerata (a medium-sized city of central Italy) may well be at the top (according to a survey carried out) of the 'liveable' cities table for physical conditions and income (see Ch. 8, para. 2), but no-one decides to go and live there thus abandoning the larger cities, and many of its more qualified residents are continuing to migrate, out of a desire for urban quality, towards the less 'liveable' metropolitan centres; the same goes for the vast majority of intermediate (Italian) cities.

11   From those of Project 80 (Ri, Ministero del Bilancio e della Programmazione Economica, 1969) to those of the 'Venetian City' (Archibugi, 1970c), of the Commission for Studies on Urban Systems in the Mezzogiorno of the Ministry for the Mezzogiorno (Ri, Ministero per il Mezzogiorno, 1983), and those of the General Transport Plan (Archibugi, 1987), all cases of territorial planning which have seen further progress in Italy in the urban systems inaugurated by Project 80.

12   For their geographical identification, see Map 1.

Chapter Sources

Chapter 1 is based on Archibugi (1995): *A strategy for the modern city: research Guideline oriented to the identification of the optimal centrality* (Paper for the 9th Aesop Congress, Glasgow, 17-19 August 1995).

Chapter 2 is based on Archibugi (1989): *Une politique solidaire européenne pour l'amélioration de l'environnement urbain. Problèmes et perspectives méthodologiques* (Rapport au Colloque organise par la Commission des Communautés européennes, Avignon, 18-20 décembre 1989).

Chapter 3 is based on Archibugi (1991): *A strategy for new public spaces and centralities. The renewal of the urban environment* (Report to the EEC Conference on: 'The future of the urban environment in Europe', Madrid, 30 April 1991).

Chapter 4 is based on Archibugi (1994a): *Urban planning and ecology. What relationship?* (Paper for the 8th Aesop Congress, Istanbul, 24-27 August 1994).

Chapter 5 is based on Archibugi (1993a): *The 'urban mobility integrated basin' and its policy-oriented identification. A pre-requisite of rationality for any planning of urban transport* (Report to the 33rd scientific meeting of SIEDS, Taormina, 6-8 May 1993; republished in *European Spatial Research and Policy*, vol. 1, no. 2, 1994, pp. 61-72).

Chapter 6 is based on Archibugi (1981): *Le bassin d'emploi: aspects conceptuels et méthodologiques* (Rapport prépare pour la Commission CEE pour les 'Séminaires sur la gestion prévisionnelle de l'emploi', Bruxelles, 1981).

Chapter 7 is based on Archibugi (1994b): *An instrument for environmental planning: the land-use/resource matrix* (Paper for the 'Conference on urban planning and environment' promoted jointly by the University of Washington and the University of Groningen, Seattle, 2-5 March, 1994).

Chapter 8 is based on Archibugi (1993b): *Ecological equilibrium and territorial planning: the Italian case* (Paper for the 7th Aesop Congress, Lodz, Poland 14-17 July 1993; republished in *European Planning Studies*, vol. 2, no. 2, 1993).

Chapter 9 is based on Archibugi (1992): *The 'urban environment' programme of the Italian Government ten-year plan for the environment* (Paper for the Urban Environment Group of Experts of the EEC, Session, October 1992).

Bibliography

Alexander, E.R. (1986), *Approaches to Planning: Introducing Current Planning Theories, Concepts, and Issues*, Gordon and Breach: New York.

Alonso, W. (1964), *Location and Land Use*, Harvard University Press: Cambridge.

Alonso, W. (1971), 'The Economics of Urban Size', *Papers and Proceedings of the Regional Scence Association*, Vol. 24.

Alonso, W. (1973), 'Markets and Planning Regions for Transportation', in De Salvo, J.S. (ed.), *Perspectives on Regional Transportation Planning*, Lexington Books: Lexington.

Alpass, J. and E. Agergaard (1978), 'The City Centre - For Whom?', in Swedish Council for Building Research (1979), *Growth and Trasformation of the Modern City*, (Stockolm Conference 1978, University of Stockolm): Stockholm.

Anderson, S. (ed.) (1967), *Planning for Diversity and Choice; Possible Futures and their Relations to the Man-Controlled Environment*, MIT Press: Cambridge.

Andranovich, G.D. and G. Riposa (1993), *Doing Urban Research*, Sage: Newbury Park, Ca.

Appleyard, D. (1986), 'Evaluating the Social and Environmental Impacts of Transport Investment', in De Boer, E. (ed.), *Transport Sociology: Social Aspects of Transport Planning*, Pergamon: Oxford.

Appleyard, D. and M. Lintell (1986), 'The Environmental Quality of City Streets: The Resident's Viewpoint', in De Boer, E. (ed.), *Transport Sociology: Social Aspects of Transport Planning*, Pergamon: Oxford

Archibugi, F., (1966a), 'L'analisi ecologica per la delimitazione di aree di programmazione' ['Ecological Analysis for the Delimitation of Planning

Areas'], in Giannotti, G., *L'analisi ecologica; Panorama della letteratura* Quaderni del Centro di studi e piani economici, Boringhieri: Turin.

Archibugi, F. (1966b) (ed.), *La Città-Regione in Italia. Premesse culturali, Ipotesi programmatiche* [The City-Region in Italy. Cultural Premises, Policy-Oriented Hypotheses], Quaderni del Centro di studi e piani economici, Boringhieri: Turin.

Archibugi, F. (1966c), 'L'idea di città: alcune annotazioni' ['The Idea of the City: Some Notes'], in Archibugi, F. (ed.), *La Città Regione in Italia; premesse culturali, ipotesi programmatiche* [The City Region in Italy; Cultural Premises, Programmatic Hypotheses], Boringhieri: Turin.

Archibugi, F. (1969), 'Strategy of National Development and Its Implications for Physical Planning', prepared for the UN Center for Housing, Building and Planning Interregional Seminar on 'Physical Planning for Urban, Regional and National Development', Bucharest, 22 Sept-7 Oct. 1969.

Archibugi, F. (1970a), 'La Planificacion fisica y economica en el desarollo nacional', *Ciudad y Territorio*, No.1, Jan.-Mar. 1970.

Archibugi, F. (1970b), *Une experience de regionalisation: les systemes metropolitaines du Progetto 80*, (Report for the 'Colloque Franco-Italien sur la Regionalisation', Fondation National des Sciences Politiques), St Vincent, 1-3 July 1970.

Archibugi, F. (1970c), *Il Progetto 80 e la 'Città Veneta'*, [Project 80 and the 'Venetian City'], Study Workshops, Venice-Mestre, 26 Sept. 1970.

Archibugi, F. (1973), *La 'struttura di programma', base operativa sistematica della programmazione*, [Programme Structuring, the Systematic Operational Base of Planning], General Report No. 2 for the 'Progetto Quadro', Ministero del Bilancio e della Programmazione Economica: Rome.

Archibugi, F. (1974), 'The "Quality of Life" in a Method of Integrated Planning (Aspects of an Italian Research Project "Progetto 80")', *Socio-Economic Planning Sciences*, Vol. 8, No. 6.

Archibugi, F. (1977), *Critica del terziario: saggio su un nuovo metodo di analisi delle attività terziarie*, [Critique of the Tertiary Sector: Contribution for a New Method of Analysis of Tertiary Activities], Centro di studi e piani economici: Rome.

Archibugi, F. (1978), 'Capitalist Planning in Question', in Holland, S. (ed.), *Beyond Capitalist Planning*, Blackwell: Oxford.

Archibugi, F. (1979[1]-82[2]), *Principi di pianificazione regionale* [Principles of Regional Planning], Angeli: Milan.

Archibugi. F. (1983a), *La Politica della Città* [City Policy], (Relazione al XXIII Congresso Geografico Italiano - Report to the XXIII Italian

Geographic Congress, Catania, 9-13 May 1983), Proceedings, Vol.. II, No. 1.

Archibugi, F. (1983b), 'Criteri di misura dei bisogni residenziali nella logica di sviluppo dei sistemi urbani' ['Measurement Criteria for Residential Needs in the Logic of the Development of Urban Systems'], *Rivista Italiana di Economia, Demografia e Statistica*, Vol. XXXVIII, No. 4, 1984.

Archibugi, F. (1984), 'Per una tassonomia della domanda di trasporto nell'ambito della pianificazione dei trasporti' ['For a Taxonomy of Transportation Demand in the Ambit of Transportation Planning'], in CNR-Pft, *La ricerca sui trasporti in Italia: primi risultati del Progetto CNR*. [Research into Transportation in Italy: First Results of the CNR Project], Angeli: Milan.

Archibugi, F. (1985a), 'La misura dei fabbisogni di servizi sanitari e i criteri di distribuzione territoriale della spesa sanitaria' ['Measurement of Needs for Health Services and Criteria for Territorial Distribution of Health Expenditure'], (Relazione al XXVII Riunione scientifica della SIEDS, Selva di Fasano, Bari, 24-27 Mar. 1981), *Rivista Italiana di Economia, Demografia e Statistica*, Vol. XXXIX, Nos 1-3.

Archibugi, F. (1985b), *Metodologia per la delimitazione programmatica di bacini integrati di mobilità urbana*, [Methodology for the Policy-oriented Delimitation of Integrated Basins of Urban Mobility], Contributo al III Convegno Nazionale del Progetto Finalizzato Trasporti, Taormina, May 1985.

Archibugi, F. (1986a), *La politica dei sistemi urbani* [Urban-Systems Policy], Centro di studi e piani economici, Report No. 86.3, Rome.

Archibugi, F. (1986b), *Per una metodologia di valutazione multi-criteri dei Programmi FAI*, [Multi-criteria Evaluation Methodology for the FAI Programmes], Centro di studi e piani economici: Rome.

Archibugi, F. (1987), *I sistemi urbani in Italia*, [The Urban Systems in Italy], Centro di studi e piani economici, Report No. 87, 1-4: Rome.

Archibugi, F. (1988a), *La domanda programmatica di trasporto: conclusioni di una analisi metodologica* [Policy-Oriented Demand for Transportation: Conclusions of a Methodological Analysis], Centro di studi e piani economici: Rome.

Archibugi, F. (1988b), *La matrice di uso del territorio, strumento di valutazione dei piani* [The Land-Use Matrix, An Instrument of Plan Evaluation], Paper to an International Seminar 'Plan Evaluation Techniques in Town-Planning', University of Rome, 18-19 Mar. 1988, Centro di studi e piani economici: Rome.

Archibugi, F. (1989a), *An EEC Strategy for the Improvement of the Urban Environment: Problems of Methodological Perspectives*, Seminar of the Commission, DG XI, Avignon, 18-20 Dec., 1989.

Archibugi, F. (1989b), 'Comprehensive Social Assessment: an Essential Instrument for Environmental Policy-Making', in Archibugi, F. and P. Nijkamp (eds), *Economy and Ecology: Towards Sustainable Development*, Kluwer Academic Press: Dordrecht.

Archibugi, F. (1990a), 'Nuovi strumenti per la valutazione integrata dell'impatto ambientale' ['New Instruments for the Integrated Analysis of Environmental Impact'], in Beato, F. (ed.), *La valutazione di impatto ambientale: un approccio integrato [Environmental Impact Evaluation: An Integrated Approach]*, Angeli: Milan.

Archibugi, F. (1990b), *L'Eco-sistema urbano: suo concetto, sua utilizzabilità nella politica del territorio e dell'ambiente* [The Urban Ecosystem: Its Concept and Utilisation in Land and Environment Policy], Report to the CNR Seminar 'Uomo-ambiente', Rome, 21 Dec. 1990.

Archibugi, F. (1991a), *A Strategy for New Public Spaces and Centralities: The Renewal of the Urban Environment*, Report to the EC Conference on 'The Future of the Urban Environment in Europe', Madrid, 29-30 April 1991, Planning Studies Centre: Rome.

Archibugi, F. (1991b), 'Rome: A New Planning Strategy', *Lazioricerche, IRSPEL*, No. 4: Rome (Italian version), Planning Studies Centre, Report No. 94.1, 1994 (English edition forthcoming from Gordon and Breach, New York).

Archibugi, F. (1992a), *The Urban Environment Programme of the Italian Government Ten Year-Plan for the Environment*, Paper prepared for the Urban Environment Group of Experts of the Commission of the European Community, October.

Archibugi, F. (1992b), *The Quadroter Project: An Ecological Reading of the Italian Territory*, Paper given at a conference on the theme 'The Ecological Aspects of Land-Use Planning' organized by the Department of Territory Science, Polytechnic of Milan, 12-13 Nov. 1992.

Archibugi, F. (1993a), 'The "Urban Mobility Integrated Basin" and its Policy-Oriented Identification: A Prerequisite of Rationality for Planning of Urban Transport', Report to the XXXIII SIEDS Scientific Meeting, Taormina, May 1993, *European Spatial Research and Policy*, Vol. 1, No. 2, 1994, pp. 61-72.

Archibugi, F. (1993b), 'Ecological Equilibrium and Territorial Planning: the Italian Case', Paper given at the VII Congress of the AESOP (Association of European Schools of Planning), Lodtz, Poland, 14-17 July, *European Planning Studies*, Vol. 2, No. 2, 1994.

Archibugi, F. (1993c), *Regional Science and the Policy-Oriented Approach: A Critical Issue*, Paper delivered at the 34th European Congress of the Regional Science Association, Groningen, 23-26 Aug. 1994.

Archibugi, F. (1994a), *The Basic Issues of Ecological City Planning*, Background paper presented at the International Symposium on 'Urban Planning and Environment', Seattle, 2-5 Mar. 1994.

Archibugi, F. (1994b), *Urban Planning and Ecology: What Relationship?*, Paper for the VIII AESOP Congress, Istanbul, 24-27 Aug. 1994.

Archibugi, F. (under the direction of) (1994c), *I sistemi urbani in Italia; una proposta di riorganizzazione urbana e di riequilibrio territoriale ed ambientale a livello regionale/nazionale*, Vol.1 'Scenario italiano generale', Vol. 2 'Scenari per singoli Ecosistemi urbani', [The Urban Systems in Italy; a Proposal for Urban Reorganisation and Territorial and Environmental Riequilibrium at the Regional and National Level, Vol. 1, 'The General Italian Scenario', Vol. 2, 'Scenarios for Single Urban Eco-systems'], CNR, Progetto strategico 'Quadroter', Rome.

Archibugi, F. (1995), *Theory of Urbanistics: Lectures on a Reappraisal of City Planning Methodology*, Textbook, Academic Year 1994/95, University of Naples (English edition: Rome Summer Course at the Planning Studies Centre in cooperation with the University of Pennsylvania [Philadelphia] and the University of Southern California [Los Angeles], June 1995).

Archibugi, F. (1996), 'Program Indicators: Their Role and Use in the Integrated Social or Community Programming', in *Social Indicator Research* (forthcoming).

Archibugi, F. and P. Bisogno (eds) (1994), *Per una teoria della pianificazione* [Toward a Theory of Planning] (Una selezione dei contributi alla 1° Conferenza mondiale sulla Scienza della Pianificazione [A Selection of Papers of the 1st World Conference on Planning Science], Palermo, Sept. 1992.

Archibugi, F. and G. Las Casas (1985), *Metodologia per la delimitazione programmatica di bacini integrati di mobilità urbana* [Methodology for the Policy-Oriented Delimitation of Integrated Basins of Urban Mobility], Contribution for Third National Meeting of the Transport Project, Taormina, May, 1985; Centro di studi e piani economici: Rome.

Archibugi, F. and P. Nijkamp (eds) (1989), *Economy and Ecology: Toward Sustainable Development*, Kluwer Academic Press: Dordrecht.

Arnott, R.J. (1979), 'Optimal City Size in a Spatial Economy', *Journal of Urban Economics*, Vol. 6, pp. 65-89.

Atkinson, A. (1991), *Principles of Political Ecology*, Belhaven Press: London.

Basta, D.J. and B.T. Bower (eds) (1982), *Analyzing Natural Systems: Analysis for Regional Residuals and Environment Quality* Management, Resources for the Future, John Hopkins University Press: Washington DC.

Batty M. and B. Hutchinson (eds) (1983), *Systems Analysis in Urban Policy-Making and Planning*, Plenum Press: New York.

Beckmann, M.J. (1973), 'Equilibrium Models of Residential Land-Use', *Regional and Urban Economics*, Vol. 3, pp. 361-368.

Begovic, B. (1991), 'The Economic Approach to Optimal City Size', *Progress in Planning*, Vol. 36, No. 2.

Beguinot, C. (ed.) (1987), *La città cablata. Lo stato dell'arte nella ricerca scientifica* [The Wired City: The State of the Art in Scientific Research], CNR-IPIGET and DIPIST, University of Naples.

Beguinot, C. (1989), *La città cablata: una enciclopedia* [The Wired City: An Encyclopaedia], CNR-IPIGET and DIPIST, University of Naples.

Beguinot, C. and U. Cardarelli (eds) (1992), *Città cablata e nuova architettura* (3 vols) [The Wired City and New Architecture], CNR-IPIGET and DIPIST, University of Naples.

Berger, M. *et al.*, (1987), 'A Revealed Preference Ranking of Quality of Life for Metropolitan Areas', *Social Science Quarterly*, Vol. 68.

Berry, B.J.L. (1966), 'Reflections on the Functional Economic Areas', in W.R. Maki and B.J.L. Berry, *Research and Education for Regional and Area Development*, Iowa State University Press: Ames.

Berry, B.J.L. (1972a), 'Population Growth in the Daily Urban Systems of the US', in Sara Mills Mazie (ed.), *Population Distribution and Policy, Research Report of US Commission on Population Growth and the American Future*, Vol. V, GPO: Washington DC.

Berry, B.J.L. (1972b), 'Latent Structure of the American Urban System, with International Comparison', in B.J.L. Berry, *City Classification Handbook*, Wiley: New York.

Berry, B.J.L. (1973), *Growth Centers in the American Urban System*, Vols 1 and 2, Ballinger: Cambridge, Mass.

Berry, B.J.L. (1976), 'The Counterurbanization Process: Urban America since 1970', in Berry, B.J.L. (ed.), *Urbanization and Counterurbanization*, Sage: Beverly Hills.

Berry, B.J.L. (1977), *The Changing Shape of Metropolitan America 1960-1970*, Ballinger: Cambridge, Mass.

211

Berry, B.J.L., P.G. Goheen and H. Goldstein (1969), *Metropolitan Area Definition: A Reevaluation of Concept and Statistical Practice*, US Bureau of the Census (Working Paper 28), reissued slightly revised 1969.

Bertuglia, C.S., G.P. Clarke and A.G. Wilson (eds) (1994), *Modelling the City: Performance, Policy and Planning*, Routledge: London.

Bird, J. (1978), *Centrality and Cities*, Routledge: London.

Blancher, M., E. Jacquet-Lagrèze and B. Roy (1977), *Elaboration de Crytères permettants une integration de divers aspects liés au temps dans l'aide à la decision en matiere de transports*, Sema.

Blunden, W.R. (1971), *The Land-Use/Transport System - Analysis and Synthesis*, Pergamon Press: Oxford (2nd edition with J.A. Black, 1984).

Boeventer, E.V. and J. Hampe (1988), *Oekonomische Grundlagen der Stadtplanung: Eine Einfuehrung in die Stadtoekonomie* (Beitraege de Akademie fuer Raumforschung und Landesplanung, No. 112), Hannover.

Booth, A. (1976), *Urban Crowding and its Consequences*, New York.

Boscacci, F. and R. Camagni (eds) (1994), *Tra città e campagna: periurbanizzazione e politiche territoriali* [Between Town and Country: Periurbanisation and Land Policies] (Fondazione Cariplo), Il Mulino: Bologna.

Bower, B.T. (ed.) (1977), *Regional Residuals Environmental Quality Management Modeling*, Resources for the Future, John Hopkins University Press: Washington DC.

Boyden, S., S. Millar *et al.* (1981), *The Ecology of a City and its People: the Case of Hong Kong*, Australian National University Press: Canberra.

Bradbury, K.L. *et al.* (1982), *Urban Decline and the Future of American Cities*, Brookings: Washington DC.

Breheny, M.J. (ed.) (1992), *Sustainable Development and Urban Form*, Pion: London.

Breheny, M.J. (1993) 'Planning the Sustainable City Region', *Town and Country Planning*, Vol. 62, No. 4.

Brotchie, J. *et al.* (eds) (1985), *The Future of Urban Form: the Impact of New Technologies*, Routledge: London.

Brown, L.A. and J. Holmes (1971), 'The Delimitation of Functional Regions, Nodal Regions, and Hierarchies by Functional Distance Approaches', *Journal of Regional Science*, No. 11, pp. 57-72.

Bullinger, D. (1986), 'Das Konzept der Optimalen Stadtroesse', *Jahrubuch fuer Sozialwissenschaft*, Vol. 37, pp. 105-122.

Burnell, J.D. and G. Galster (1992), 'Quality of Life Measurement and Urban Size: An Empirical Note', *Urban Studies*, Vol. 29.

Ca (Government of Canada) (1990), *Canada's Green Plan for a Healthy Environment.*

Camagni, R., (ed.) (1991), *Computer Network: Mercati e prospettive delle tecnologie della comunicazione* [Computer Network: Markets and Perspectives of the Communication Technologies], Etas: Milan.

Camagni, R. (1992), *Economia Urbana: Principi e Modelli Teorici* [Urban Economics: Principles and Theoretical Models], La Nuova Italia: Rome.

Camagni, R. and R. Rabellotti (1990), 'Advanced Technology Policies and Strategies in Developing Regions', in Ewers, H.J. and J. Allesh (eds), *Innovation and Regional Development*, de Gruyer.

Camagni, R. and R. Capello (1991), 'Le caratteristiche delle nuove tecnologie e loro interazione con la domanda' ['The Characteristics of New Technologies and their Interaction with Demand], in Camagni, R. (ed.), *Computer Network: Mercati e prospettive delle tecnologie della comunicazione*, Etas: Milan.

Camhis, M. and S. Fox (1993), 'Urban Networking in the Context of the Development of the European Community's Territory', in Getimis, P. and G. Kafkalas (eds), *Urban and Regional Development in the New Europe*, Topos: Athens.

Carpenter, R.A. and S. Sani (1983), 'Urban Air Pollution', in Carpenter, R.A. (ed.) (East-West Environment and Policy Institute), *Natural Systems for Development*, McMillan.

Carver, H. (1965[2]), *Cities in the Suburbs*, University of Toronto Press: Toronto.

Castells, M. (ed.) (1985), *High Technology, Space, and Society*, Sage: Beverly Hills.

Centre d'études sur les réseaux, les transports, l'urbanisme et les constructions publiques (1989), *Les études de prévision de trafic en milieu urbain,* Centre d'études sur les réseaux, les transports, l'urbanisme et les constructions publiques: Lyon.

Centre d'études sur les réseaux, les transports, l'urbanisme et les constructions publiques (1993a), *Evolution démographique croissance urbaine et mobilité,* Centre d'études sur les réseaux, les transports, l'urbanisme et les constructions publiques: Lyon.

Centre d'études sur les réseaux, les transports, l'urbanisme et les constructions publiques (1993b), *Mobilité quotidienne et structure spatiale de la ville: Toulouse et Bordeaux,* Centre d'études sur les réseaux, les transports, l'urbanisme et les constructions publiques: Lyon.

Centre d'études sur les réseaux, les transports, l'urbanisme et les constructions publiques (1994), *Les enjeux des politiques de déplacement dans une stratégie urbaine*, Centre d'études sur les réseaux, les transports, l'urbanisme et les constructions publiques: Lyon.

Centre d'études sur les réseaux, les transports, l'urbanisme et les constructions publiques (1996), *Plans de déplacement urbains*, Centre d'études sur les réseaux, les transports, l'urbanisme et les constructions publiques: Lyon.

Centro di studi e piani economici (Planning Studies Centre) (1971a), *Le proiezioni territoriali del Progetto 80. Ricerca e modelli di base* [The Territorial Projections of Project 80. Basic Research and Models] (3 vols.), Ministero del Bilancio e della Programmazione Economica: Rome.

Centro di studi e piani economici (Planning Studies Centre) (1971b), *Le proiezioni territoriali del Progetto 80 (Sintesi)* [The Territorial Projections of Project 80, A Summary], special issue of *Urbanistica*.

Centro di studi e piani economici (Planning Studies Centre) (1985), *Indicatori di qualità urbana discussi in sede OCSE* [Urban Quality Indicators Discussed in the OECD], Centro di studi e piani economici: Rome.

Centro di studi e piani economici (Planning Studies Centre) (1992), *Una prima rassegna sistematica di indicatori ambientali urbani e naturali in funzione dei Programmi del Piano Decennale per l'Ambiente (Decamb)*, [A First Systematic Review of Urban and Natural Indicators with reference to the Ten-Year Plan for the Environment] (3 vols), Centro di studi e piani economici: Rome.

Chadwick, G. (1971), *A System View of Planning*, Pergamon: Oxford.

Chapin, S.F. Jr. (1965), *Urban Land Use Planning*, University of Illinois Press: Urbana.

Chapin, S.F. Jr. and E. Kaiser (1985), *Urban Land Use Planning* (3rd edition), University of Illinois Press: Urbana.

Cherry, G.E. (1986), *Settlement Planning and the Regional City*, in Gordon, G. (ed.), *Regional Cities in the UK 1890-1980*, Harper: Lindon.

Cheshire, P. (1995), 'A New Phase of Urban Development in Western Europe? The Evidence for the 1980s', *Urban Studies*, Vol. 32, pp. 1045-1063.

Cheshire, P.C. and D.G. Hay (1989), *Urban Problems in Western Europe*, Unwin Hyman: London.

Christaller, W. (1933), *Die Zentrale Orte in Suddeutschland, Jena 1933* (Eng. Trans., Englewood Cliffs: US [1965]; It. Trans., Angeli: Milan [1980]).

Cipolletta, I. (1991), 'Dal decentramento alla ripolarizzazione' ['From Decentralisation to Repolarisation], in Gottmann, J. and C. Muscarà (eds),

La città prossima ventura [The City of the Near Future], Laterza: Rome-Bari.

Clark, W.A.V. and M. Kuijpers-Linde (1994), 'Commuting in Restructuring Urban Regions', *Urban Studies*, Vol. 31, pp. 465-483.

Clark, W.C. and R.E. Munn (eds) (1986), *Sustainable Development of the Biosphere. International Institute for Applied Systems Analysis*, Cambridge University Press: Cambridge.

Clavel, P. (1986), *The Progressive City: Planning and Participation, 1969-1984*, Rutgers: New Brunswick, NJ.

Conti, S. (1990), 'Innovazione tecnologica e territorio' ['Technological Innovation and Territory'], in Conti, S. and Spriano (eds), *Effetto città* (Vol. 1) *Sistemi urbani e innovazione: prospettive per l'Europa degli anni '90*, [City Effect, Vol. 1, Urban Systems and Innovation: Perspectives for Europe in the 1990s], Fondazione Agnelli: Turin.

Cooke, P. (1993), 'Regional Innovations Systems: An Evaluation of six European Cases', in Getimis, P. and G. Kafkalas, *Urban and Regional Development in the New Europe*, Topos: Athens.

Curti, F. (1986), 'Declino metropolitano e riurbanizzazione selettiva: ipotesi esplicative da modelli noti e implicazioni normative', [Metropolitan Decline and Selective Reurbanisation: Explanatory Hypotheses from Known Models and Regulatory Implications'], *Archivio di studi Urbani e Regionali*, No. 27.

DATAR (Delegation a l'amenagement du territoire de l'action regionale) (1988), *La lettre de la DATAR - Les villes et l'aménagement du territoire*, (special edition, Aug.-Sept. 1988) No. 119: Paris.

Davée, M. and G. Marotel (1983), *Travailler à Paris, Vivre à 100 km*, Irt (Note d'Information No. 27).

Davies, H.W.E. (1981), 'The Inner City in Britain', in Schwartz, G.G. (ed.), *Advanced Industrialisation and the Inner Cities*, Lexington Books: Lexington, Mass.

Davison, A. and J. Barnes (1992), 'Patterns of air pollution: critical loads and abatement strategies', in Newson, M. (ed.), *Managing the Human Impact on the Natural Environment*, Belhaven Press: London.

Deelstra, T. (1993), 'The Quest for Sustainability in Urban Development and Design', in Rautsi, J. (ed.), *The European City Today: The Helsinki Round Table on Urban Improvement Strategies* (pp. 9-27), Ministry of the Environment: Helsinki.

de Finetti, B. (1965), 'Econometristi allo spettroscopio', ['Econometricians in the Spectroscope], *La Rivista Trimestrale*, Nos 15-16.

de Finetti, B. (1969) *Un matematico e l'economia*, [A Mathematician and Economics], Angeli: Milan.

de Finetti, B. (ed.) (1973), *Requisiti per un Sistema Economico Accettabile in Relazione alle Esigenze della Collettività* [Requirements for an Economic System Acceptable from the Point of View of Collective Needs], Angeli: Milan.

De Roo, G. (1993), 'Environmental Zoning: The Dutch Struggle Towards Integration', in *Environmental Planning Studies*, Vol. 1, No. 3.

De Salvo, J.S. (ed.) (1973), *Perspectives on Regional Transportation Planning*, Lexington Books: Lexington.

Deutsch, K.W. (1971), 'On Social Communication and the Metropolis', in Bourne, L.S. (ed.), *Internal Structure of the City*, Oxford University Press: New York.

Dickey, J. (1985), 'Urban Impacts of Information Technology', in Brotchie, J. *et al.* (eds), *The Future of Urban Form: the Impact of New Technologies*, Routledge: London.

Douglas, I. (1983), *The Urban Environment*, Arnold: London.

Doxiadis, K.A. (1966-70), *Emergence and Growth of an Urban Region*: Vol. 1 'Analysis' (1966); Vol. 2 'Future Alternatives' (1967); Vol. 3 'A Concept for Future Development' (1970), Edison: Detroit.

Doxiadis, K.A. (1968), *Ekistics, An Introduction to the Science of Human Settlements*, Hutchinson: London.

Doxiadis, K.A. (1970), *Hearing on: National Transportation Act*, Commerce Committee, 91st Congress, 2nd Session, S. 924 and S. 2425, Serial 91-69, GPO: Washington DC.

Doxiadis, K.A. (1972), 'Ekistics - The Science of Human Settlements', in Mesarovic, M.D. and A. Reisman (eds), *Systems Approach and the City*, North-Holland: Amsterdam.

Drewett, R. and A. Rossi (1984), *Urban Europe: Settlement Structure and Change 1959-1980*, Gower: Aldershot.

Drewett, R., R. Knight, U. Schubert (1992), *The Future of European Cities*, Part I, A Report to the Commission of EU, FAST, DGXII.

Duncan, O.D. *et al.* (1960), *Metropolis and Region*, John Hopkins Press: Baltimore.

Dziewonski, K. (1964), 'Economic Regionalisation', *Geographia Polonica*, Vol. 1, pp. 171-185.

EC Commission (1983), *Les europeens et leur environnement*, EC: Brussels.

EC Commission (1990), *Green Paper on the Urban Environment, Communication from the Commission to the Council and Parliament*, EC: Brussels.

EC Commission (1992), *Community Activities in Urban Matters*, EC: Brussels.

EC Commission (1994-99) *Urban: An EU Initiative Program in Urban Field; Statements and Resolutions (1994-1999)*, EC: Brussels.

EC Commission (1994a), *Toward a Better Liveable City* (City Action RDT Programme, Background Paper), EC: Brussels.

EC Commission (1994b), *Technology and the Future of Cities. Responding to the Urban Malaise: An Agenda for the European Union* (by Ugo L. Businaro, Fast FOP 380), EC: Brussels.

EC Commission Expert Group on the Urban Environment (1994c), *European Sustainable Cities*, Report for the 'European Conference on Sustainable Cities and Towns', Aalborg, Denmark, 24-27 May 1994.

EC Commission (1994d), *Charter of European Cities and Towns Toward Sustainability (The 'Aalborg Charte')*, EC: Brussels.

Edmunds, S. and J. Letey (1973), *Environmental Administration*, McGraw-Hill.

Eldredge, W. (ed.) (1967), *Taming Megalopolis:* Vol. 1 'What Is and What Could Be'; Vol. 2 'How to Manage an Urbanized World', Anchor: New York.

Elgin, D. *et al.* (1974), *City Size and Quality of Life*, Stanford Research Institute: Menlo Park.

Elkin, T. *et al.* (1991), *Reviving the City: Toward Sustainable Urban Development*, Friends of the Earth: London.

Eurocities, Car Free Cities Club (1994), 'Toward Sustainability', in van Wijk, F. and H. Bouma (eds), Conference Papers, Amsterdam, 24-25 Mar. 1994.

European Foundation for the Improvement of Living and Working Conditions (1993), *Innovations for the Improvement of the Urban Environment: A European Overview*, Luxembourg.

European Foundation for the Improvement of Living and Working Conditions (1994), *Visions and Actions for Medium-Sized Cities*, Alicante: Volos.

Evans, A.W. (1972), 'The Pure Theory of City Size in an Industrial Economy', *Urban Studies*, Vol. 1, pp. 49-77.

Evans, A.W. (1985), *Urban Economics: An Introduction*, Blackwell: Oxford.

Ewald, W.R. Jr. (ed.) (1967), *Environment for Man. The Next Fifty Years*, Indiana University Press: Bloomington.

Ewald, W.R. Jr. (ed.) (1968a), *Environment and Change. The Next Fifty Years*, Indiana University Press: Bloomington.

Ewald, W.R. Jr. (ed.) (1968b), *Environment and Policy. The Next Fifty Years*, Indiana University Press: Bloomington.

Faludi, A. (1973a), *Planning Theory*, Pergamon: Oxford.

Faludi, A. (ed.) (1973b), *A Reader in Planning Theory*, Pergamon: Oxford.

Faludi, A. (ed.) (1986), *Critical Rationalism and Planning Methodology*, Pion: London.

Fischer, M.M. (1982), 'Some Fundamental Problems in Homogeneous and Functional Regional Taxonomy', in Kuklinski, A. (ed.), *Societies, Regions, Boundaries* (New Babylon: Studies in Social Sciences), Unrisd and Mouton.

Fox, K.A. (1965), 'The Functional Economic Area: Delineation and Implications for Economic Analysis and Policy', *Regional Science Association Papers*, Vol. 10, pp. 57-85.

Fox, K.A. (1967), 'Functional Economic Areas and Consolidated Urban Regions of the United States', in *Social Science Research Council, ITEMS 21*.

Fox, K.A. (1973), 'Delimitation of Regions for Transportation Planning', in De Salvo, J.S. (ed.), *Perspectives on Regional Transportation Planning*, pp. 91-140, Lexington Books: Lexington.

Fox, K.A. (1974), 'Elements of an Operational System II: Cities and Regions' (Ch. XII), in Fox, K.A., *Social Indicators and Social Theory, Elements for an Operational System*, Wiley: New York.

Fox, K.A. (1985), *Social System Accounts: Linking Social and Economic Indicators through Tangible Behavior Setting*, D. Reidel Publ. Co.: Dordrecht.

Frieden, B.J. and W.W. Nash (eds) (1969), *Shaping an Urban Future*, MIT Press: Cambridge.

Frieden, B. and L. Segalyn (1989), *Downtown, Inc.: How America Builds Cities*, MIT Press: Cambridge.

Friedmann, J. and J. Miller (1965), 'The Urban Field', *Journal of the American Institute of Planners*, Vol. XXXI, No. 4, pp. 312-320.

Friedmann, J. and B. Stuckey (1973), *The Territorial Basis of National Transportation Planning*, in De Salvo, J.S. (ed.), *Perspectives on Regional Transportation* Planning, Lexington Books: Lexington.

Frisch, R. (1962), 'Preface to the Oslo Channel Model: A Survey of Types of Economic Forecasting and Programming', in Frisch, R. (1976), *Economic Planning Studies, A Collection of Essays* (Long, F. [ed.]), Reidel: Dordrecht.

Frisch, R. (1964), 'Economic Planning and the Role of Econometrics', *Statsoekonomisk Tidsskrift*, Vol. 78.

Frisch, R. (1970a), 'Econometrics in the Midst of Analytical and Social Turmoils', in *Scientists at Work. Festschrift in honour of Herman Wold*, pp. 249-259.

Frisch, R. (1970b), 'From Utopian Theory to Practical Applications: The Case of Econometrics', in Frisch, R. (1976), *Economic Planning Studies, A Collection of Essays* (Long, F. [ed.]), Reidel: Dordrecht.

Frisch, R. (1971), 'Cooperation Between Politicians and Econometricians on the Formalization of Political Preferences', in Frisch, R. (1976), *Economic Planning Studies, A Collection of Essays* (Long, F. [ed.]), Reidel: Dordrecht.

Frisch, R. (1976), *Economic Planning Studies, A Collection of Essays* (Long, F. [ed.]), Reidel: Dordrecht.

Fujita, M. (1989), *Urban Economic Theory: Land Use and City Size*, Cambridge University Press: Cambridge.

Fujita, M. and T.E. Smith (1987), 'Existence of Continuous Residential Land-Use Equilibria', *Regional Science and Urban Economics*, Vol. 17, pp. 549-594.

Garbesi, K. *et al.* (eds) (1989), *Controlling Summer Heat Island*, Lawrence Berkeley Laboratory: Berkeley.

Garreau, J. (1991), *Edge City*, Doubleday: Garden City, NY.

Gb (Government of Great Britain) (1990), *This Common Heritage: Britain's Environment Strategy*, (presented to Parliament by the Secretaries of State for Environment, Trade and Industry, Health, Education and Sciences, Scotland, Transport, Energy, and Northern Ireland; the Minister of Agriculture, Fisheries and Food, and the Secretaries of State for Employment and Wales), HMSO: London.

Geddes, P. (1899), *Regional Survey*, London.

Geddes, P. (1904), *City Development*, Edinburgh.

Geddes, P. (1915), *Cities in Evolution: An Introduction to the Town Planning Movement and to the Study of Civics*, William and Norgate.

Gehl, J. (1993), 'Human Quality in the City', in Rautsi, J. (ed.), *The Helsinki Round Table on Urban Improvement Strategies* (pp. 42-46), Ministry of the Environment: Helsinki.

Getimis, P. and G. Kafkalas (eds) (1993), *Urban and Regional Development in the New Europe: Policies and Institutions for the Development of Cities and Regions in the Single European Market*, Topos: Athens.

Giannotti, G. (1966), L'analisi ecologica. Panorama della letteratura [Ecological Analysis. Panorama of the Literature]. Introduzione di F. Archibugi. Boringhieri: Torino.

Girardet, H. (1992a), *Cities: New Directions for Sustainable Urban Living*, Gaia Books: London.

Girardet, H. (1992b), *The Gaia Atlas of Cities: New Directions for Sustainable Urban Living*, Anchor Books: New York.

Giura, T. (1992), *Tecnologia e communicazioni in urbanistica*, [Technology and Comunications in Town Planning], DIPIST, Collana di studi di urbanistica, No. 13, University of Naples.

Goldfield, D.R. and B.A. Brownell (1979), *Urban America: from Downtown to NoTown*, Houghton Mifflin: Boston.

Goodland, R., H.C. Daly and S. El Serafy (eds) (1992), *Population, Technology and Lifestyle: the Transition to Sustainability*, Island Press: Washington DC.

Gorschboth, F.F. (1972), 'Systems Analysis of Urban Air Pollution', in Mesarovic, M.D. and A. Reisman (eds.), *Systems Approach and the City*, North-Holland: Amsterdam.

Gottmann, J. (ed.) (1980), *Centre and Periphery: Spatial Variations in Politics*, Sage: Beverly Hills, CA.

Gottmann, J. (1988), *La città invincibile: una confutazione dell'urbanistica negativa* [The invincible city: a confutation of negative town-planning], Angeli: Milano.

Gottmann, J. and C. Muscarà (eds) (1991), *La città prossima ventura*, [The City of the Near Future], Laterza: Rome-Bari.

Graham, S. and S. Marvin (1994), 'Telematics and the Convergence of Urban Infrastrucure: Implications for Contemporary Cities', *Town Planning Review*, Vol. 65, pp. 227-242.

Grayson, L. and K. Young (1994), *Quality of Life in Cities*, London Research Centre, The British Library: London.

Gruen, V. (1964), *The Hearth of our Cities; the Urban Crisis: Diagnosis and Cure*, Simon and Shuster: New York.

Gruen, V. (1973), *Centers for the Urban Environment; Survival of the Cities*, Van Nostrand: New York.

Haeussermann, H. and W. Siebel (1992), 'Urbanitaet', *Beitraege zur Stadtforschung, Stadtentwicklung, Stadtgestaltung*, No. 37, Vienna.

Hahn, E. (1991), *Ecological Urban Restructuring. Theoretical Foundation and Concept of Action*, WZB Papers (FS, II, 91-402).

Haimes, Y.Y. (1972), 'Pollution and Ecology', in Mesarovic, M.D. and A. Reisman. (eds.), *Systems Approach and the City*, North-Holland: Amsterdam.

Hall, P. (1977), *Europe 2000*, Duckworth: London.

Hall, P. (1978), 'The European City in the Year 2000', in Swedish Council for Building Research (1979), *Growth and Trasformation of the Modern City.* (Stockolm Conference 1978, University of Stockolm): Stockholm.

Hall, P. (1980), *Great Planning Disasters,* Weidefeld and Nicolson: London.

Hall, P. (1988), *Cities of Tomorrow: An Intellectual History of City Planning in the Twentieth Century,* Blackwell: Oxford.

Hall, P. and D. Hay (1980), *Growth Centres in the European Urban System,* Heinemann Educational Books: London.

Handley, J.F. (1984), 'Ecological requirements for decision-making regarding medium-scale developments in the urban environment', in Roberts, R.D. and T.M. Roberts (eds) (1984), *Planning and Ecology,* Chapman and Hall: London-New York.

Harris, B. (1986), 'Post-Industrial Urban Policy: Reviewing the Background', in Hutchinson, B. and M. Batty (eds), *Advances in Urban Systems Modelling,* Elsevier Science Publishers: Amsterdam.

Harris, C. (1965), 'Methods of Research in Economic Regionalization', *Geographia Polonica,* Vol. 4.

Harrison, R.M. (ed.) (1990), *Pollution: Causes, Effects and Control,* Royal Society of Chemistry: Cambridge.

Henderson, J.V. (1977), *Economic Theory and the Cities,* Academic Press: New York (2nd edition, 1985).

Herington, J. (1984), *The Outer City,* Harper and Row: London.

Heripret, C. (1989), *L'amenagement integré des zones urbaines: sa place dans la politique communitaire de l'environnement,* Association pour le developpement et la Diffusion des Etudes Foncières (Etude realisée pour la CEE): Paris.

Herson, L.J.R. and J.M. Bolland (1990), *The Urban Web,* Nelson-Hall: Chicago.

Hill, M. (1973), 'Planning for Multiple Objectives, An Approach to Evaluation of Transportations Plans', Regional Science Research Institute (Monograph series No. 5): Philadelphia.

Hill, M. and Y. Tzamir (1972), 'Multidimensional Evaluation of Regional Plans Serving Multiple Objectives', *Regional Science Association Papers,* Vol. 29, pp. 139-165.

Hirschorn, L. (1979), 'The Urban Crisis: A Post-Industrial Perspective', *Journal of Regional Science,* No. 19.

HRB (1968), *Urban Development Models,* Proceedings of a Conference held in Dartmouth College, Hanover, New Hampshire, 26-30 June 1967, Highway Research Board: Washington DC.

Hutchinson, B. and M. Batty (eds) (1986), *Systems Analysis in Urban Policy-Making and Planning*, Plenum Press: New York.

Institut d'Urbanisme, University of Montreal (1988), *Les indicateurs d'environnement urbain*, Ministry of the Environment of Quebec.

Indovina, F. *et al.* (1990), *La città diffusa*, Daest: Venice.

Indovina, F. *et al.* (1992), 'Il consumo della qualità urbana', ['Consumption of Urban Quality'], in Salzano, E., *La città sostenibile*, [The Sustainable City], Edizioni delle Autonomie: Rome.

Isard, W. (1956), *Location and Space Economy*, MIT Press: Cambridge.

Isard, W. (1960), *Methods of Regional Analysis: An Introduction to Regional Science*, MIT Press: Cambridge.

Jacobs, J. (1977), *The Death and Life of Great American Cities*, Vintage Books: New York.

Jap (Government of Japan) - Environment Agency (1986), *Long-Term Plan for Environmental Protection: In Pursuit of a Healthy and Enriched Relationship Between Human Beings and the Environment*, Tokyo.

Johansen, L. (1977), *Lectures on Macroeconomic Planning*, North-Holland: Amsterdam.

Kanemoto, Y. (1980), *Theories of Urban Externalities*, North-Holland: Amsterdam.

Kanemoto, Y. (1987), 'Externalities in Space', in Miyao, T. and Y. Kanemoto (eds), *Urban Dynamics and Urban Externalities*, pp. 43-103, Harwood: Chur.

Klaassen, L.H. (1978), 'Désurbanisation e Réurbanisation en Europe Occidentale' in Paelinck, J.H.P. (ed.), *La structure urbaine en Europe occidentale*, Takefield: Farnborough.

Klaassen, L.H. (1985), 'Transport Energy Interactions', in Brotchie, J. *et al.* (eds), *The Future of Urban Form*, Routledge: London.

Klaassen, L.H. (1987), 'The Future of Larger European Towns', *Urban Studies*, Vol. 24, pp. 251-257.

Klaassen, L.H., W. Molle and J. Paelink (eds) (1981), *Dynamics of Urban Development*, Gower, Aldershot.

Knight, R.V. (1992a), *The Future of the European Cities* (The Role of Science and Technology, Part IV), Report to the Commission of EU, FAST, DGXII.

Knight, R.V. (1992b), *Global and Local Cities*, Paper for the Summer School of Applied Social Science, Iuav, Daest, Venice (It. trans. in Perulli, P. [1993]).

Knox, F. (1973), *Planning and the City: The Optimum Size of Cities*, Unit 27, Open University Press: Milton Keynes.

222

Koehler, M. (1985), 'Kriterien der Innenstadtbegruenung', in *Stadtoekologie*, DBV-Jugend Schriftenreihe 3: Reutlingen.

Kuik, O. and H. Verbruggen (1991), *In Search of Indicators of Sustainable Development*, Kluwer: Dordrecht.

Kunzmann, K. and M. Wegener (1991), *The Pattern of Urbanization in Western Europe*, Institut fuer Raumplanung Universitaet Dortmund, 15 Mar. 1991 (also in *Ekistics*, Vol. 58, Nos 350-351).

Las Casas, G. and S. Lombardo (1978), *Proposta di un Metodo per la Delimitazione dei Bacini di traffico* [Proposal for a Method for the Delimitation of Traffic Basins], Conference Proceedings, Airo, Segesta, Urbino.

LeRoy, S.F. and J. Sonstelie (1983), 'Paradise Lost and Regained: Transportation Innovation, Income, and Residential Location', *Journal of Urban Economics*, Vol. 13, pp. 67-89.

Lichfield, N., P. Kettle and M. Whitebread (1975), *Evaluation in the Planning Process*, Pergamon Press: Oxford.

Lichfield, N. (1996), *Community Impact Evaluation*, UCL Press: London.

Lineberry, R. and I. Sharkansky (1978), *Urban Politics and Urban Policy*, Harper and Row: New York.

Lipietz, A. (1993), 'Il locale e il globale: personalità regionale o interregionale?' [Local and Global: Regional and Interegional Personality?], in Perulli, P., *Globale/Locale: il contributo delle scienze sociali*, [Global/Local: The Contribution of Social Sciences], Angeli: Milan.

Loeckx, A. (1993), 'The City Out of Place. Questioning the Peripheries: Taxonomy, Theory, Design', in Getimis, P. and G. Kafkalas (eds), *Urban and Regional Development in the New Europe*, Topos: Athens.

Loesch, A. (1940), *Die Raeumliche Ordnung der Wirtschaft*, Fischer: Jena (Eng. Trans. *The Economics of Location*, Yale University Press: New Haven, 1954).

Lowe, M.D. (1990), *Alternative to the Automobile: Transport for Livable Cities*, Worldwatch Institute: Washington DC.

Lowry, I.S. (1968), 'Seven Models of Urban Development: A Structural Comparison', in *Urban Development Models*, Proceedings of a Conference, Dartmouth College, Hanover, New Hampshire, 26-30 June 1967, Highway Research Board: Washington DC.

Macka, M. (ed.) (1967), *Economic Regionalization*, Publishing House of the Czechoslovak Academy of Sciences: Prague.

Mammarella, L. (1976), *Insediamenti umani e condizioni ambientali* [Human Settlements and Environmental Conditions], Bulzoni: Rome.

223

Mammarella, L. (1978), 'L'atmosfera urbana e le sue contaminazioni' ['The Urban Atmosphere and its Contamination'], in Nicoletti, M. (ed.), *L'ecosistema urbano* [The Urban Ecosystem], Dedalo Libri: Bari.

Mandeville, T. (1983), 'The Spatial Effects of Information Technology', in *Futures*, 65-70.

Masser, I. and J. Scheurwater (1980), 'The Functional Regionalization of Spatial Interaction Data: An Evaluation of Some Suggested Strategies', *Environment and Planning A.*, No. 12, pp. 1357-82.

Mazzoleni, C. (1993), 'Città locale/città globale: dallo spazio dei luoghi allo spazio dei flussi e delle reti' [Local City/Global City: From the Space of Places to the Space of Flows and Networks'], in Perulli, P., *Globale Locale: il contributo delle scienze sociali*, [Global/Local: The Contribution of Social Sciences], Angeli: Milan.

McConnell, S. (1981), *Theory for Planning*, Heinemann, London.

Mega, V. (1993), 'Introduction', in European Foundation for the Improvement of Living and Working Conditions, *Innovations for the Improvement of the Urban Environment: A European Overview*, Luxembourg.

Meier, R.L. (1962), *A Communications Theory of Urban Growth*, MIT Press: Cambridge.

Meier, R.L. (1972), 'Communications Stress', *Annual Review of Ecology and Systematics*, No. 3, pp. 289-313.

Meier, R.L. (1974), *Planning for an Urban World: The Design of Resource-Conserving Cities*, MIT Press: Cambridge.

Meier, R.L. (1985), 'Telecommunications and Urban Development', in Brotchie, J. *et al.* (eds), *The Future of Urban Form. The Impact of New Technology*, Groom Helm.

Meltzer, J. (1984), *Metropolis to metroplex*, John Hopkins University Press: Baltimore.

Mesarovic, M.D. and A. Reisman (eds) (1972), *System Approach and the City*, North-Holland: Amsterdam.

Mestre, V.E. and D.C. Wooten (1980), 'Noise Impact Analysis' in Rau, J.G. and D.C. Wooten (eds), *Environmental Impact Analysis Handbook*, University of California at Irvine, McGraw Hill: New York.

Mills, E.S. (ed.) (1987), *Handbook of Regional and Urban Economics*, North-Holland: Amsterdam.

Mills, E.S. and de Ferranti, D.M. (1971), 'Market Choices and Optimum City Size', *American Economic Review, Papers and Proceedings*, Vol. 61, pp. 340-45.

Mirrlees, J.A. (1972), 'The Optimum Town', *Swedish Journal of Economics*, Vol. 74, pp. 114-135.

Murie, A. (1994), *Cities and Housing after the Welfare State*, Ame (Amsterdam study centre for the metropolitan environment): Amsterdam.

Muscarà, C. (1968), *Una regione per il programma* [A Region for the Programme], Marsilio: Padua.

Neiman, M. (1975), *Metropology*, Sage: Beverly Hills.

Neutze, G.M. (1965^1-68^3), *Economic Policy and the Size of Cities*, Reprint by Kelley: New York.

Newton, P.W. and M.A.P. Taylor (1984), *The Impact of Technological Change on Urban Form: Report of the CIB Futures Study*, CSIRO Division of Building Research: Melbourne.

Newton, P.W. and M.A.P. Taylor (1985), 'Probable Urban Futures', in Brotchie, J. *et al.* (eds), *The Future of Urban Form*, Routledge: London.

Nicholson-Lord, D. (1987), *The Greening of the Cities*, Routledge and Kegan: London.

Nicoletti, M. (ed.) (1978), *L'ecosistema urbano* [The Urban Eco-system], Dedalo: Bari.

Nijkamp, P. (1977), *Theory and Application of Environmental Economics*, North-Holland: Amsterdam.

Nijkamp, P. (1986), 'Qualitative Methods for Urban and Regional Impact Analysis', in Hutchinson, B. and M. Batty (eds), *Advances in Urban Systems Modelling*, North-Holland: Amsterdam.

Nijkamp, P. and U. Schubert (1985), 'Urban Dynamics', in Brotchie, J. *et al.* (eds), *The Future of Urban Form*, Routledge: London.

Nijkamp, P. and H. Voogd (1983), *Multicriteria Analysis for Development Planning*, International Institute for Applied System Analysis (Collaborative Paper), Laxenburg, A. (mimeo).

Nl (Government of the Netherlands) (1988-89), *National Environmental Policy Plan (NEPP), To Choose or to Lose*, Second Chamber of the States General Session: The Hague.

Nl (Government of the Netherlands) (1990), *National Environmental Policy Plan Plus (NEPP-Plus)*: The Hague.

Nl (Government of the Netherlands), Ministry of Housing, Physical Planning and Environment (1991), *Essential Environmental Information, The Netherlands 1991*, Ministry of Housing, Physical Planning and Environment: Holland.

Norton, R.D. (1979), *City Life Cycles and American Urban Policy*, Academic Press: New York.

Odum, H.T. (1983), *System Ecology: An Introduction*, Wiley: New York.

OECD (1971a), *Le bruit dû à la circulation urbaine*, OECD: Paris.

OECD (1971b), *The Urban Transportation Planning Process*, OECD: Paris.

OECD (1973), *List of Social Concerns Common to most OECD Countries*, OECD: Paris.

OECD (1974), *Social Indicators Development: Approaches, Principles and Concepts*, OECD: Paris.

OECD (1976), *Mésure du bien-être social: un rapport sur les progrès d'élaboration des indicateurs sociaux*, OECD: Paris.

OECD (1978), *Indicateurs d'environnement urbain*, OECD: Paris.

OECD (1979), *Les transports urbains et l'environnement*, 4 vols, OECD: Paris.

OECD (1982), *The List of Social Indicators*, OECD: Paris.

OECD (1986), *Environmental Effects of Automotive Transport*, The OECD Compass Project, OECD: Paris.

OECD (1988a), *Les villes et leurs transports*, OECD: Paris.

OECD (1988b), *Transport and the Environment*, OECD: Paris.

OECD (1990), *Environmental Policies for Cities in the 1990s*, OECD: Paris.

OECD (1995), *Urban Governance in the OECD Countries* (Discussion Document).

Oke, T.R. (1973), 'City size and urban heat island', *Atmospheric Environment*, Vol. VII, pp. 769-79.

Openshaw, S. (1977), 'Optimal Zoning Systems for Spatial Interaction Models', *Environment and Planning*, A. 9, 1977, pp. 169-184.

Owens, S. (1986), *Energy, Planning and Urban Form*, Pion: London.

Owens, S. (1991), *Energy-conscious Planning. The Case for Action*, Council for the Protection of Rural England: London.

Papageorgiou, G.J. (1978), 'Spatial Externalities. First: Theory, Second: Applications', *Annals of the Association of American Geographers*, Vol. 68, pp. 465-492.

Parkinson, M. *et al.* (1992), *Urbanisation and the Function of Cities in the European Community* (A Report to the Commission of the European Communities, DGXVI, from the European Institute of Urban Affairs, Liverpool John Moores University).

Pasquini, F. *et al.* (eds) (1990), *Modelli d'analisi e d'intervento per un nuovo regionalismo* [Models of Analysis and Intervention for a New Regionalism], Angeli: Milan.

Perloff, H.S. (1969a), 'A Framework for Dealing with the Urban Environment: Introductory Statement', in Perloff, H.S. (ed.), *The Quality of the Urban Environment. Essays on 'New Resources' in an Urban Age*, Resources for the Future, John Hopkins University Press: Washington DC.

Perloff, H.S. (ed.) (1969b), *The Quality of the Urban Environment. Essays on 'New Resources' in an Urban Age*, Resources for the Future, John Hopkins University Press: Washington DC.

Perloff, H.S. (1980), *Planning the Post-Industrial City*, Planners Press (APA): Washington DC.

Perulli, P. (1992), *Atlante metropolitano: il mutamento sociale nelle grandi città* [Metropolitan Atlas: Social Change in the Large Cities], Il Mulino: Bologna.

Perulli, P. (ed.) (1993), *Globale/Locale: il contributo delle scienze sociali*, [Global/Local: The Contribution of Social Sciences], Angeli: Milan.

Platt, R.H., R.A. Rowentree and P.C. Muick (eds) (1994), *The Ecological City: Preserving and Restoring Urban Biodiversity*, University of Massachusetts Press: Amherst.

Pred, A. (1977), *City-Systems in Advanced Economies*, Wiley: New York.

Pred, A. (1980), *Urban Growth and City-Systems in the US*, Harvard University Press: Cambridge.

Prescott, J.R. *et al.* (1994), *Urban-Regional Economics, Social System Accounts, and Eco-Behavioural Science: Selected Writings by Karl A. Fox*, Iowa State University Press: Ames.

Prince of Wales, The (1989), *A Vision of Britain*, Carrick.

Prince of Wales' Institute of Architecture, The (1993), *The Sustainable City* (Report on the 1993 Summer School, London).

Rapoport, A. (1977), *Human Aspects of Urban Form: Toward a Man-Environment Approach to Urban Form and Design*, Pergamon: Oxford.

Rau, J.G. and D.C. Wooten (eds) (1980), *Environmental Impact Analysis Handbook*, University of California at Irvine, McGraw Hill: New York.

Ravetz, A. (1978), 'The Relation of the Centre to the Suburbs in the City Structure', in Swedish Council for Building Research (1979), *Growth and Trasformation of the Modern City*, (Stockolm Conference 1978, University of Stockolm), Stockholm.

Ravetz, A. (1986), *The Government of Space: Town Planning in Modern Society*, Faber: London.

Rf (Secretariat d'Etat aupres du PM chargé de l'Environnement et de la Prevention des Risques Technologiques) (1990), *Plan national pour l'Environnement: Rapport preliminaire en vue du debat d'orientation* (Chabason, L. and J. Theys): Paris.

Ri (Ministero dell'Ambiente) (Ministry of the Environment) (1989a), *Relazione sullo stato dell'ambiente, Nota aggiuntiva* [Report on the State of the Environment, Adjunct]: Rome.

Ri (Ministero dell'Ambiente) (Ministry of the Environment) (1989b), *Rapporto al Ministro dell'Ambiente sulle linee di politica ambientale a medio e lungo termine* [Report to the Minister of the Environment on the Guidelines of Environmental Policy to Medium and Long Term], Gruppo di riflessione presieduto dal Prof. Franco Archibugi [Reflection Team directed by Prof. Franco Archibugi]: Rome.

Ri (Ministero dell'Ambiente) (Ministry of the Environment) (1992), *Piano decennale dell'Ambiente (Decamb)* [Ten-Year Plan for the Environment]:Rome.

Ri (Ministero dell'Ambiente - Consiglio Nazionale delle Ricerche) [Ministry of the Environment - National Research Council] (1991a), *Quadro territoriale di riferimento per la politica ambientale (Quadroter)* [Territorial Frame of Reference for Environmental Policy]: Rome.

Ri (Ministero dell'Ambiente - Consiglio Nazionale delle Ricerche) [Ministry of the Environment - National Research Council] (1991b), *Quadro territoriale di riferimento per la politica ambientale (Quadroter), Rapporto n. 3 'Organizzazione del territorio alla scala di ciascun Eco-sistema urbano'* [Territorial Framework of Reference for Environmental Policy, Report No. 3 'Land Organisation at the Urban Ecosystem Scale'] (3 issues): Rome.

Ri (Ministero del Bilancio e della Programmazione Economica) [Ministry of Budget and Economic Planning] (1969), *Progetto 80. Rapporto preliminare al programma economico nazionale* [Preliminary Report to the National Economic Programme] 1971-1975: Rome.

Ri (Ministero del Bilancio e della Programmazione Economica) [Ministry of Budget and Economic Planning] (1971), *Le proiezioni territoriali del Progetto 80. Ricerca e modelli di base* [Territorial Projections of Project 80. Research and Basic Models] (3 vols): Rome.

Ri, Ministero per il Mezzogiorno, Commissione di studio per un Programma dei Sistemi urbani nel Mezzogiorno [Ministry for Special Intervention in Southern Italy, Study Commission for a Programme of Urban Systems] (1983), *La politica dei sistemi urbani nel Mezzogiorno* [Urban Systems Policy in Southern Italy], Cassa per il Mezzogiorno: Rome (pp. 168, including maps).

Richardson, H.W. (1972), 'Optimality in City Size, Systems of Cities and Urban Policy: a Sceptic's View', *Urban Studies*, Vol. 9.

Richardson, H.W. (1977), *The New Urban Economics: and Alternatives*, Pion: London.

Richardson, H.W. (1983), *The Economics of Urban Size*: London.

Roberts, R.D. and T.M. Roberts (eds) (1984), *Planning and Ecology*, Chapman and Hall: London-New York.

Rodwin, L. (ed.) (1961), *The Future Metropolis*, Daedalus: Fall.

Ross, S.L. (1993), 'Dimensions of Urban Structure: An Example of Construct Validation', *Urban Studies*, Vol. 30, No. 7.

Ryding, S.O. (1992), *Environmental Management Handbook*, Ios Press: Amsterdam.

Salzano, E. (ed.) (1992), *La città sostenibile* [The Sustainable City], Edizioni delle Autonomie: Rome.

Samuelsen, G.S. (1980), 'Air Quality Impact Analysis', in Rau, J.G. and D.C. Wooten (eds), *Environmental Impact Analysis Handbook*, University of California at Irvine, McGraw Hill: New York.

Sengupta, J.K. and K.A. Fox (1969), *Optimization Techniques in Quantitative Economic Models*, North-Holland: Amsterdam.

Simmie, J. (1993), *Planning at the Crossroads*, UCL Press: London.

Simoncini, G. (1970), *Il futuro e la città: Urbanistica e problemi di previsione urbana*, [The Future and the City: Town Planning and Problems of Urban Forecasting], Il Mulino: Bologna.

Sjoberg, G. (1964), 'The Rise and Fall of Cities: A Theoretical Perspective', *International Journal of Comparative Sociology*, No. 4, pp. 107-20.

Solow, R.M. (1973), 'On Equilibrium Models of Urban Locations', in Parkin, J.M. (ed.), *Essays in Modern Economics*, Longman: London.

Steger, W.A. and T.R. Lakshmanan (1968), 'Plan Evaluation Methodologies: Some Aspects of Decision Requirements and Analytical Response', in HRB, *Urban Development Models: Proceedings of a Conference held Dartmouth College, Hanover, New Hampshire, 26-30 June 1967*, Highway Research Board: Washington DC.

Sternlieb, G. and W.J. Hughes (1975), *Post-industrial America: Metropolitan Decline and Interregional Job Shifts*, Rutgers University: New Brunswick.

Stren, R.E., R.R. White and J.B. Whitney (eds) (1992), *Sustainable Cities: Urbanization and the Environment in International Perspective*, Westview Press: Boulder.

Swedish Council for Building Research (1979), *Growth and Trasformation of the Modern City*, (Stockolm Conference 1978, University of Stockolm): Stockholm.

Tabb, W.K. and L. Sawers (eds) (1984), *Marxism and the Metropolis*, Oxford University Press: Oxford.

Taylor, M.A.P. and P.W. Newton (1983), 'Exploring the Impact of Technology Change on Urban Form', in *Proceedings of the Second*

International Conference on New Survey Methods in Transport, Pokolbin, NSW, Sept. 1983.

(Un-Ece) United Nations, Economic Commission for Europe (1988), *Regional Strategy for Environmental Protection and the Rational Use of Natural Resources in ECE Member Countries Covering the Period up to the Year 2000 and beyond*: Geneva.

Vallega, A. (1976), *Regione e Territorio* [Region and Territory], Mursia: Milan.

Van den Berg, L. *et al.* (eds) (1982), *Urban Europe: A Study of Growth and Decline*, Pergamon Press: Oxford.

Van den Berg, L. *et al.* (eds) (1989), 'Revitalisation of the European City. Structural Changes and New Requirements', in Eurocities Conference, *Eurocities* (Barcelona), pp. 79-90.

Vernon, R. (ed.) (1962), *Myth and Reality of the Present Urban Problems*, Joint Center for Urban Studies, Harvard and MIT: Cambridge.

Vining, R. (1953), 'Delimitation of Economic Areas: Statistical Conception in the Study of the Spatial Structure of an Economic System', *Journal of American Statistical Association*, Vol. 48, pp. 44-64.

Vonk, F.P.M. (1993), 'Urban Economic Regeneration: an International Comparison of Medium-Sized Cities' Policy Making', in Getimis, P. and G. Kafkalas (eds), *Urban and Regional Development in the New Europe: Policies and Institutions for the Development of Cities and Regions in the Single European Market*, Topos: Athens.

Voogd, H. (1983), *Multicriteria Evaluation for Urban and Regional Planning*, Pion: London.

Warner, S.B. Jr. (ed.) (1966), *Planning for a Nation of Cities*, MIT Press: Cambridge.

Warner, S.B. Jr. (ed.) (1978), 'The Public Invasion of Private Space and the Private Engrossment of Public Space', in Swedish Council for Building Research (1979), *Growth and Trasformation of the Modern City*, (Stockolm Conference 1978, University of Stockolm): Stockholm.

Waste, R. (1989), *The Ecology of City Policy Making*, Oxford University Press: Oxford.

WCED - World Commission on Environment and Development (1987), *Our Common Future*, Oxford University Press: Oxford.

Webber, M.J. (1982), *Information Theory and Urban Spatial Structure*, Croom Helm: London.

Webber, M.M. (1963), 'Order in Diversity: Community without Propinquity', in Lowdon Wingo Jr. (ed.), *Cities and Space, The Future Use of Urban Land*, John Hopkins Press: Baltimore.

230

Webber, M.M. (1964), 'The Urban Place and the Non-Place Urban Realm', in Webber, M.M. *et al., Explorations into Urban Structure*, University of Pennsylvania Press: Philadelphia.

Webber, M.M. (1982), Urban Growth: What are its Sources?, in *Cities - The Forces that Shape them*, Cooper-Hewitt Museum, Rizzoli: New York.

Wengert, N. (1973), 'Political and Administrative Realities of Regional Transportation Planning', in De Salvo, J.S. (ed.), *Perspectives on Regional Transportation Planning*, Lexington Books: Lexington.

Wettmann, R.W. and W.R. Nicol (1980), *Politiche di decongestionamento dei centri urbani nella Comunità europea* [Policies for Decongestion in the Urban Centres of the European Community], Collezione studi, Serie politica regionale, No. 18, Brussels.

Wheaton, W.C. (1974), 'A Comparative Static Analysis of the Urban Spatial Structure', *Journal of Economic Theory*, Vol. 9, pp. 223-237.

Whitby, M. and J. Ollerenshaw (eds) (1988), *Land Use and the European Environment*, Belhaven Press: London.

White, R.R. (1994), *Urban Environmental Management: Environmental Change and Urban Design*, Wiley: Chichester.

White, R.R. and I. Burton (eds) (1983), *Approaches to the Study of the Environmental Implications of Contemporary* Urbanization, MAB Technical Notes, Unesco: Paris.

White, R.R. and J.B. Whitney (1992), *Cities and Environment: An Overview*, in Stren, R.E., R.R. White and J.B. Whitney (eds), *Sustainable Cities: Urbanization and the Environment in International Perspective*, Westview Press: Boulder.

WHO-UNEP (World Health Organization and United Nations Environment Programme) (1992), *Urban Air Pollution in the Megacities of the World*, Blackwell: Oxford.

Wilson, A.G. *et al.* (1977), *Models of Cities and Regions: Theoretical and Empirical Developments*, Wiley: New York.

Wirth, L. (1938), 'Urbanism as a Way of Life', *American Journal of Sociology*, July 1938.

Wolman, H. (1990), *Urban Development and Urban Ecology in the Federal Republic of Germany* (European Conference 'Environment and Urban Development', Bremen, Jan. 1990).

Index

—D—

Doxiadis, Costantin 70, 107

—E—

East European cities 52
ecological city 38
ecology 101
economic advantages 55
  comparative 55
economic rationale 17
economic resources 105
economies of scale 24
eco-plans 175
Edmunds and Letey 161
effectiveness
  of policies 18
electricity 25
energy activities 107
environment 4
  amenities 21
  compatibility 33
  future of urban environment 7
  urban 2, 4, 11
  urban degradation 1, 46, 53
environmental
  malaise as an imbalance between
    demand and supply for
    environmental resources 153
  safeguards 164
environmental equilibrium 11
  ambit of 4
  city size 20
  competitive 22
  imbalance 110
  measurement 107
environmental planning 47
  field of 104
  pluriennial 2
environmental policy
  identified with land-use policy 180
  instrumental components of 103
environmentalism 101
  history of 1
EPA 2
  Federal policy for the environment 2
epistemology 28
equilibrium
  ecological 4, 102, 109
  ecological urban 108

Europe 9, 13, 51
European cities 52, 55
European Commission 18, 47
  Directorate for the Environment DGXI
    5
  green paper 5
  inter-services coordination 5
  programmes of action 5
    for the environment 5
  Regional Policy 5
  Research Directorate 5
  Social Affairs 5
  Transport Directorate 5
  Urban Environment Group 113
European Community. See European
  Union. See European Union
European countries 51
European Economic Community 1
European Foundation for the
  Improvement of Living and Working
  Conditions 7
European Sustainable Cities 116
European territory 35
European Union 7
  Committee of Intergovernmental
    Experts 5
  Council of Ministers 5
  Urban Environment Experts 116
evaluation 135
  methods of 113
  of environmental equilibrium 107
  of plans 157
exchange efficiency 50
exhaust fumes 98
experts
  masquerading as politicians 113
externalisation
  of the cost of urban equilibrium 58
externality 24, 26
  intangible 25
  negative 26
  overload 26
  positive 26

—F—

factor of agglomeration 26
fast lanes 50
FEA, Functional Economic Area 70

flora and fauna 1
Florence 191
focal areas or points
    alternative 98
    secondary 92
forum 91
Fox, Karl 70, 118, 133
frame
    of the system of objectives 61
frame of reference 114
France 2
France (Secretariat auprès du PM chargé
    de l'Environnement...) 6
free area 33
frequency of use 146
Frisch, Ragnar 28
functional economic areas 133
Functional Economic Areas (FEA) 118
functions
    of the city 108

—G—

garagisation 50, 98
garden cities 17, 36
gas 25
gebiet einheiten 118
Geddes, Patrick 115
General Plan for Transport 68, 172
Genoa 191
gentrification 54, 96
geomorphological conditions 105
giganticness
    of service structures 125
global village effect 94
Goal Achievement Matrix 135
goals 15, 47
    of urban policy 15
    their relationships 112
    typologies of 112
Great Britain, Government of 2, 6
green spaces 1
greenery 2, 33
greyhound 3, 15
Groningen, University of 7
Gropius, Walter 17
Gruen, Victor 99

—H—

health services 123
heat island 48
heating emissions 2, 34, 49
heavy clouding 48
historic
    centre 14, 170
    urban centres 50
historic superficiality 66
historical criticism 97
holding capacity standard 112
holistic approach 109
hospitals 25, 96
household 26
    structure of 22
housing
    minimum units of 36
Howard, Ebenezer 17, 67
human behaviour 28
human preferences
    cultures 28
    groups 28
    individuals 28
    nations 28
humidity 48
hyper-congestion
    of traditional centres 185

—I—

identity 14, 60
    local 33
    personal 60
IIASA, Laxenburg 115
impact area 107
impact assessment 2
income 30
indicators 27, 36, 53, 61
    as a variable of the general model 112
    environmental 65
    lack of homogeneity as a dangerous
        pitfall in environmental planning
        114
    of achievement 112
    of action 112
    of loading capacity 111
    of result 112
    of state 112

241

242